IMAGES
of America

SANDOWN

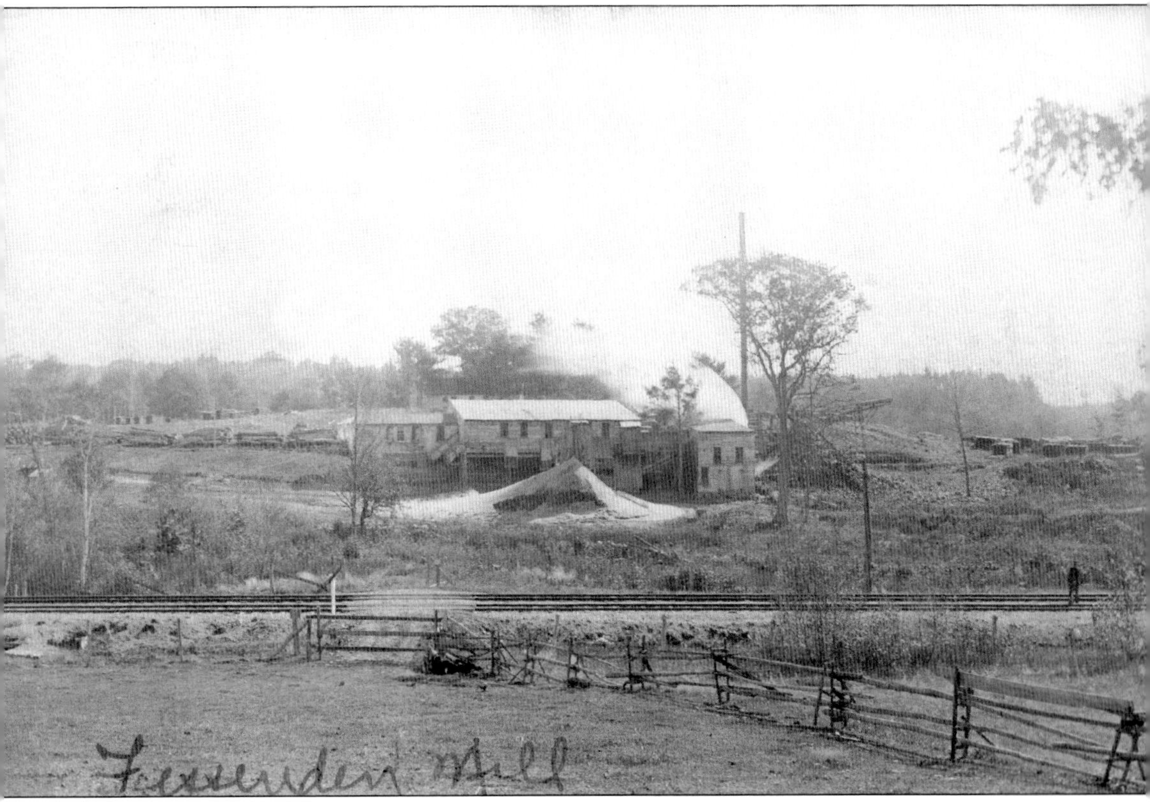

In 1905, the Fessenden mill, a steam-powered lumber mill, opened for business. The largest of the mills in town, it was located east of the railroad station on Depot Road, near the present-day sanitation area. Millions of board feet of lumber were produced during the mill's years of operation. Unfortunately, in 1918, a fire in the boiler destroyed the entire structure. A much smaller operation continued into the 1920s. (Courtesy of Eleanor Bassett.)

On the Cover: In 1956, one of the most enjoyable events at Sandown's 200th anniversary celebration was the children's parade. Youth of all ages went to great lengths to decorate anything with wheels. Pictured with the covered wagon are Alan MacGregor and his brother Malcolm. In front of them, Beth Lessard rides her tricycle and Richard Lessard pushes his brother Lawrence in a stroller. (Courtesy of the Sandown Historical Society.)

IMAGES
of America

SANDOWN

Arlene F. Bassett and
Barbara A. Lachance

ARCADIA
PUBLISHING

ISBN 978-1-4671-2056-2

Published by Arcadia Publishing
Charleston, South Carolina

Printed in the United States of America

Library of Congress Control Number: 2013937538

For all general information, please contact Arcadia Publishing:
Telephone 843-853-2070
Fax 843-853-0044
E-mail sales@arcadiapublishing.com
For customer service and orders:
Toll-Free 1-888-313-2665

Visit us on the Internet at www.arcadiapublishing.com

We dedicate this book to our husbands, Jerry Lachance and Carroll Bassett. We appreciate their patience and understanding during the many months spent preparing this volume.

Contents

ACKNOWLEDGMENTS

The authors are so grateful to all of those who were willing to assist with this project. A special thank you to author Richard Holmes for his hours of telephone advice and for his permission to use *A View From Meeting House Hill: A History of Sandown, New Hampshire*, to glean historical facts. Thanks to John Cameron for sending amazing photographs taken long ago by his father, Mal Cameron Sr.

For loaning us photographs and helping with identifications of people and places, we thank the Sandown Fire Department, the Sandown Police Department, the Sandown Public Library, Sandown Town Hall, curator Bertha Deveau and the Sandown Historical Society and Museum, St. Matthews United Methodist Church, the Old Meeting House Historical Association, Suzanne Anderson, Eleanor Bassett, Juliana Ball, Dorothy Batchelder, Jacqueline Burke, Ann Cabral, David Drowne, Susan Dupouy, Michael Harnois, Marion Jean, Lillian Loring, June McNally, Robert and Lois MacKinnon, Virginia Morris, Lisa Peterson, Michelle Short, Linda Torre, and Alden True.

We would also like to thank our editor at Arcadia Publishing, Caitrin Cunningham, for her gentle prodding and optimistic outlook as we compiled our work. We could not have done it without each and every one of you.

INTRODUCTION

Thanks to author Richard Holmes's book *A View From Meeting House Hill: A History of Sandown, New Hampshire*, much is known about the early history of Sandown. The town had its beginnings as part of an enormous tract of land that over the years has been divided many times. As these smaller tracts of land continued to divide, towns came into their own. One of these towns was Kingston, which eventually voted to let the parcel of land now known as Sandown cut away from its western border. It then took five years for Gov. Benning Wentworth to approve the separation, in 1756.

Living in a more compact area was an advantage to the early settlers. It meant that they did not have to travel miles and miles on foot or by horse to attend church or buy goods. They had the right to assemble and could elect their own officials. As for the name, it is said that it was personally selected by Governor Wentworth. During his many trips to England, it is believed that he visited the community of Sandown on the Isle of Wight, borrowing that name for this New Hampshire town, which had been waiting, not so patiently, to be named. To this day, Sandown, England, and Sandown, New Hampshire, continue to be the only towns in the world with the name.

One of the most interesting early events took place in 1675. Native American chief King Phillip waged a terrible war against the settlers. He looked to the other local tribes for support and is said to have met with Chief Passaconaway on the shores of a Sandown lake to plan the total destruction of the white man. Some claim that this story is pure legend, but it has been passed down through the generations for over 300 years. Sandown's Lake Phillip inherited its name from this event.

As the Old Meeting House was being constructed in 1774, the workers looked forward to each day's ration of rum. Alas, one day, the rum barrel was empty. Selectman Stephen Batchelder was then dispatched to Newburyport, Massachusetts, to fetch another supply of rum. Meanwhile, back at the meetinghouse, the men refused to do any work during the two days it took Batchelder to return with the rum. Gov. Francis Murphy declared it to be the first labor strike in the state and maybe even the country.

In 1976, when the United States celebrated its 200th birthday, the national bicentennial committee made a motion picture showing scenes from America's history. The first several minutes of the film were of Sandown's meetinghouse. A craftsman was hired to fashion a replica of the south door of the meetinghouse and thousands of visitors to the bicentennial exhibit passed through it.

During the Great Depression, Henry Ford offered $40,000 to purchase the Old Meeting House. It was a tempting offer and a great deal of money, but Ford wanted to take the building apart and move it to his museum in Dearborn, Michigan, where it would be reassembled and used as a tourist attraction. Sandown residents had enough foresight to say no to Ford.

Sandown's first preacher was Rev. Josiah Cotton, who came from a long line of great preachers, including his grand uncle Cotton Mather, made famous by the Salem Witch Trials.

Sandown's location in southern New Hampshire makes it a convenient drive to a number of interesting places. Within two hours in any direction, travelers can land in one of five New England states: Maine, Vermont, Massachusetts, Rhode Island, and Connecticut. Within an hour's drive are the historic cities of Boston, Portsmouth, and Concord, New Hampshire's state capital.

The population of Sandown remained about 500 for most of its first 200 years. The population dipped to 229 people in the 1930 census before slowly increasing until the 1960 census. As with most towns in southern New Hampshire that have a close proximity to Boston, a combination of improved highways and large landowners subdividing their land for housing developments created a population boom in Sandown beginning in the 1970s and continuing today. The once rural farming town changed quickly into a bedroom community, with workers residing in Sandown and commuting throughout the region.

This transition brought a need for increased community services. Educating the children of Sandown meant a change from the four one-room schools that had educated all eight grades to one central elementary school in 1956. As more families moved into town, a number of additions were built to the central school. However, even that was not enough, and in 1966, Sandown joined the Timberlane Regional School District. Today, there are two elementary schools, with kindergarten through third grade in the North School and grades four and five at the Central School. Students in grades 6 through 12 attend Timberlane Regional Middle and High School in Plaistow.

Other town services have changed as well. The board of selectmen grew from a three-member board to a five-member board to handle increased governing responsibilities. In 1974, the first town library building was erected. Today, the police and highway departments have a number of full-time employees. The fire department remains a volunteer organization but the chief is full-time. The recreation department now has its own building as well.

Even with these changes, Sandown continues to be regarded as rural, which is attractive to residents who travel for city employment but cannot wait to come home to quiet, small-town life. There is a public library, a town hall, a fire and police station, and a post office on Main Street, but no stoplight. There is one church, several auto repair shops, a few cottage industries, one small convenience store, but no gas stations.

Throughout its history, the people of Sandown have found ways to interact with neighbors. Beginning with the Grange, clubs and organizations of all kinds have thrived. In the 1950s, there was even a women's group called the Mud Club. There have been many church and social organizations for the youth of Sandown as well.

For such a small town, Sandown was still able to produce some noteworthy citizens, including authors Richard Holmes and Eva Beede Odell, pastors Willis P. Odell and John Rea Chapman, Adm. Howard R. Shaw, and two young women who represented New Hampshire in the Miss America pageant: Laura Lourette in 1988 and Lindsay Graham in 2010. Men and women from Sandown have bravely served in all major military conflicts, including the Revolutionary War, the Civil War, World Wars I and II, the Korean War, the Vietnam War, and the current conflicts in Iraq and Afghanistan. The town holds a special Memorial Day service each year to remember all the soldiers who have served.

Between the covers of this book, there lies much of the history of this southern New Hampshire town. It is hoped that longtime residents will be surprised by some of the photographs and stories and that newer residents will learn some of the history of the town in which they chose to settle.

One

Historic Buildings

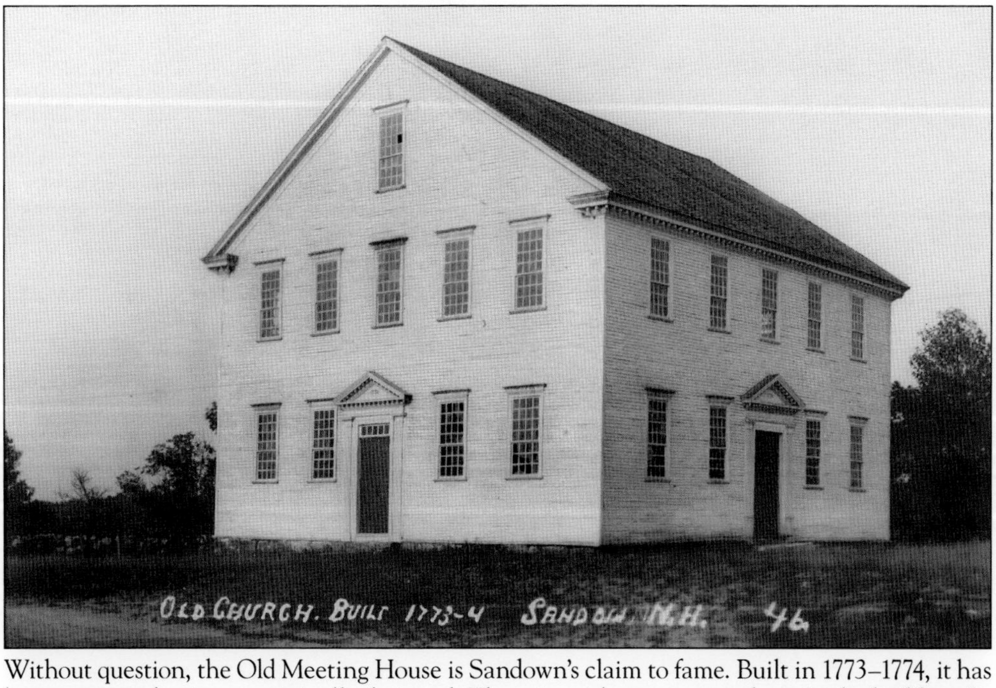

Without question, the Old Meeting House is Sandown's claim to fame. Built in 1773–1774, it has been preserved as it was originally designed. There is neither power nor heat in the building. In 1976, photographs and a video of the meetinghouse were used in the American bicentennial tour, which traveled throughout the world. Sandown is proud that the building has been placed in both the State and National Registers of Historic Places. (Courtesy of Eleanor Bassett.)

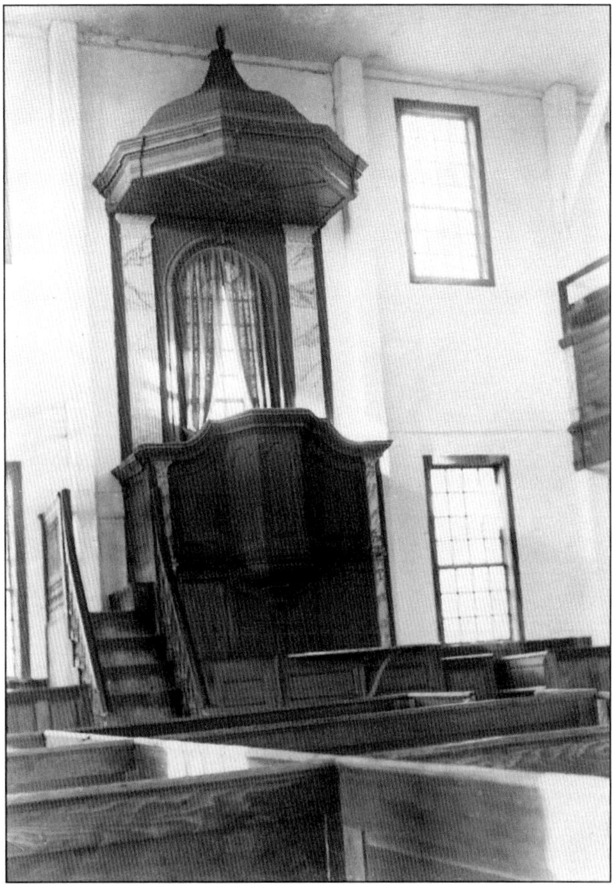

This is the Wine Goblet, or Tulip Pulpit, at Sandown's Old Meeting House. It stands 11 feet off the floor, and the speaker can be seen easily from every seat. Above the pulpit is a beautifully carved giant wooden sounding board. Its purpose is to carry the speaker's voice to the very corners of the building. (Courtesy of Eleanor Bassett.)

One of the unfortunate features of most New England meetinghouses were the slave pews. Sandown's Old Meeting House is no exception. These pews (below) were located to the left and right of the high pulpit, tucked into the corner. Men sat on one side and women on the other. These pews received little use, as there were almost no slaves this far north. However, household servants were also seated here. (Courtesy of Richard Holmes.)

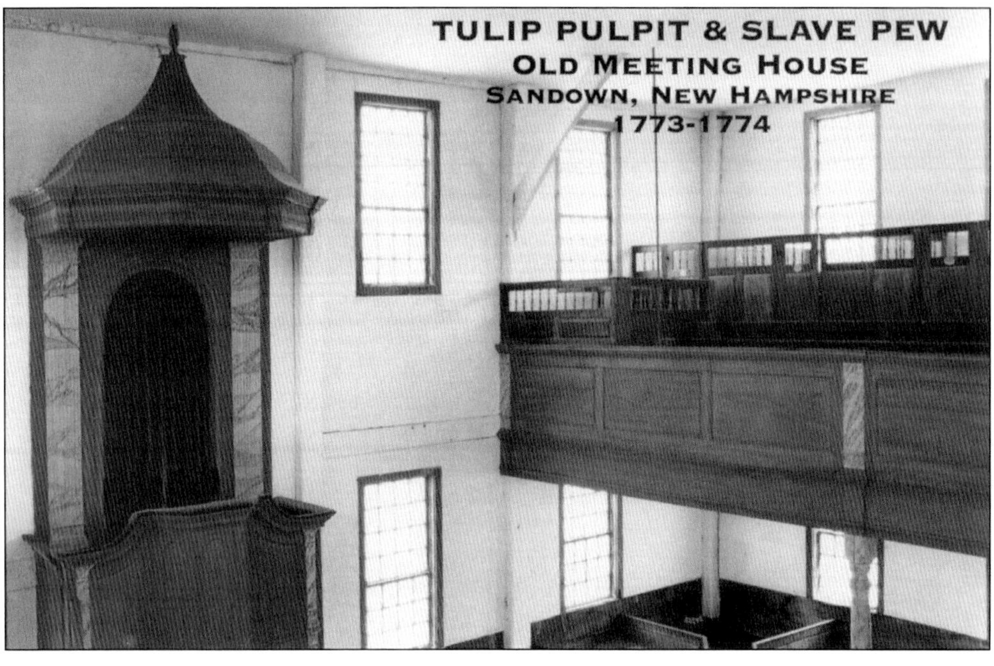

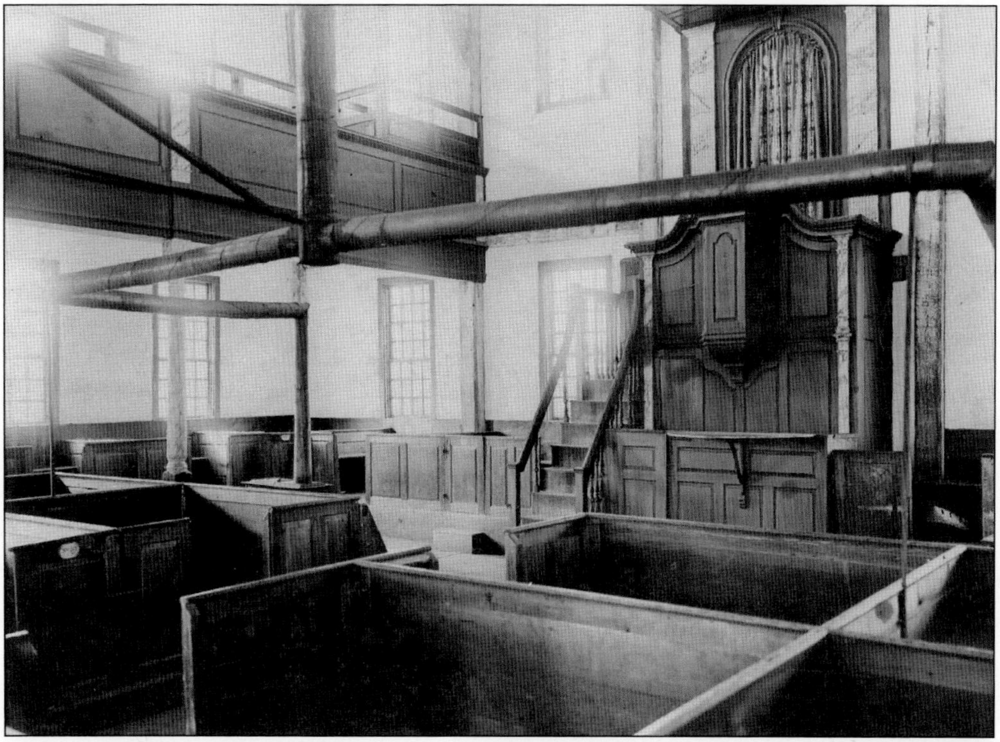

For the first 50 years, the Old Meeting House had no heat, which greatly annoyed the congregation. In 1826, a chimney was built and two stoves were added. Later, these were replaced with two new stoves. The unsightly pipes, seen above, wound around the building, but heat was now available. Fortunately, the pipes were removed when they were no longer needed, leaving only a small reminder in the ceiling. (Courtesy of Eleanor Bassett.)

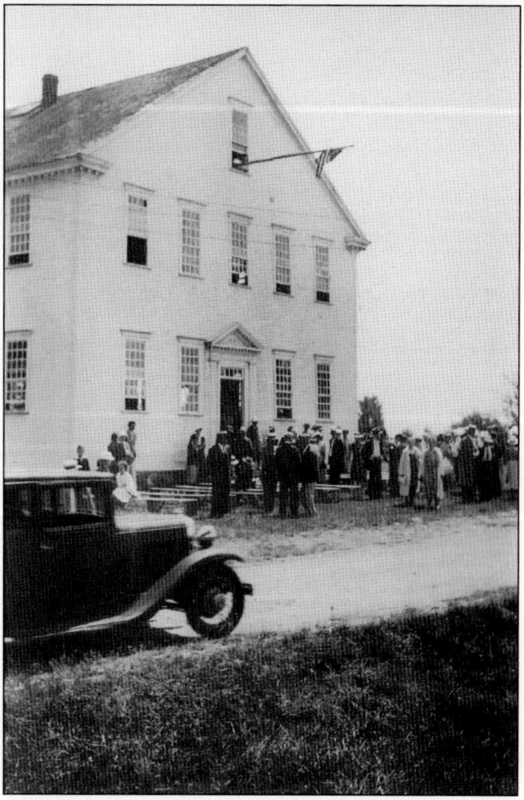

For over 70 years, an annual Old Home Day service has been held at the Old Meeting House on the second Sunday in August. The crowd at the 1938 service is seen here. Someone has climbed into the attic and is displaying an American flag. This was quite an amazing feat, considering that the person had to tightrope walk on beams to reach the window, as the attic has no floor. (Courtesy of Eleanor Bassett.)

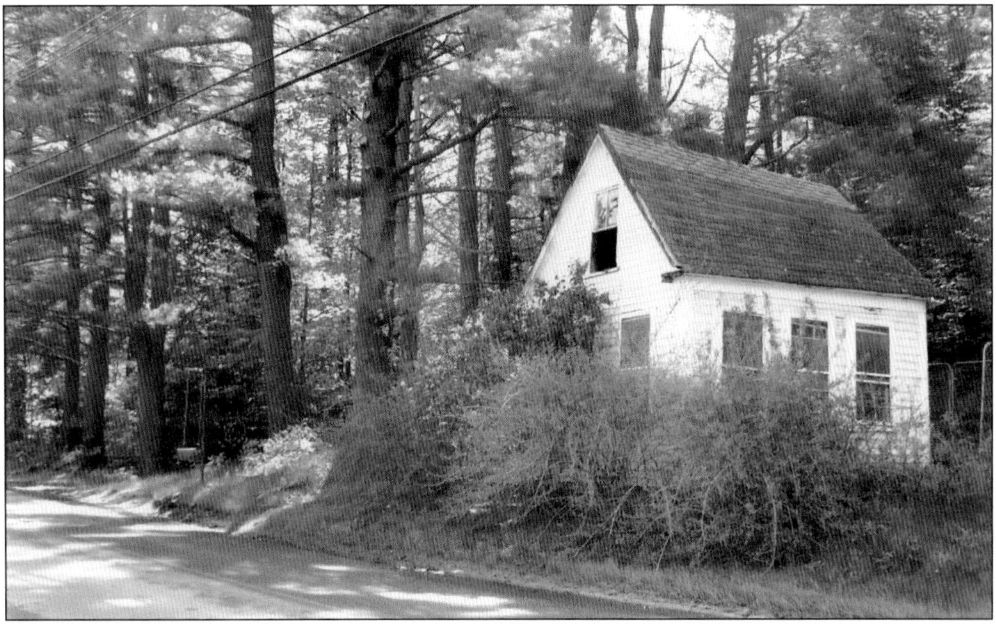

This building, on Fremont Road, was a summer home owned by the Pollard family in the 1950s. Originally, in 1774, it was used as a storage shed for the tools used to build the Old Meeting House. Also kept here was the famous rum, the lack of which stopped the construction of the meetinghouse until more could be acquired, causing what has been called the first labor strike in America. (Courtesy of the Sandown Historical Society.)

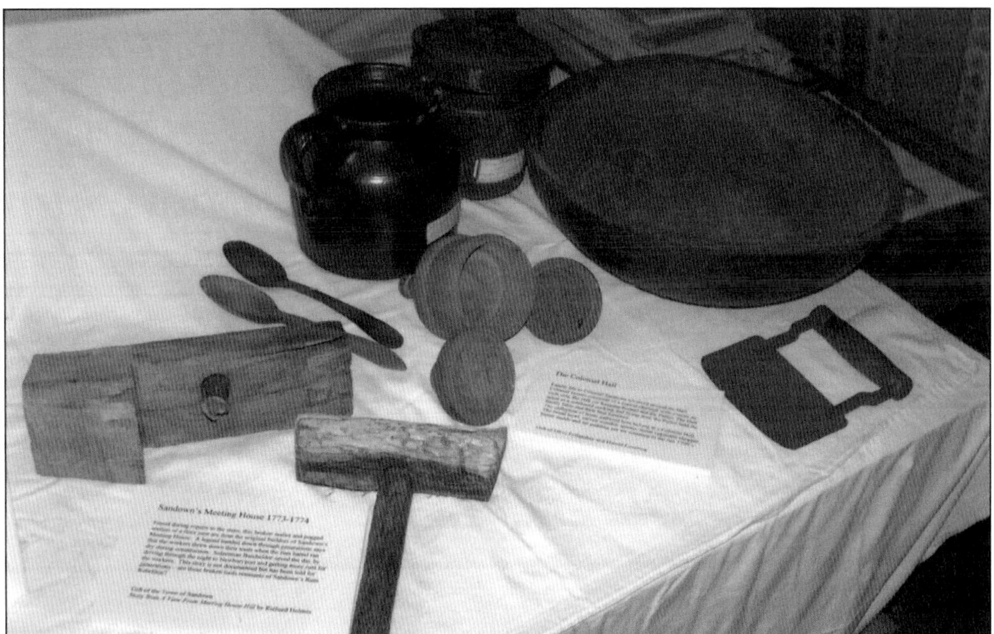

See here on the bottom left are two artifacts found at the Old Meeting House during repairs: a pegged piece of a floor joist and a wooden mallet. The mallet was used while constructing the building in 1774, but it apparently broke and was tossed under the pulpit, where it remained for 200 years. (Courtesy of the Sandown Historical Society.)

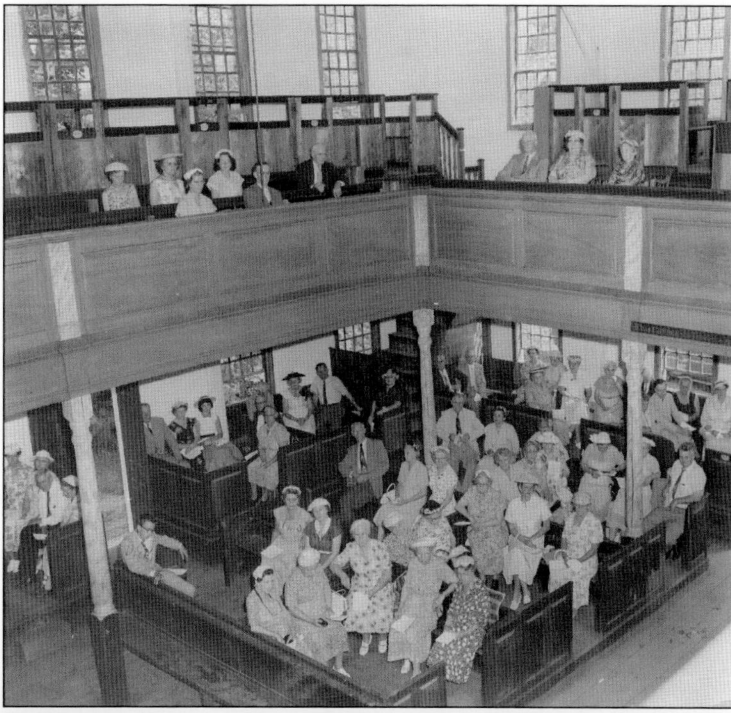

This large crowd gathered at the Old Meeting House for an event around 1955. Dresses and hats were certainly the fashion of the day. This is a wonderful view of the interior of the building, which looks exactly the same today. The meetinghouse is a popular venue for spring and summer weddings, and visitors come from far away to view this piece of New England history. (Photograph by Mal Cameron; courtesy of the Sandown Historical Society.)

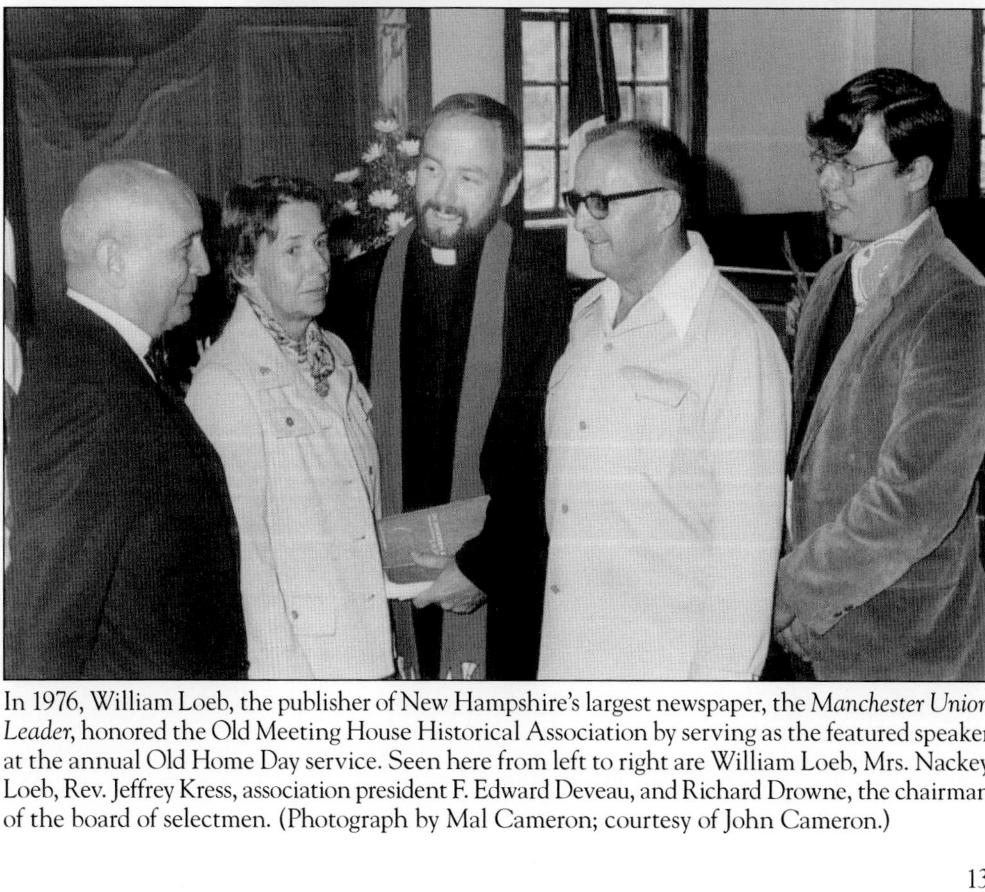

In 1976, William Loeb, the publisher of New Hampshire's largest newspaper, the *Manchester Union Leader*, honored the Old Meeting House Historical Association by serving as the featured speaker at the annual Old Home Day service. Seen here from left to right are William Loeb, Mrs. Nackey Loeb, Rev. Jeffrey Kress, association president F. Edward Deveau, and Richard Drowne, the chairman of the board of selectmen. (Photograph by Mal Cameron; courtesy of John Cameron.)

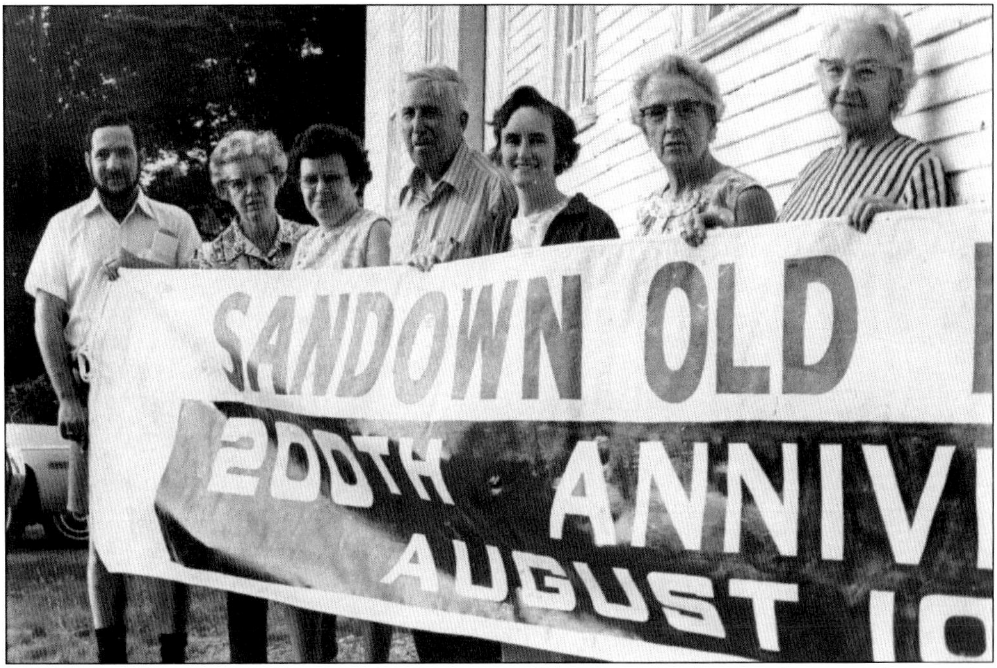

In 1974, the Old Meeting House celebrated its 200th birthday. A banner was hung to advertise the special service to be held at the historic building. Seen here from left to right are an unidentified man, Hazel Rogan, Lillian Butt, Malcolm Cameron Sr., Janet Romaine, Edna French, and Olive Follansbee. (Courtesy of the Sandown Public Library.)

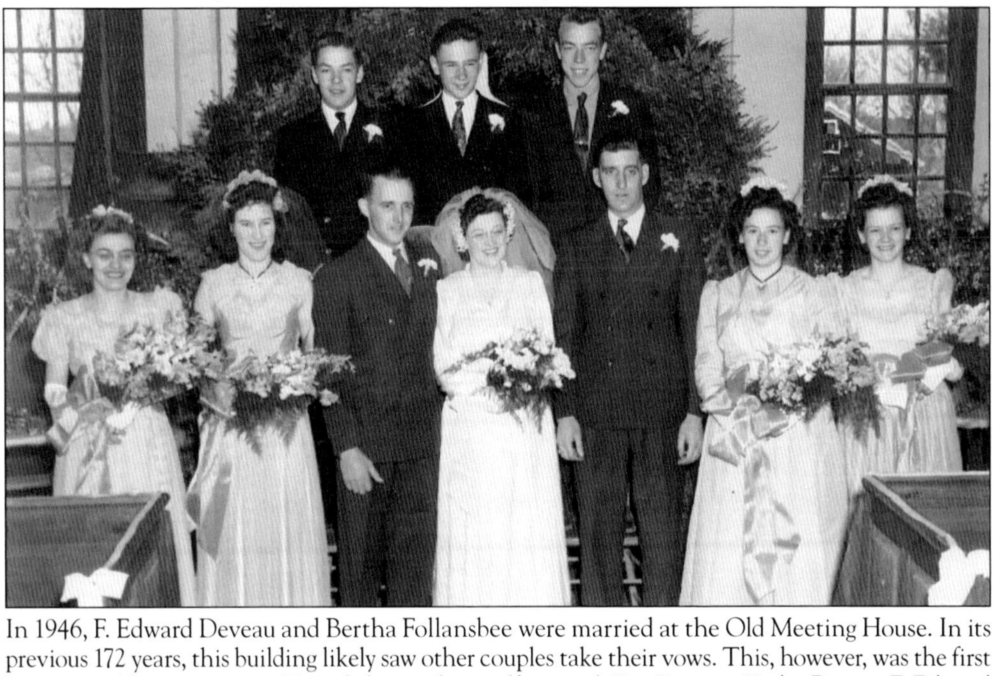
In 1946, F. Edward Deveau and Bertha Follansbee were married at the Old Meeting House. In its previous 172 years, this building likely saw other couples take their vows. This, however, was the first known wedding ceremony. From left to right are (first row) Eva Bassett, Violet Brown, F. Edward and Bertha Deveau, Leon Soule, Virginia Follansbee, and Jeanne Follansbee; (second row) Harold Venner, Norman Follansbee, and Donald Hills. (Courtesy of the Sandown Historical Society.)

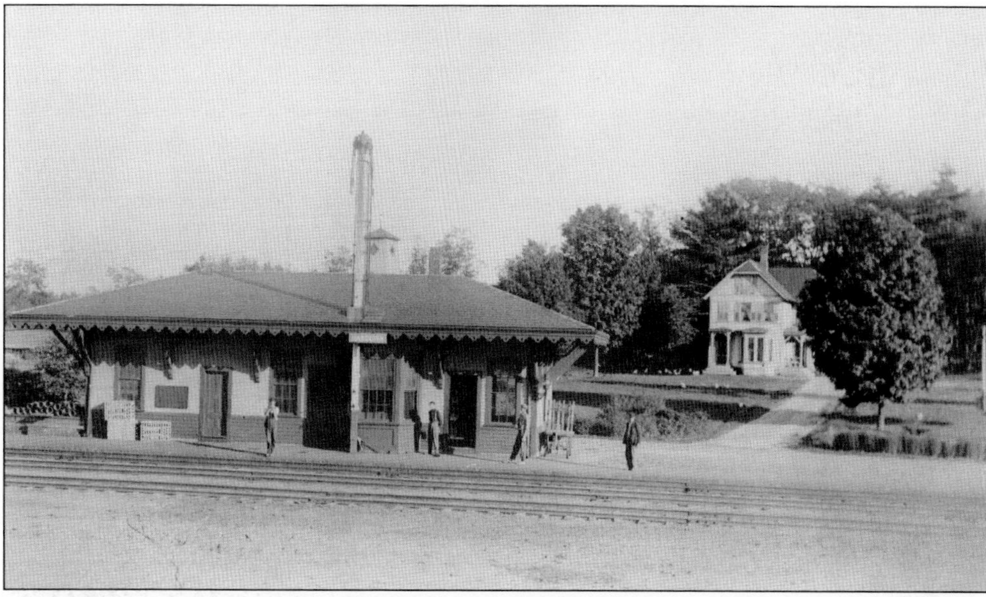

In 1981, the town approved for the Sandown Historical Society and Museum to occupy the Sandown depot as a museum for recording and displaying the history of the town. The building is now in the National Register of Historical Places. The house in the background was built by George Sanborn, who was stationmaster from 1887 to 1917. (Courtesy of Eleanor Bassett.)

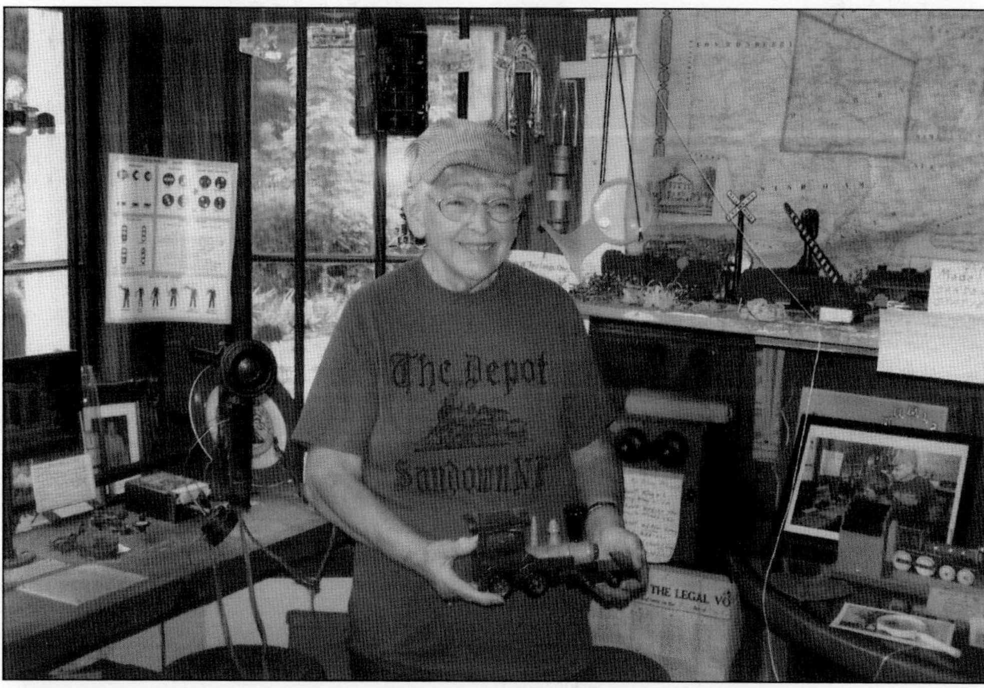

Surrounded by historical artifacts in the Depot Museum, curator Bertha Deveau continues her work to preserve Sandown's history. Deveau and her husband, F. Edward, were instrumental in forming the society in 1977. With the help of other residents, including John Harrington, the group restored the old depot, which now displays antique railroad equipment and town memorabilia. (Courtesy of the Sandown Historical Society.)

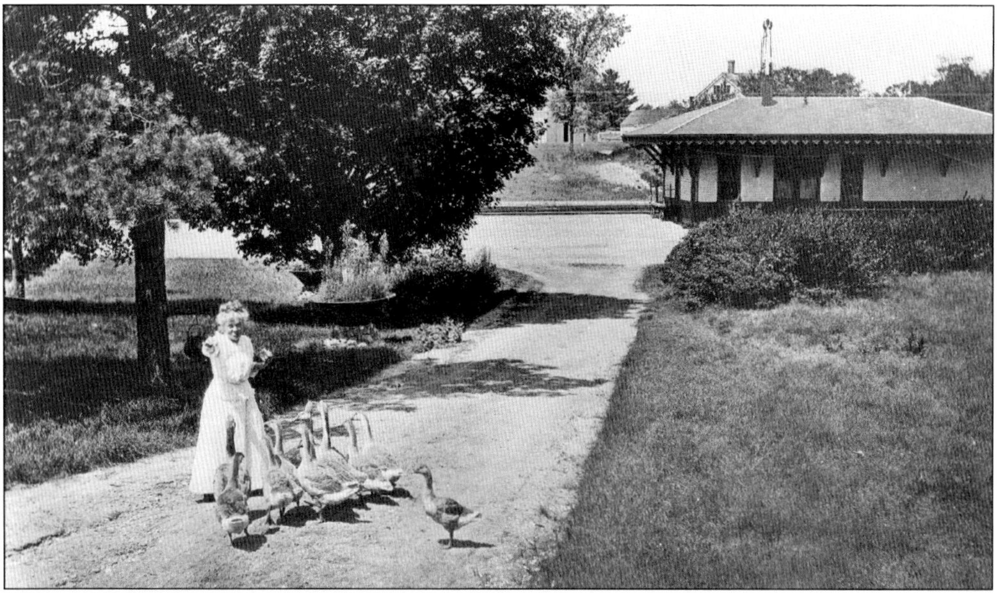

Lisette Sanborn, the wife of stationmaster George Sanborn, shoos her geese away from the busy railroad tracks. Many animals, including horses, met their doom as trains came roaring through Sandown. (Courtesy of Eleanor Bassett.)

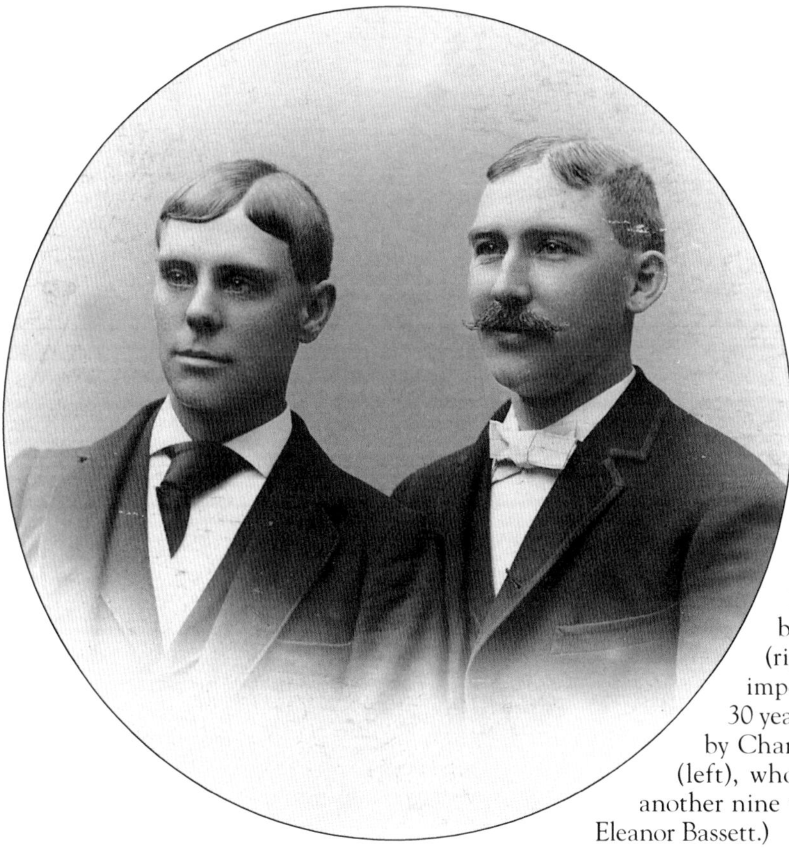

A stationmaster was a necessity at every train depot. Sandown's first stationmaster was Alvah Sanborn. He was followed by George Sanborn (right), who held this important position for 30 years. He was replaced by Charles Burton French (left), who held the job for another nine years. (Courtesy of Eleanor Bassett.)

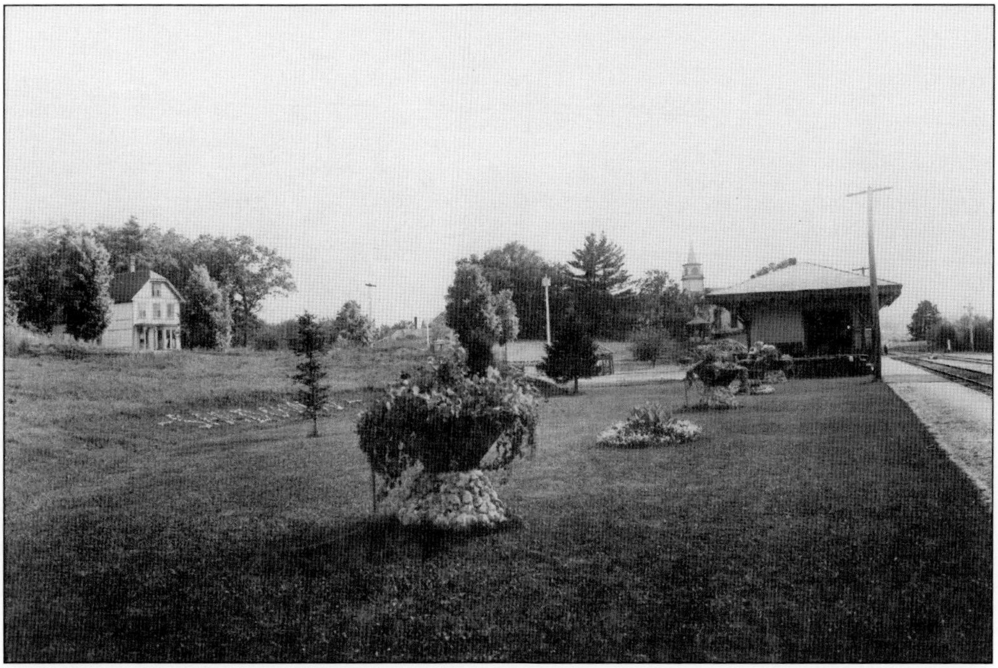

Sandown was fortunate to win the fight to route the tracks through town, bringing much-needed revenue. The trains also brought people and goods to Sandown. Visible in this photograph are the depot, stationmaster George Sanborn's home, and the Methodist church. The well-tended plants paid off when the Sandown depot won an award for having the most beautiful grounds. (Courtesy of the Sandown Historical Society.)

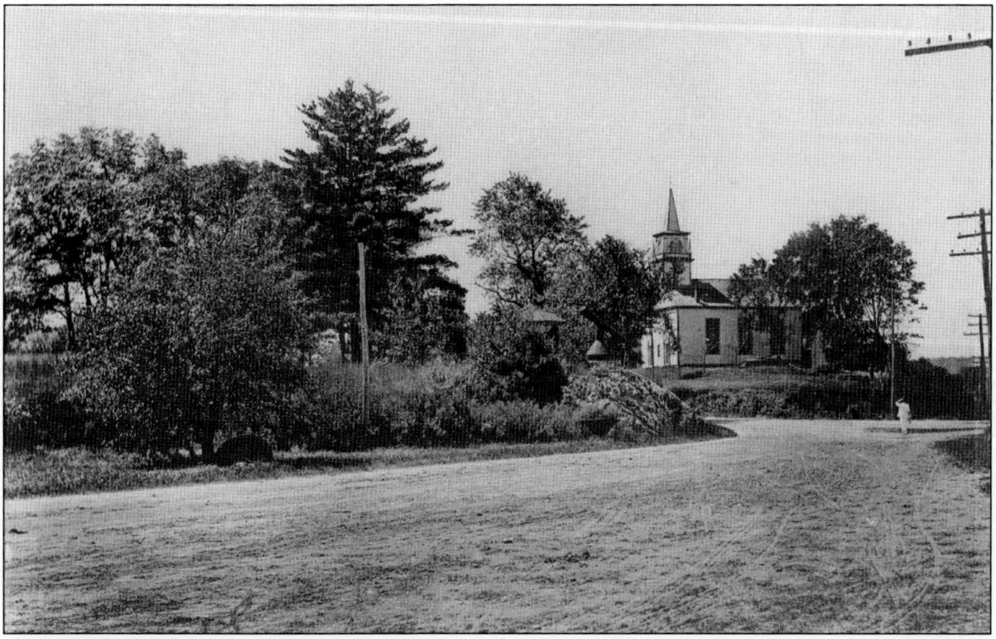

This photograph of St. Matthews Church was taken from the depot. One wonders if the photographer had just stepped off a train and thought this to be a pretty view. (Courtesy of Robert and Lois MacKinnon.)

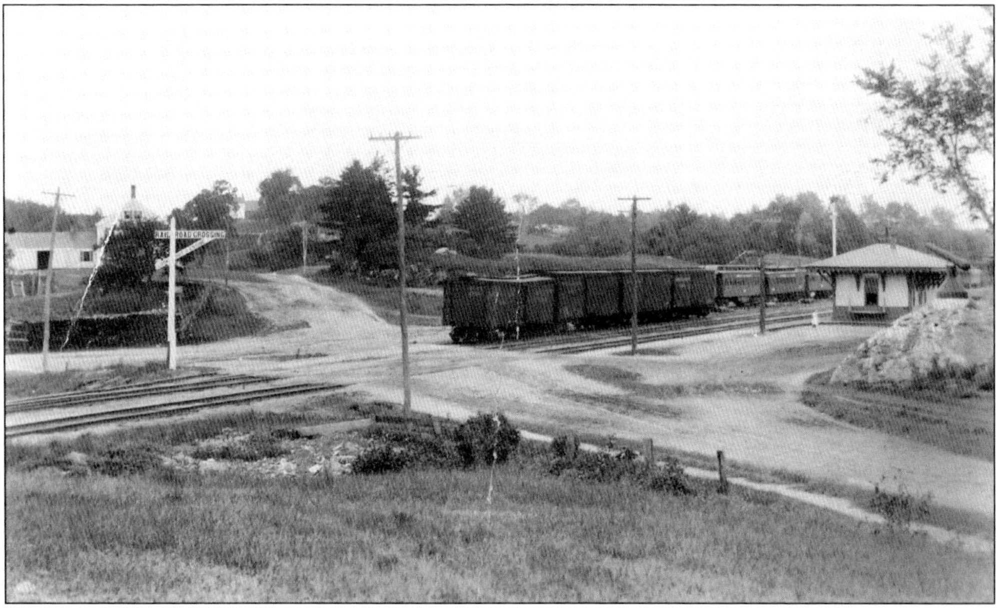

The first freight train stopped at the Sandown depot in November 1874; what an amazing sight it must have been for the residents. It was a sad day in 1934 when the last freight train made the final stop in Sandown. (Courtesy of Eleanor Bassett.)

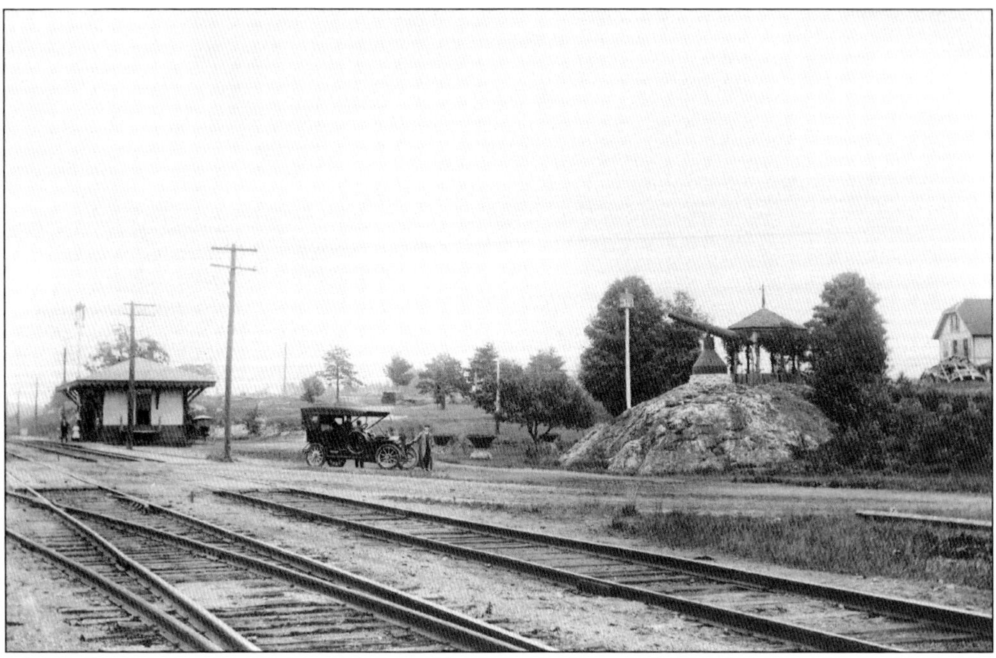

Although the depot remains standing in the center of town, the tracks were removed in 1936. The "horseless carriage" seen here by the tracks is a wonderful reminder of long-ago days when trains passed through Sandown. (Courtesy of Eleanor Bassett.)

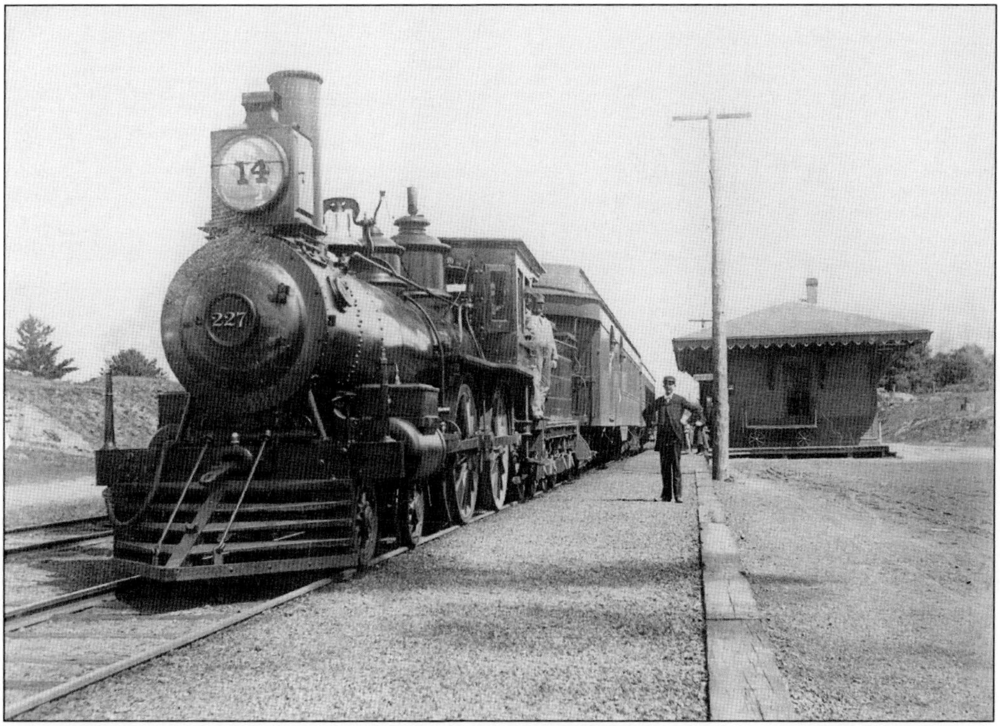

The trains ran through the towns of Nashua, Hudson, Windham, Derry, Hampstead, Sandown, Fremont, Epping, Lee, Barrington, and Rochester. This train is pulling into the Sandown depot from Fremont. (Courtesy of Eleanor Bassett.)

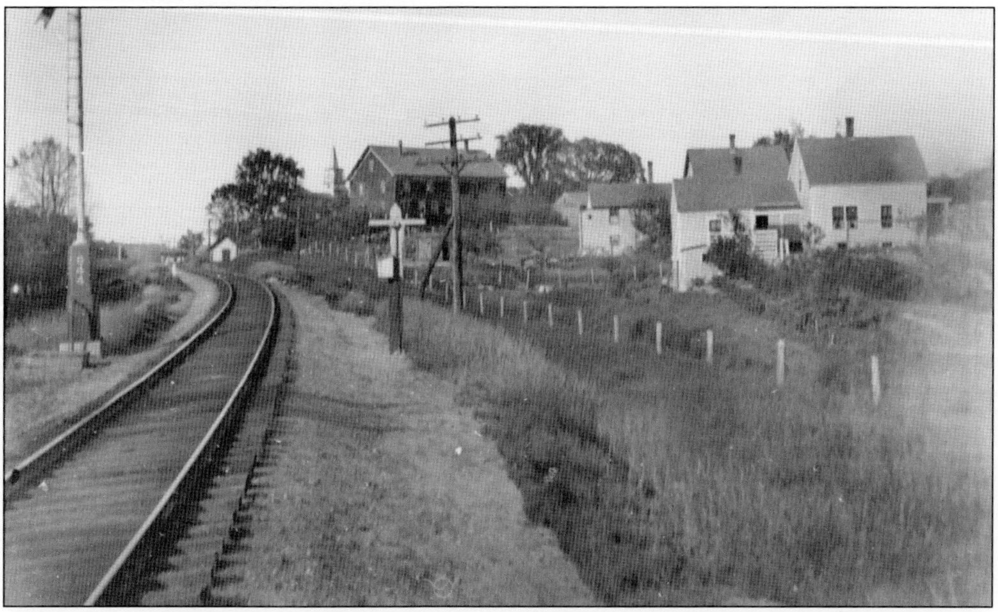

This section of track ran behind these homes on Hampstead Road. This view looks east toward the town center. The large building in the middle is Sanborn Hall, one of Sandown's early town halls. It was razed because of serious structural problems. There are very few known photographs of this piece of history. (Courtesy of Richard Holmes.)

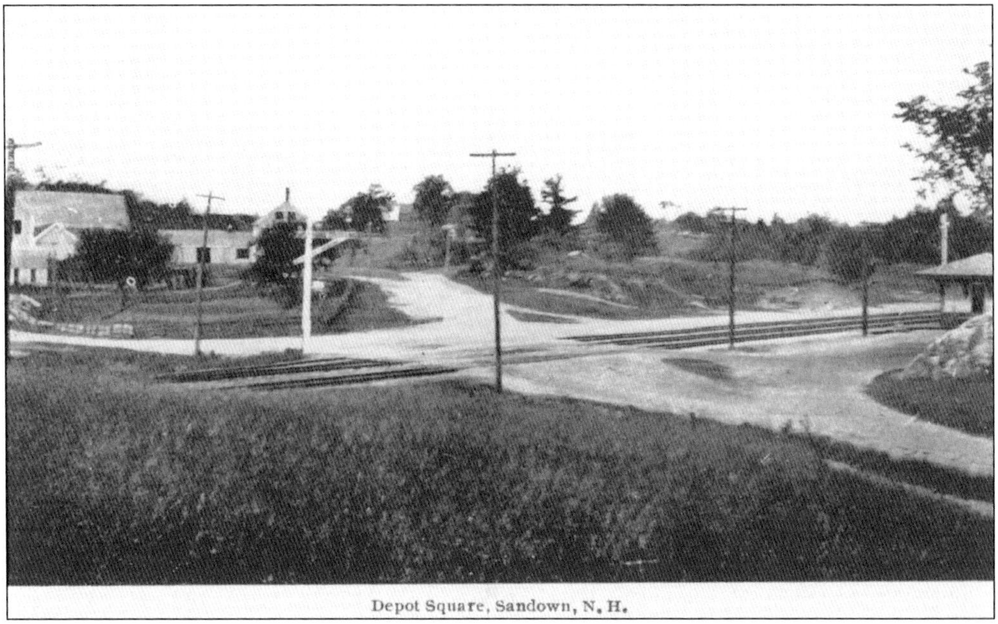

There were no paved roads during Sandown's railroad era, when this intersection was called Depot Square. The depot is on the far right, with the tracks running in front of it. The lower road on the right is Main Street (Route 121A), which continues across the tracks and bends to the left. The road heading straight ahead up the hill is Fremont Road. Most of these landmarks can still be seen today. (Courtesy of Richard Holmes.)

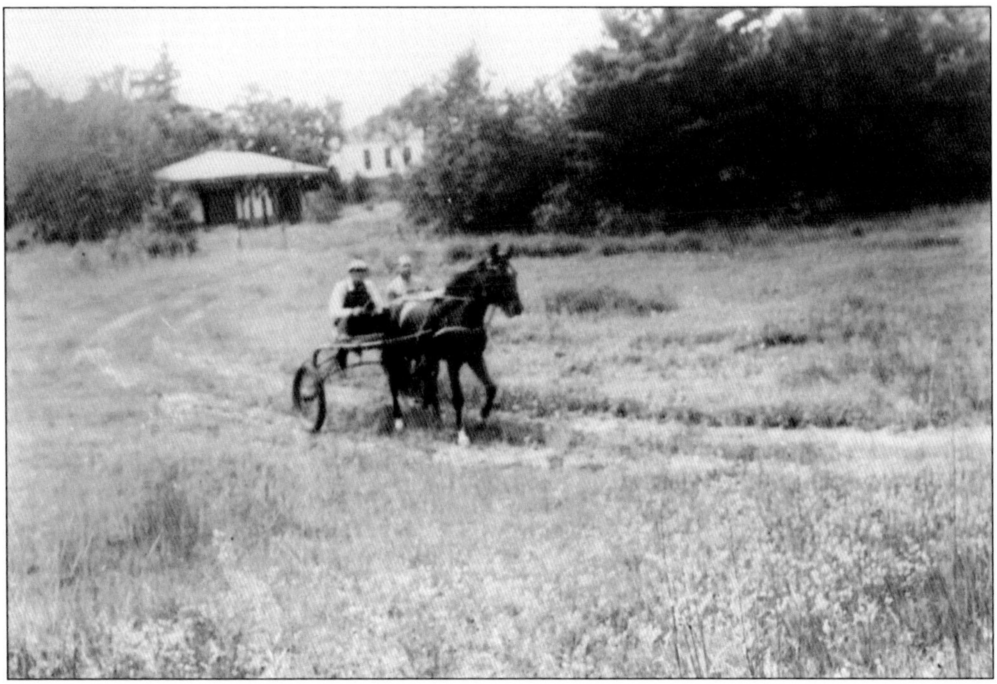

The area behind the depot was a perfect place for Harry Whitcomb to practice trotting with his horse and sulky. It appears that a crude track had been worn into the grass. (Courtesy of Robert and Lois MacKinnon.)

Two

MAKING A LIVING

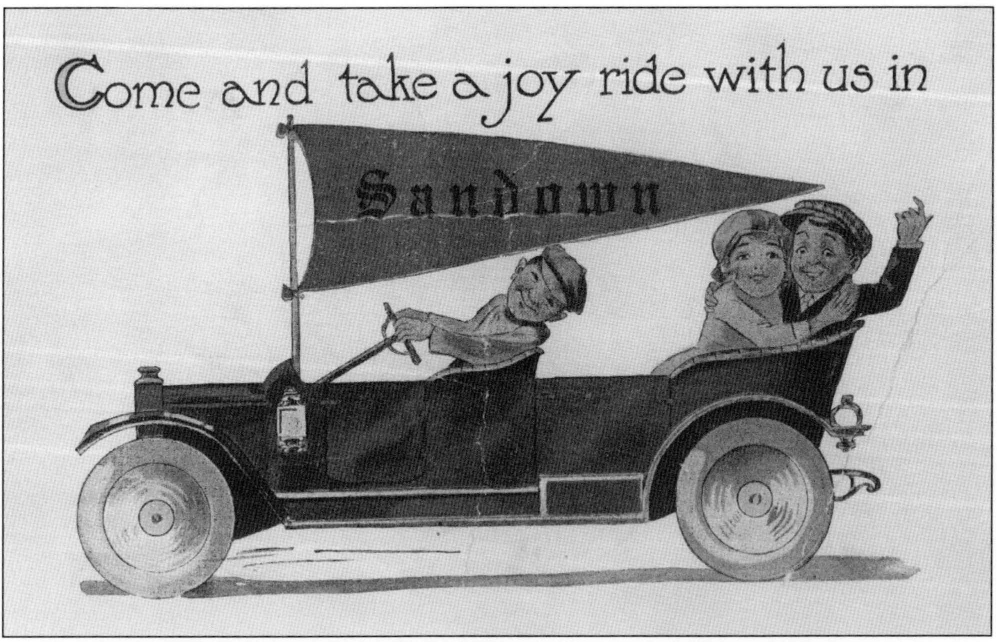

Sandown businesses used all forms of advertisement to bring tourists and visitors to the town. This postcard was one of many that depicted the area as a fun place to spend the day or the weekend. Cards like these were usually purchased in town and sent to friends and family in lieu of a lengthy letter. The local stores and hotels sold many of these cards to travelers as well. (Courtesy of Richard Holmes.)

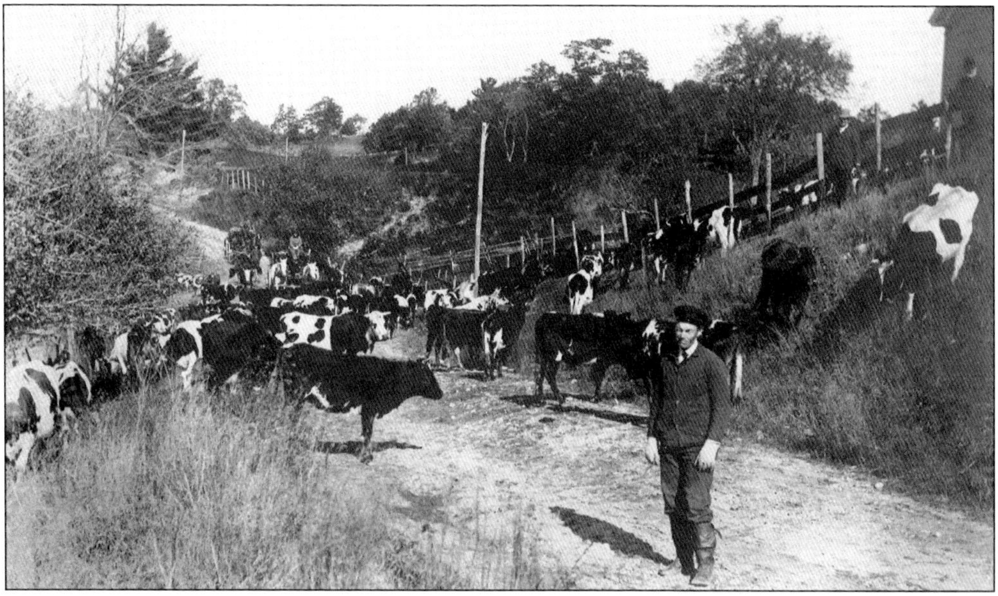

From the time of the earliest settlers, farming was the main way of making a living for residents of this rural community. This Sandown farmer stops to pose for a photograph while his herd of cattle wanders aimlessly on unpaved Main Street. Unlike today, there was no threat of speeding traffic. (Courtesy of Eleanor Bassett.)

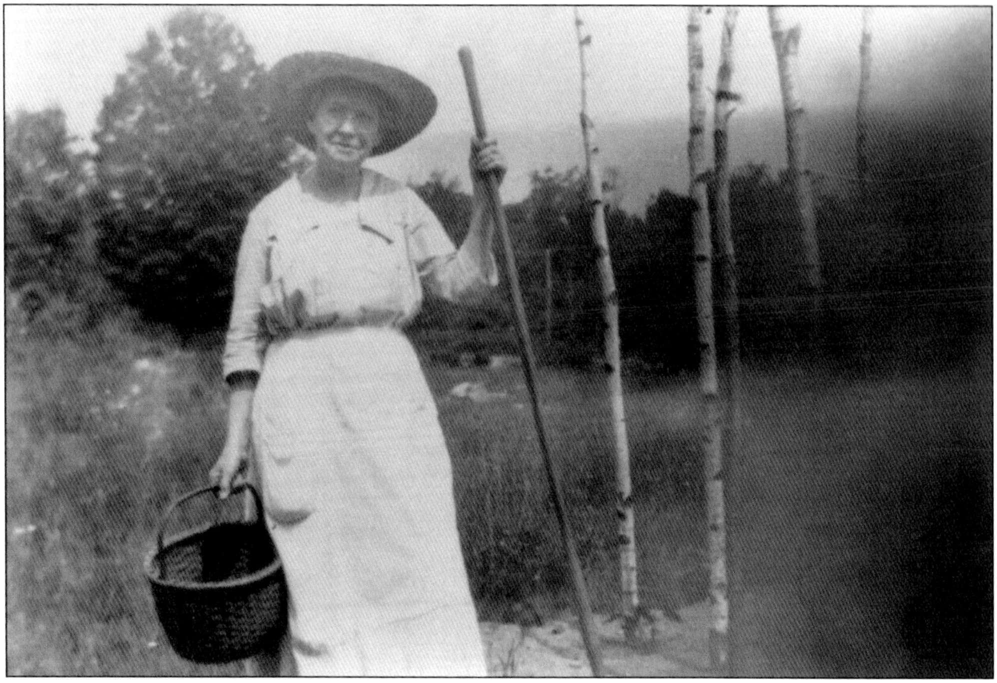

This unidentified woman holds a basket that was woven in Sandown. In the early days, itinerant basket weavers would arrive at a home where a business was operated. The weaver would stay at the home until the desired number of baskets had been made to fill the business owner's order. The basket weaver would receive room and board as a portion of his pay. (Courtesy of Suzanne Anderson.)

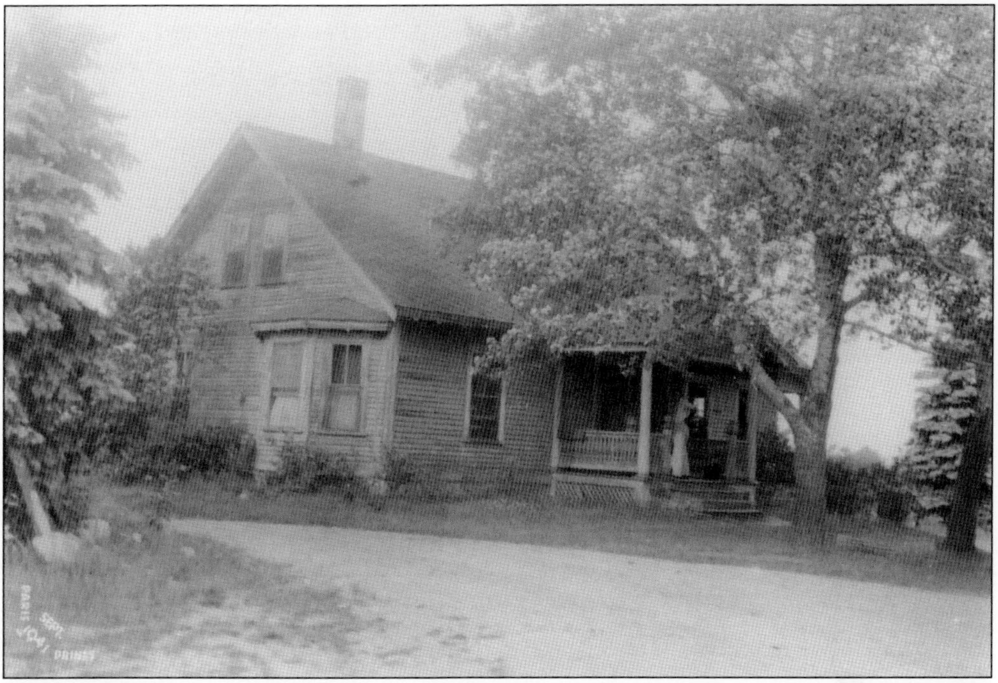

When it was owned by Clarence and Marion Merrick Drowne, this property was a working farm providing seasonal employment for much of the town's population. It was best known for its apple and peach orchards, which produced bushels of delicious fruit. It also boasted a healthy crop of potatoes each year. The home is now owned by Alvin and Lorene Atkins. (Courtesy of June McNally.)

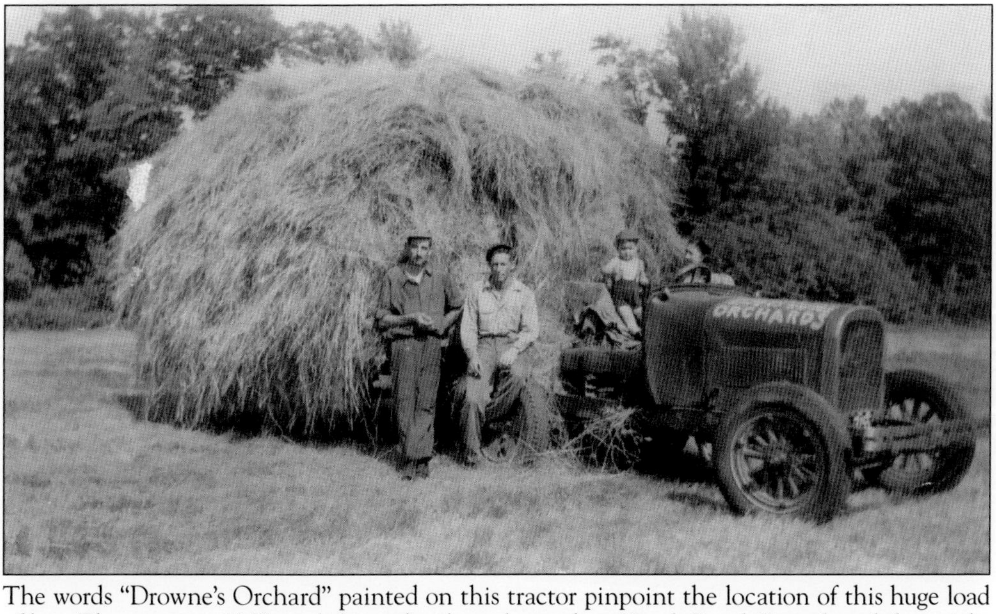

The words "Drowne's Orchard" painted on this tractor pinpoint the location of this huge load of hay. The year was 1945, and the orchard was located on North Road. Seen from left to right are Harold Lovering, Everett "Bud" Holmes, young Ralph Drowne Jr., and Ralph's mother, Pearl Drowne. (Courtesy of Suzanne Anderson.)

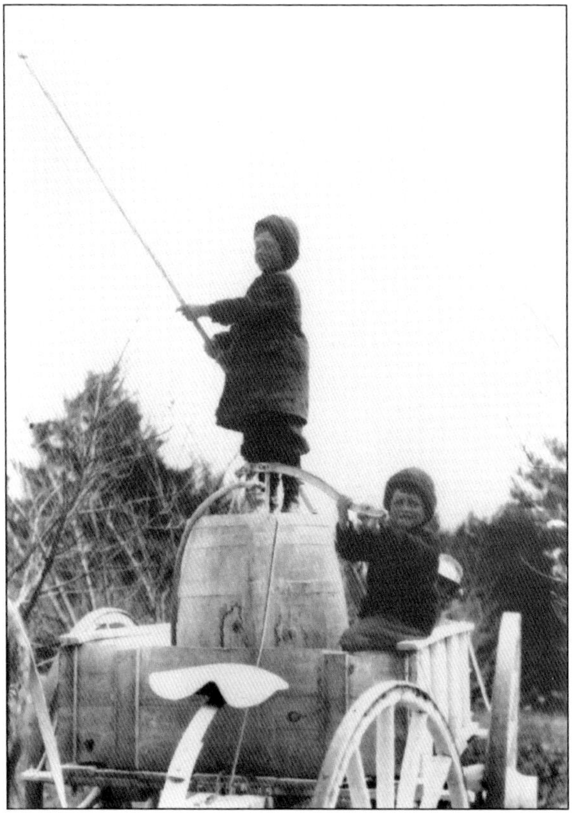

These young boys help their father, Clarence Drowne, at the apple and peach orchard on North Road. They are spraying the trees to ward off insects. Ralph is manning the pump handle while Albert aims the sprayer. This photograph, from about 1950, is surprising by today's standards, but such was the way in the good old days. (Courtesy of Suzanne Anderson.)

The peach crop at Drowne's Orchard was plentiful in the photograph below, from around 1950. Showing off the peaches are, from left to right, brothers Albert, Fred, and Ralph Drowne. (Courtesy of Suzanne Anderson.)

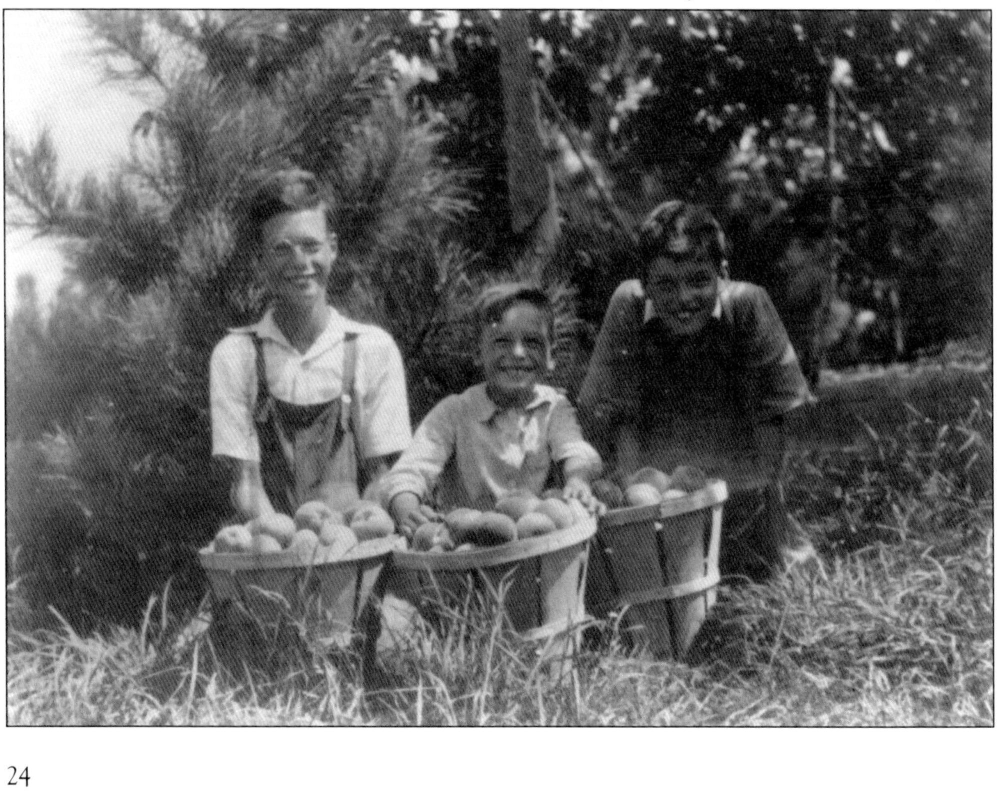

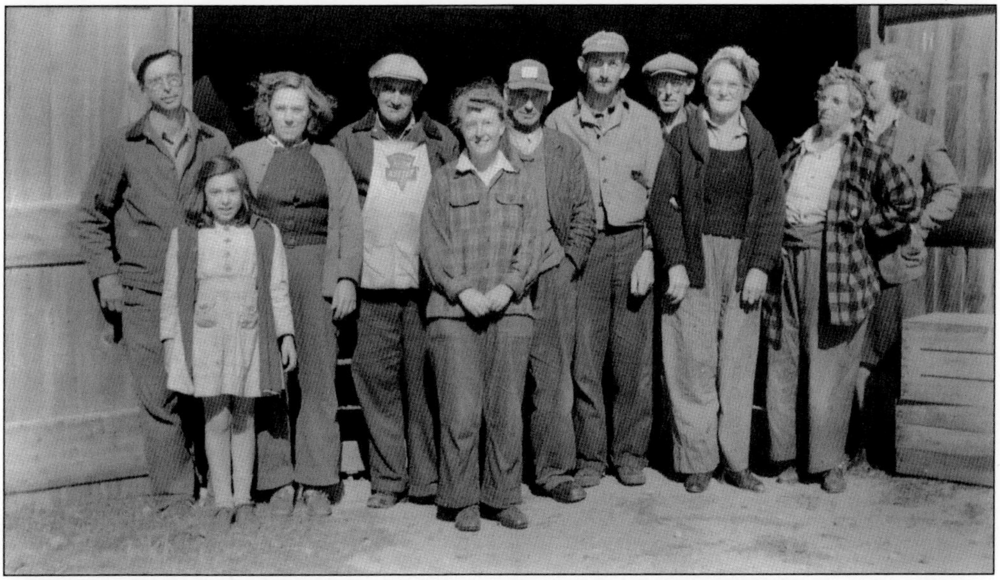

Employees of Drowne's Orchard stopped to pose for a photograph before heading out into the orchard for a day of picking fruit. From left to right are Albert and Marguerite Drowne with their daughter June, John Holmes Sr., Nellie Lovering, Fred Adams, Harold Lovering, James Paine, Charlotte Paine, Maude Holmes, and Doris Barnes. (Courtesy of June McNally.)

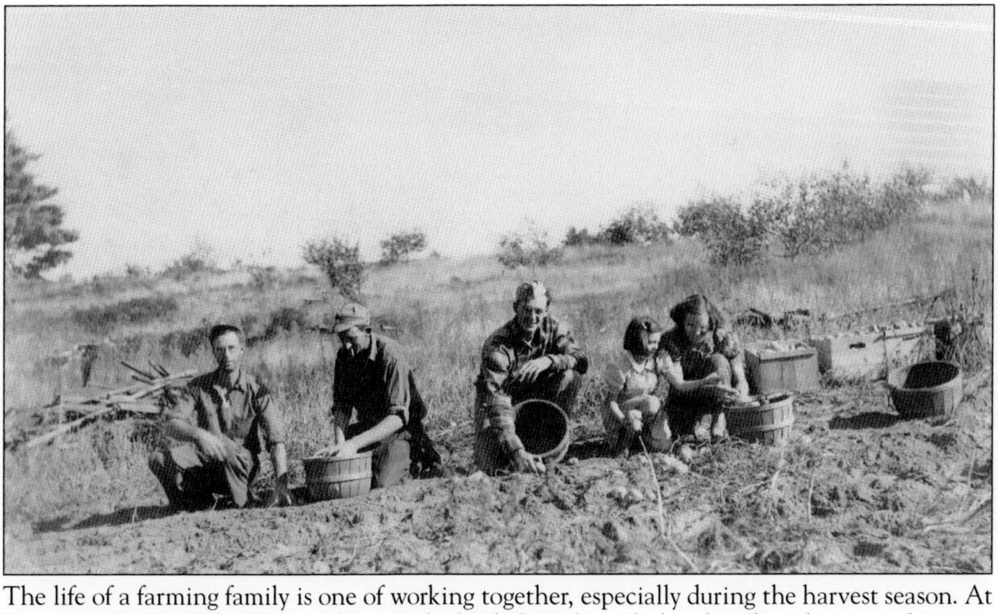

The life of a farming family is one of working together, especially during the harvest season. At Drowne's Orchard, family members worked side-by-side with farmhands to bring in the crop. Seen here from left to right are Albert Drowne, Harold Lovering, Fred Adams, June Drowne, and Marguerite Drowne. (Courtesy of June McNally.)

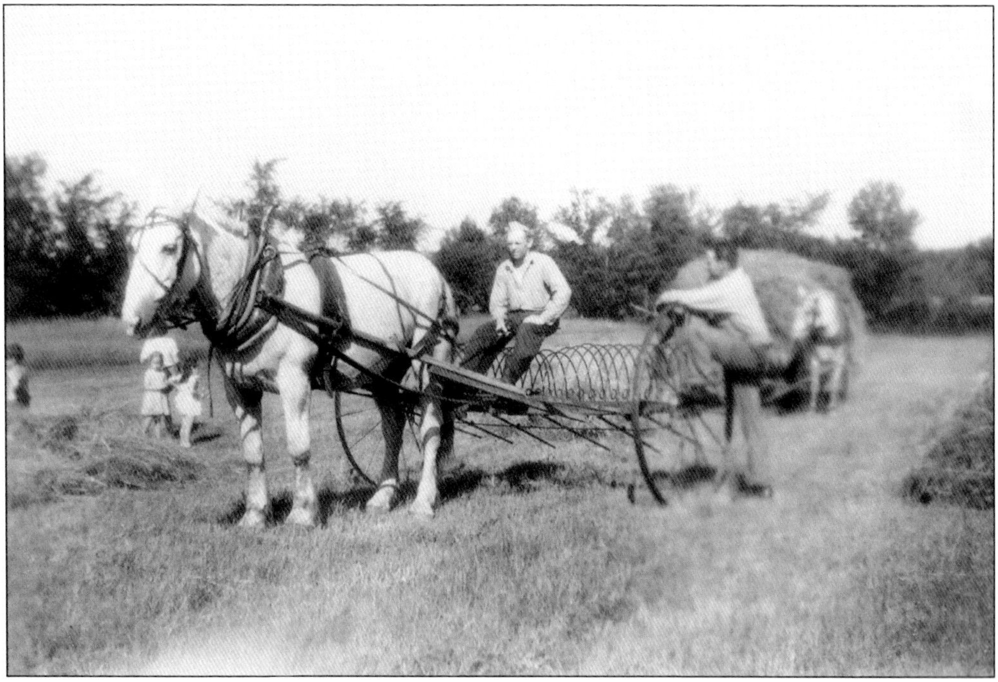

Working farms were a common sight in the 1940s and 1950s. Here, the owner of this farm, John James Pinard, drives his horse-drawn hay rake. Behind him is a load of hay, also pulled by a horse. The man on the right is unidentified. (Courtesy of Dorothy Batchelder.)

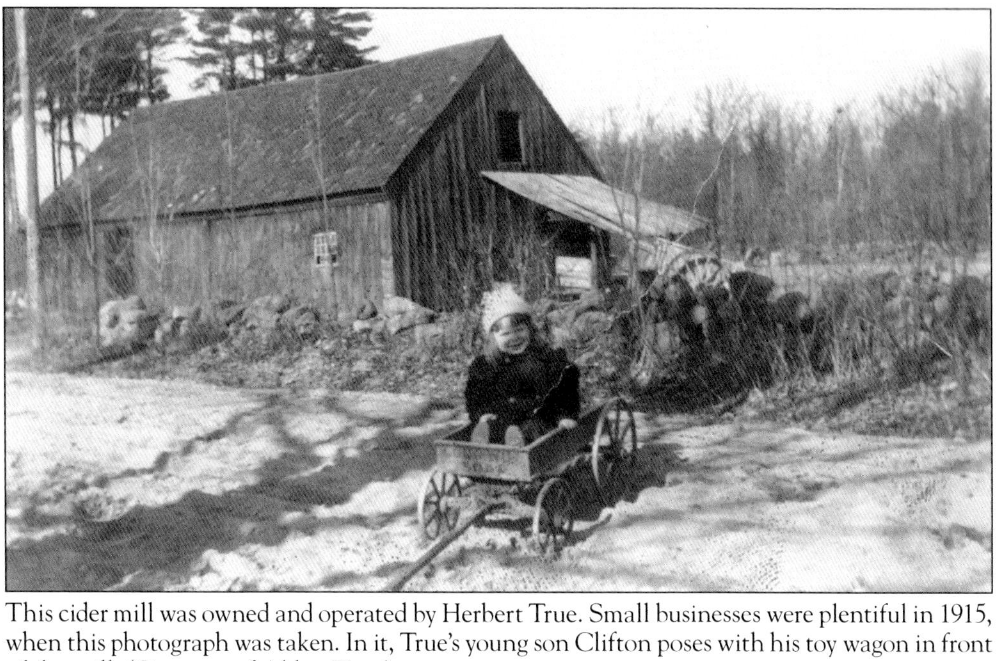

This cider mill was owned and operated by Herbert True. Small businesses were plentiful in 1915, when this photograph was taken. In it, True's young son Clifton poses with his toy wagon in front of the mill. (Courtesy of Alden True.)

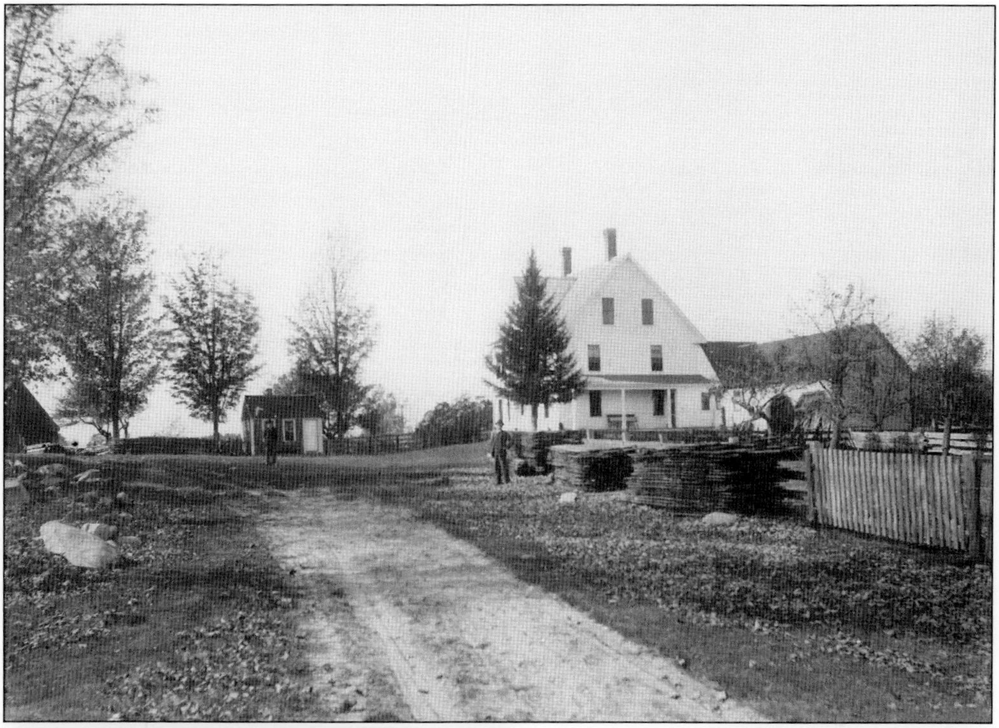

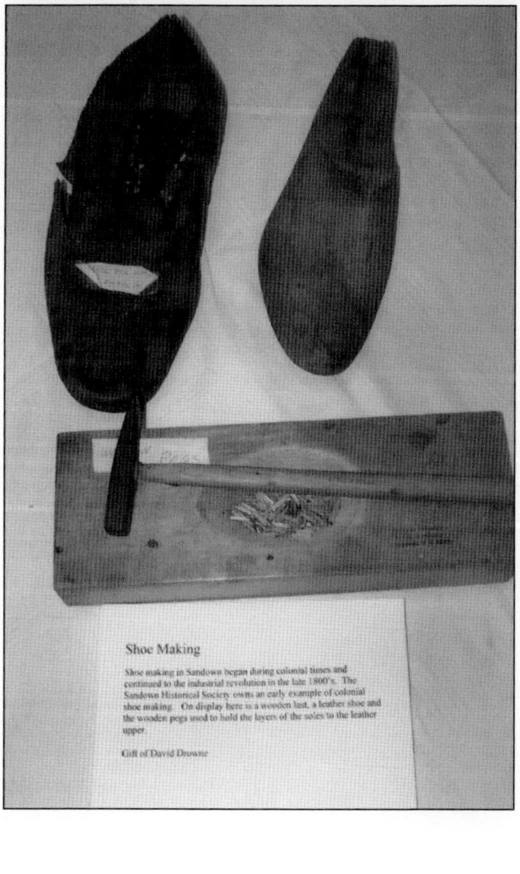

Beginning as a cottage industry, shoe making was a common side job for farmers. Above, on the Eliphlet Hunt farm, the small building to the left of the house was a one- or two-man shop that produced about 3,000 pairs of shoes a year. Once the railroad arrived, larger shoe shops such as the Elwin C. Mills shop on South Main Street arrived, which employed 60 workers and produced 3,000 pairs of shoes per day. (Courtesy of Robert and Lois MacKinnon.)

Shoe making in Sandown began during Colonial times and continued until the Industrial Revolution in the late 1800s. Seen here is a wooden last, a leather shoe, and the wooden pegs used to hold the layers of the soles to the leather upper. This exhibit can be seen at the Sandown Historical Museum. (Courtesy of the Sandown Historical Society.)

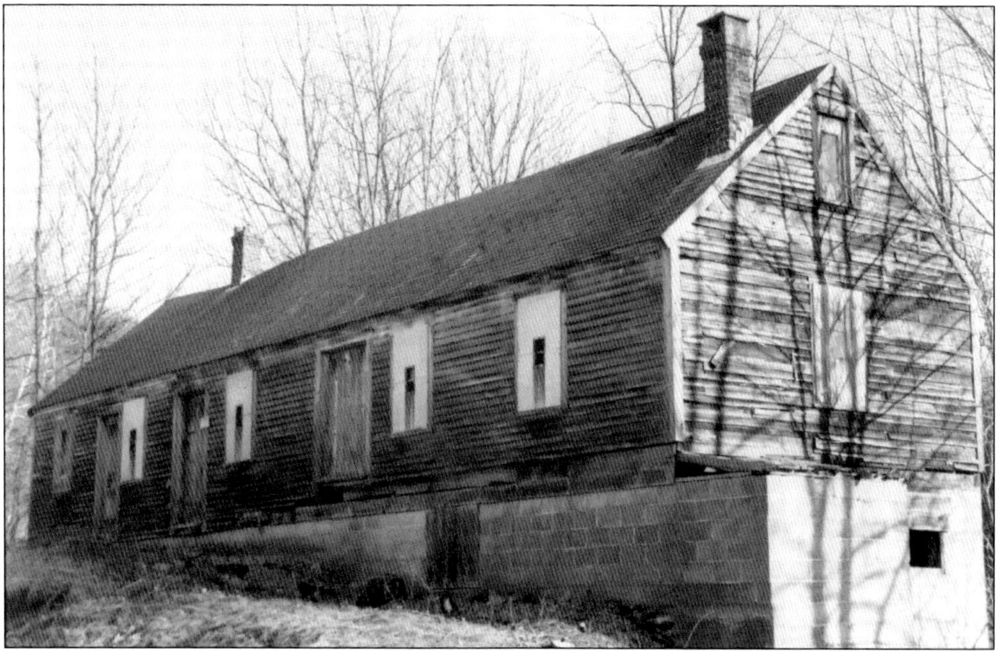

The George Fernald Griffin blacksmith shop stood at the top of what was known as Griffin's Hill on Main Street, which most town residents would now know as the beginning of the Roy L. Miller Recreational Field. In 1857, the building housed a shoe shop on the top floor and a blacksmith shop in the basement. In the 1980s, the building was razed by the fire department and replaced with the athletic fields. (Courtesy of Eleanor Bassett.)

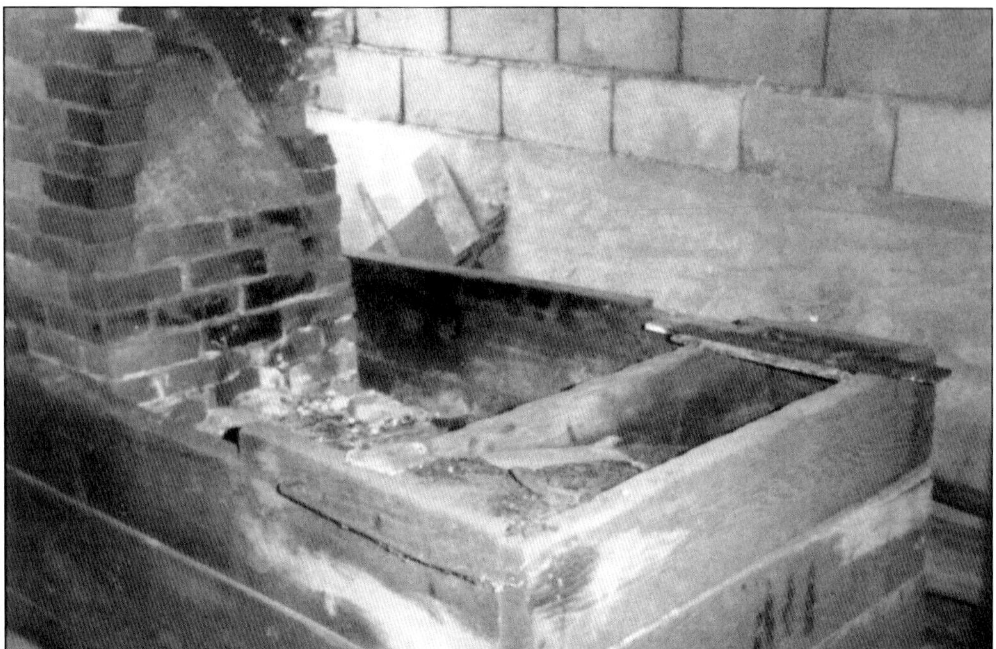

The remains of the 1850s forge used at the Griffin blacksmith shop on Main Street is seen here. The blacksmith shop was one of four in Sandown in 1857. (Courtesy of Eleanor Bassett.)

Starting with the first settler in 1736, the abundance of large trees attracted homesteaders to make a living while clearing the land for farming. Even the king of England had his cut of trees, since it was decreed that tracts of white pines were reserved for the king. In the late 1800s, the two largest mills were the Lovering mill and the Fessenden mill. Huge trees, like the one seen at right behind Leslie George (left) and Alvin Ray, were cut down and taken to a mill for processing. Unfortunately, it is rare to find trees this large in today's forests. Herbert True is seen below at his sawmill on Main Street, a fine example of the small family-owned industries that are a part of the town's history. (Right, courtesy of the Sandown Historical Society; below, courtesy of Alden True.)

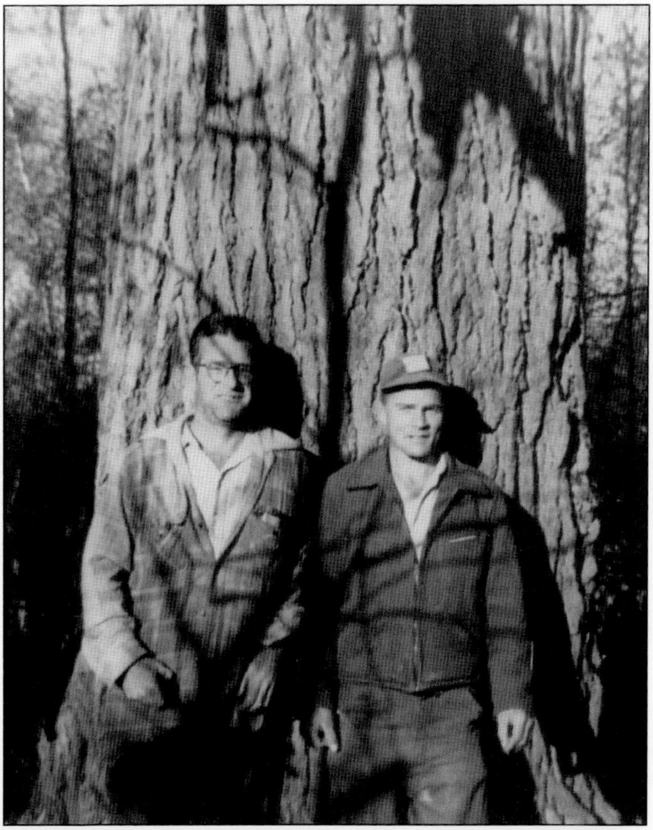

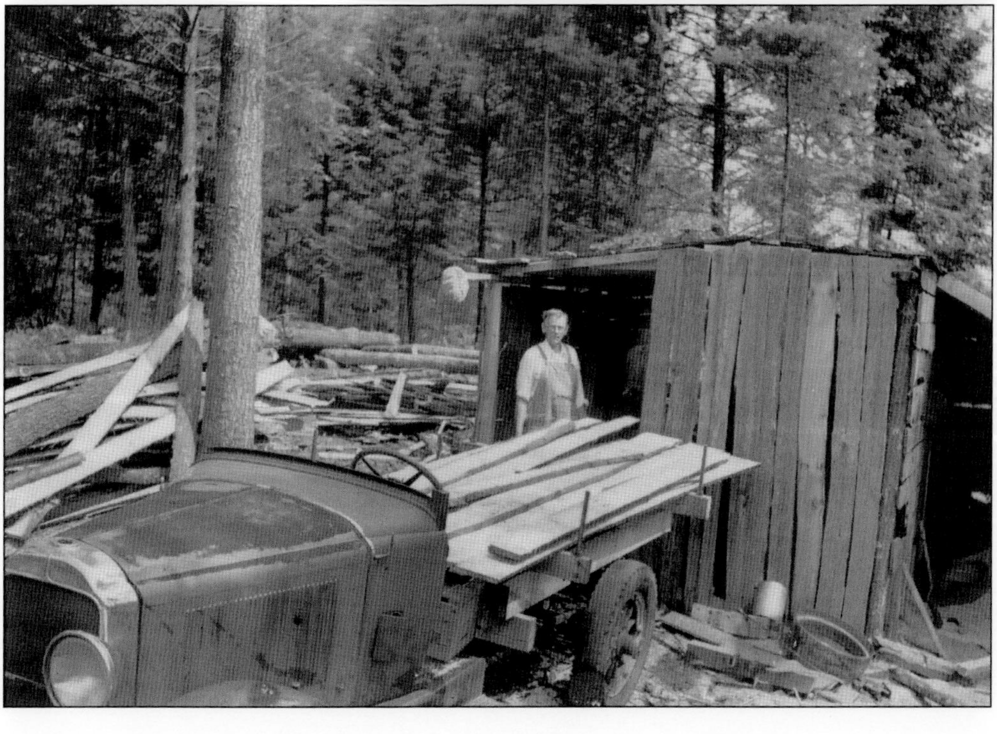

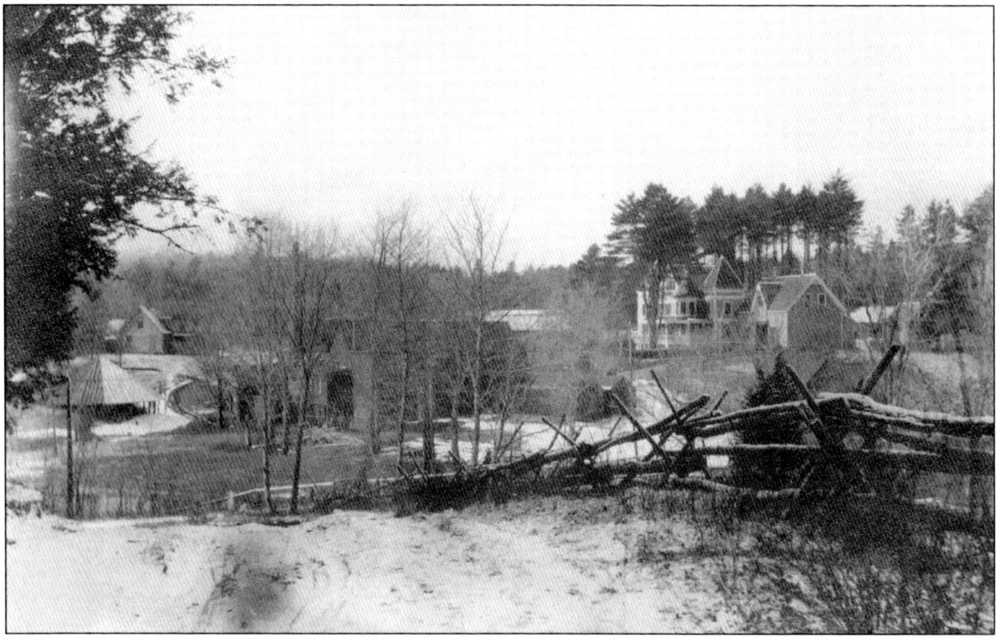

In 1877, brothers Frank and John W. Lovering started the Lovering mill on the Exeter River on North Main Street. After his brother's death a few years later, John had the foresight to diversify the sawmill to produce a variety of wood products, including buckets, washtubs, cloth boards, and even ice cream freezers. The second-largest mill in Sandown, the Lovering mill was quite successful, producing 50 tubs a day by 1890. During renovations to modernize the building in 1922, the mill was destroyed by a fire and never rebuilt. The grand home of John W. and Sarah Priscilla Lovering can be seen in the background of these two photographs, overlooking the mill. The home still stands today as a reminder of a bygone era. (Both, courtesy of Eleanor Bassett.)

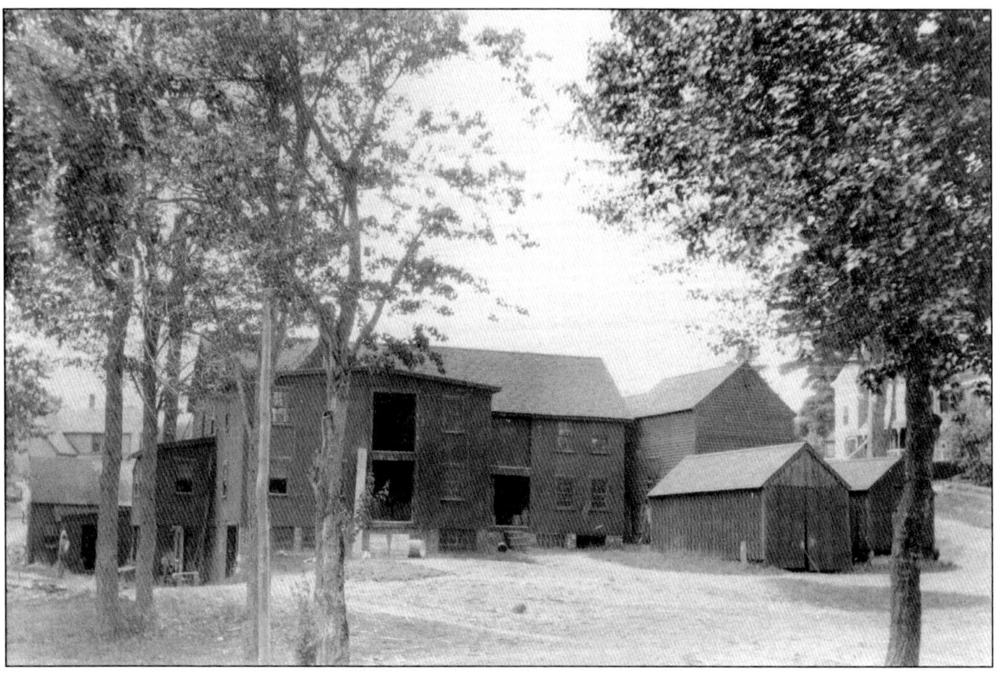

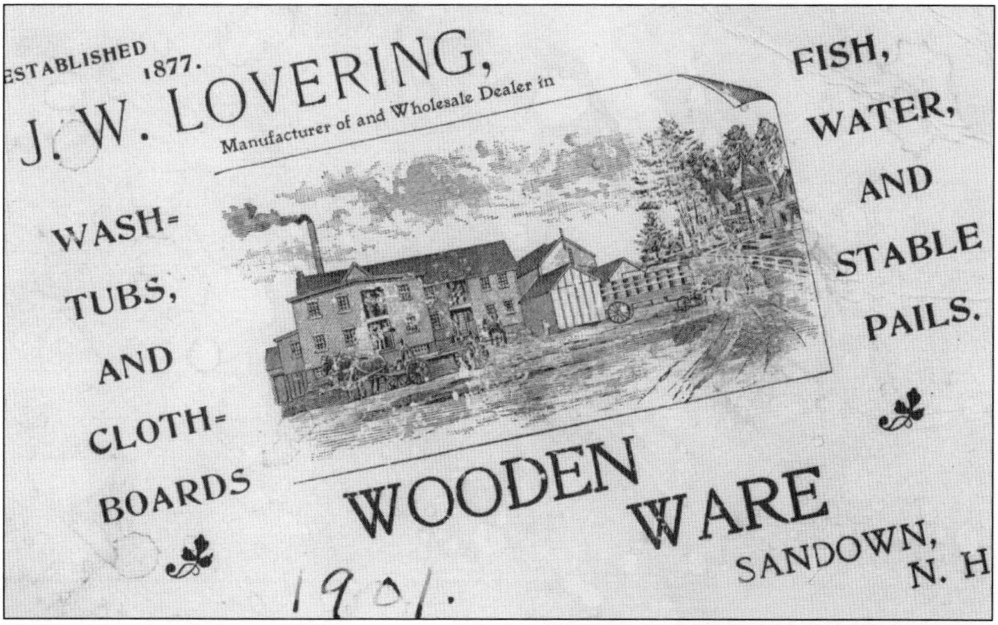

In the 1901 advertisement above, John W. Lovering promoted himself as a manufacturer and wholesale dealer of wooden ware, including washtubs, cloth boards, and pails for fish, water, and stable use. With the convenience of the railroad for transporting his goods, Lovering was able to expand his markets to the larger cities. (Courtesy of Eleanor Bassett.)

DELIVERED PRICE LIST OF TUBS.

OIL in.Tubs, 2 in nest	$1.20
" " " 3 "	1.55
" " " 8 "	2.05
" " " No. 1, per doz.	8.00
" " " " 2, "	6.50
" " " " 3, "	5.00
" " " " 0, "	10.20
PTD. in.Tubs, 2 in nest	1.15
" " " 3 "	1.45
" " " 8 "	1.95
" " " No. 1,per doz.	7.60
" " " " 2, "	6.25
" " " " 3, "	4.50

KEELERS.

OIL in.Keelers, 5 in nest	$ .80
" " " No. 1, per doz.	3.00
" " " " 2, "	2.60
" " " " 3, "	2.15
" " " " 4, "	1.55
" " " " 5, "	1.15
PTD. in Keelers, 5 in nest	,70.
" " " No. 1, per doz.	2.60
" " " " 2, "	1.90
" " " " 3, "	1.55
" " " " 4, "	1.35
" " " " 5, "	1.00

10 per cent. off on orders of 25 dollars or more value.
15 " " " " " 100 " " "

J.W.LOVERING, SANDOWN, N. H.
ESTABLISHED 1877.

According to this price list of tubs, the Lovering mill charged $1.20 for two wooden buckets that were delivered to one's home or business. A keeler was a broad, shallow wooden tub that was used mainly for cooling liquids such as cream. A set of five oiled keelers cost 80¢. (Courtesy of Eleanor Bassett.)

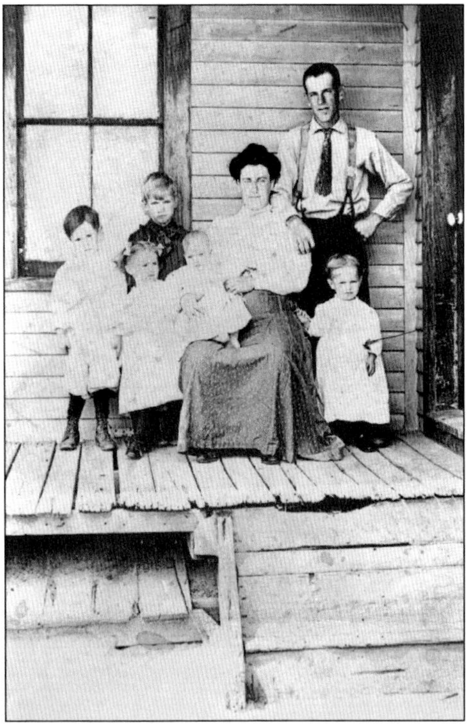

In 1905, the Fessenden mill, located on Depot Road near the railroad station, opened for business. This 1910 photograph shows mill worker Clarence George and his family. Although George died at age 40, his daughter Constance lived to the age of 101 years old. Her daughter Virginia Morris still lives in Sandown. This home, on Main Street, is now owned by David and Christine Augusta. From left to right are Kenneth, Doris, Chester, baby Leslie, Ida, George, and Constance. (Courtesy of the Sandown Historical Society.)

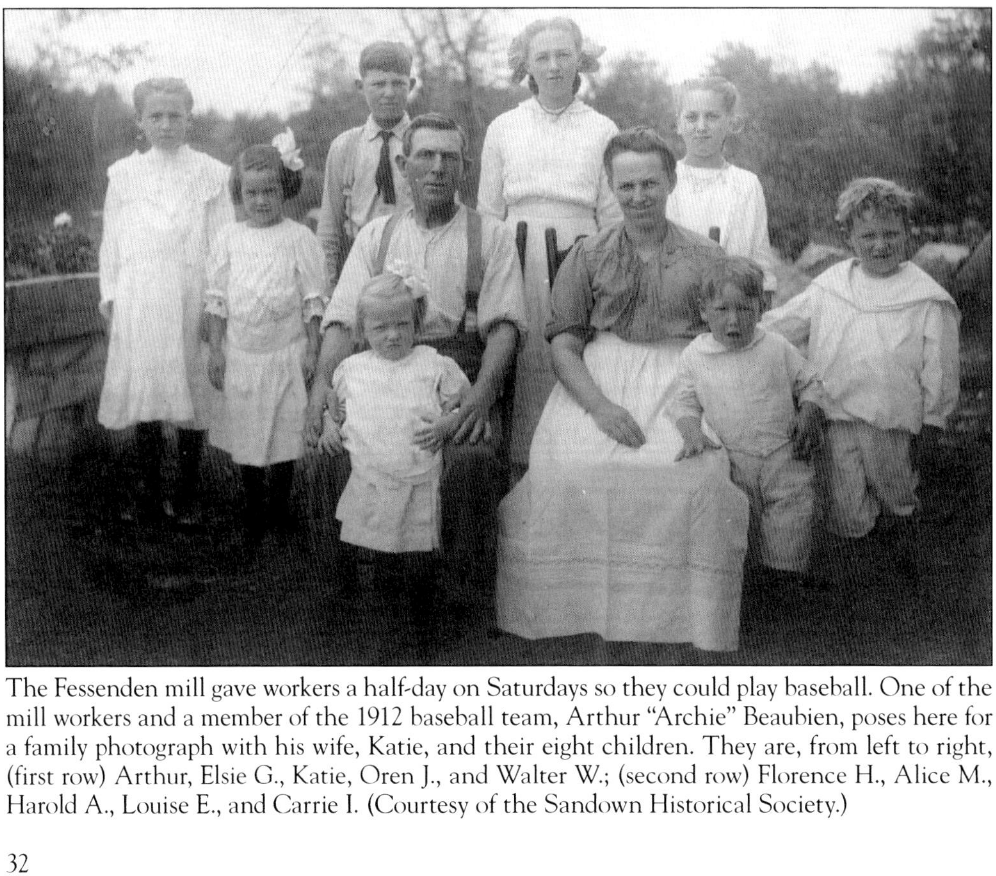

The Fessenden mill gave workers a half-day on Saturdays so they could play baseball. One of the mill workers and a member of the 1912 baseball team, Arthur "Archie" Beaubien, poses here for a family photograph with his wife, Katie, and their eight children. They are, from left to right, (first row) Arthur, Elsie G., Katie, Oren J., and Walter W.; (second row) Florence H., Alice M., Harold A., Louise E., and Carrie I. (Courtesy of the Sandown Historical Society.)

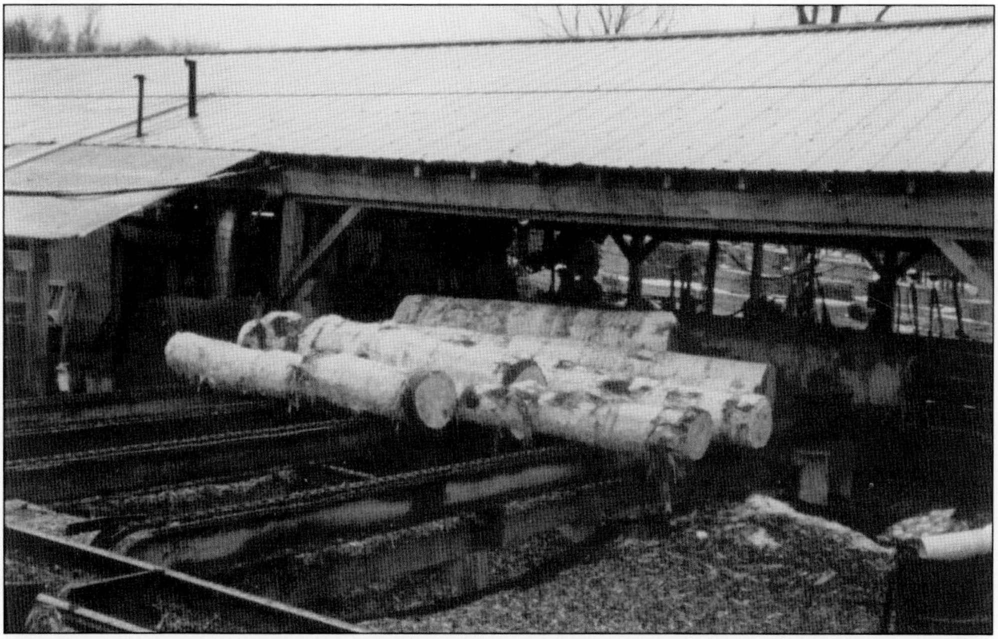

Woodbury Lane Sawmill, seen here, was a newer mill with more modern equipment that was run by electricity. It was owned and operated by Drowne Enterprises but is no longer in operation. (Courtesy of David Drowne.)

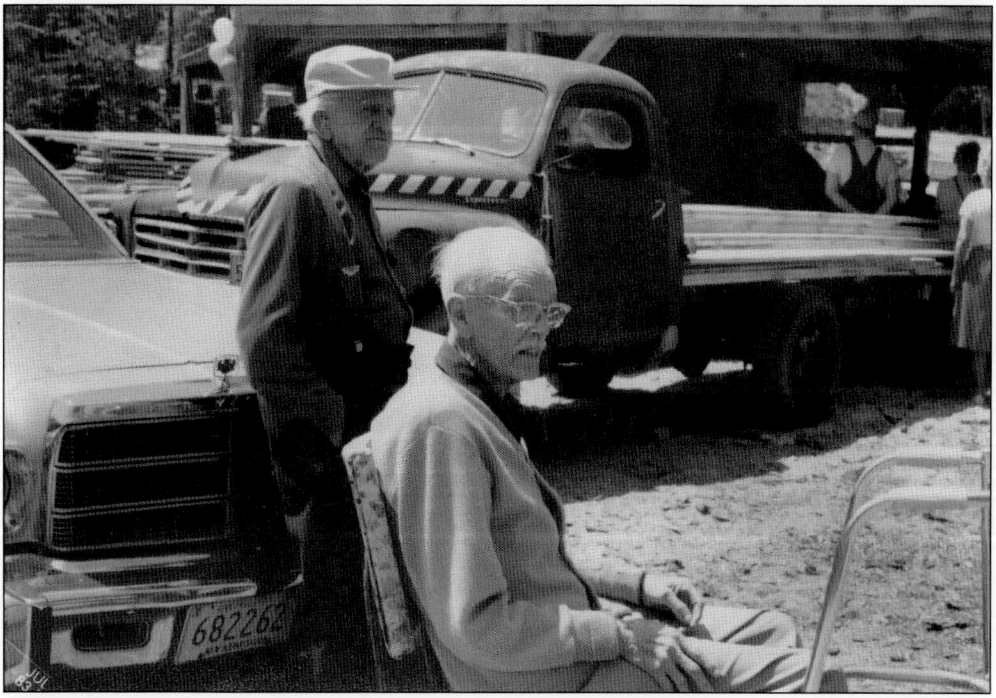

These two Sandown old-timers, Raymond Bassett and Ernest Pillsbury, attended the opening of Woodbury Lane Sawmill in the 1970s. The lumber mill was a welcome enterprise for employment in the small town, which was seeing more of its residents travel out of town for work. (Courtesy of David Drowne.)

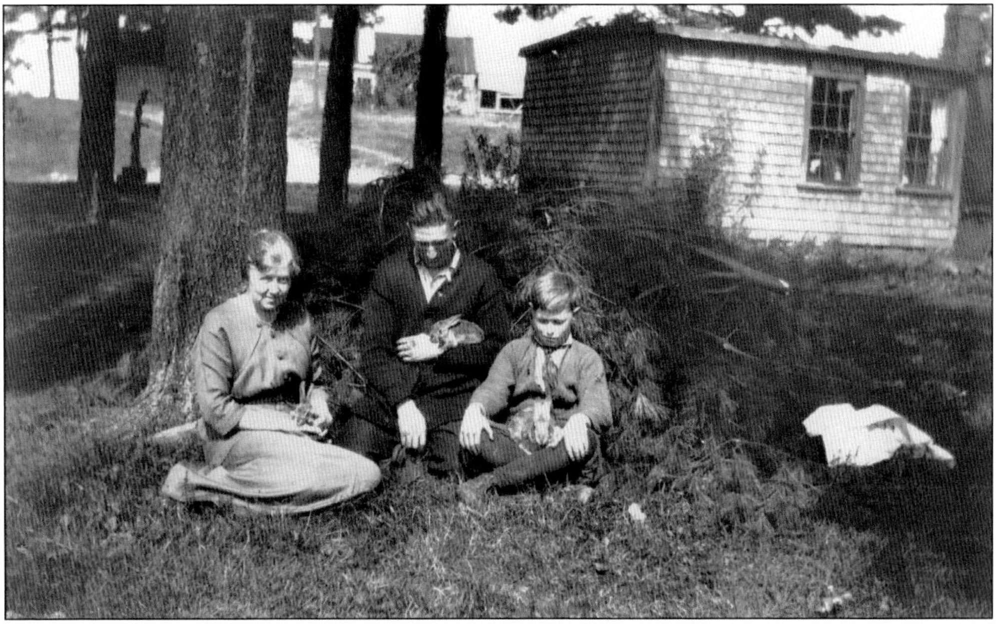

Although mills in large cities were notorious for poor working conditions, the Fessenden mill provided some housing for its workers, including a two-story tenement and small homes on the property. The mill also shut down production during the planting and harvesting seasons so that workers could take care of their farms. Here, Fessendon mill worker Leon Follansbee enjoys a day off with his wife, Bertha Louise Tenney Follansbee, and their son Ralph. (Courtesy of the Sandown Historical Society.)

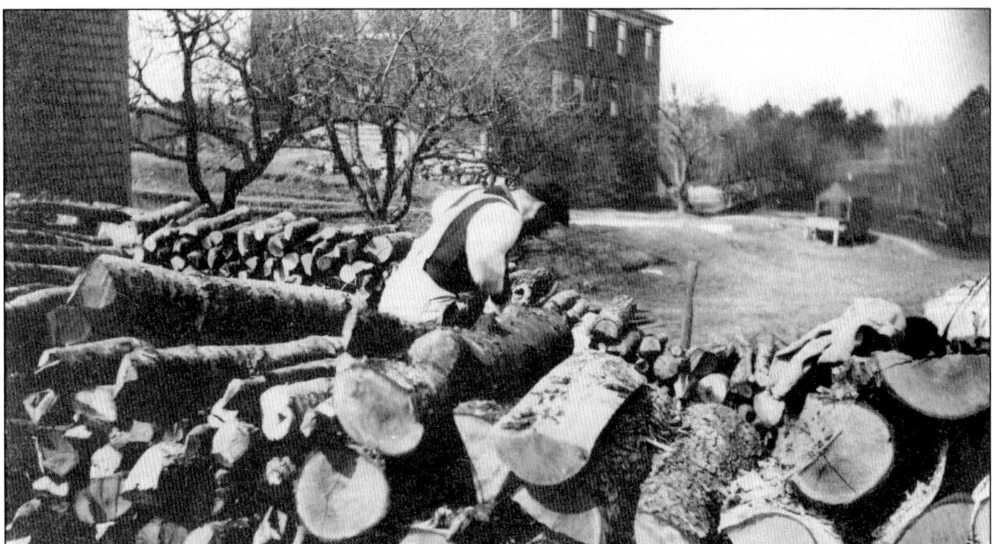

George Bassett, the proprietor of Bassett's store, cuts and stacks wood for the upcoming winter. In the background is Sanborn Hall. Bassett's store was located next to St. Matthews Church. When it burned down in 1998, it was owned by Kenneth Perrino. (Courtesy of Eleanor Bassett.)

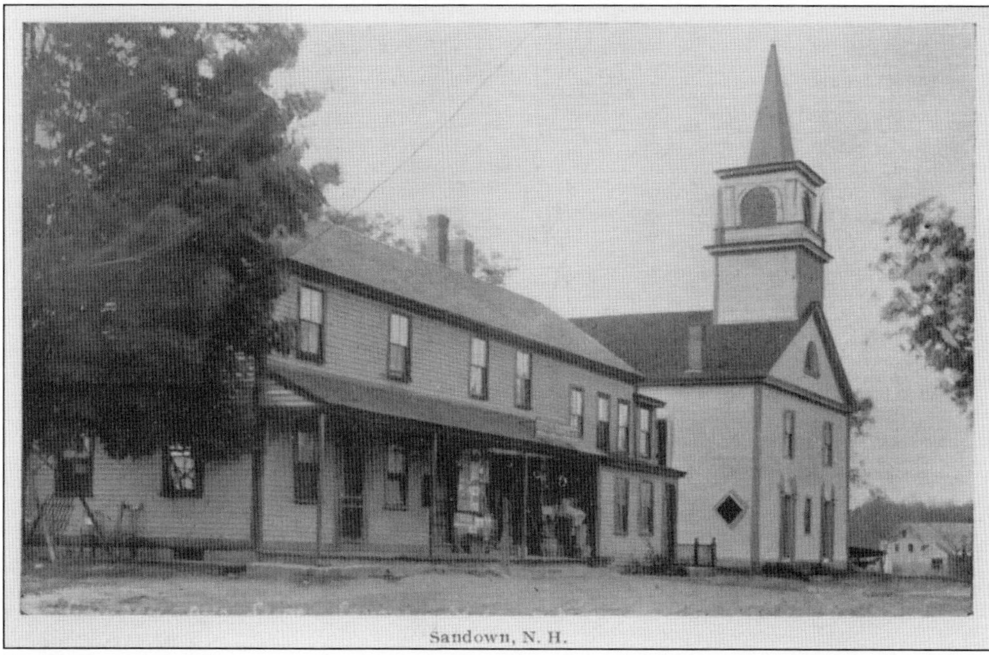

Known mostly by the name of its proprietor at the time, the "Center Store" was conveniently located on Main Street in the center of town, next to the Methodist church. As in many small towns, the store was more than a place to buy groceries. This store also housed the public library in 1892, demonstrated the first phonograph, and had the first telephone. In the 1960s, the store included a snack bar, a pinball machine, and a pool table. (Courtesy of Eleanor Bassett.)

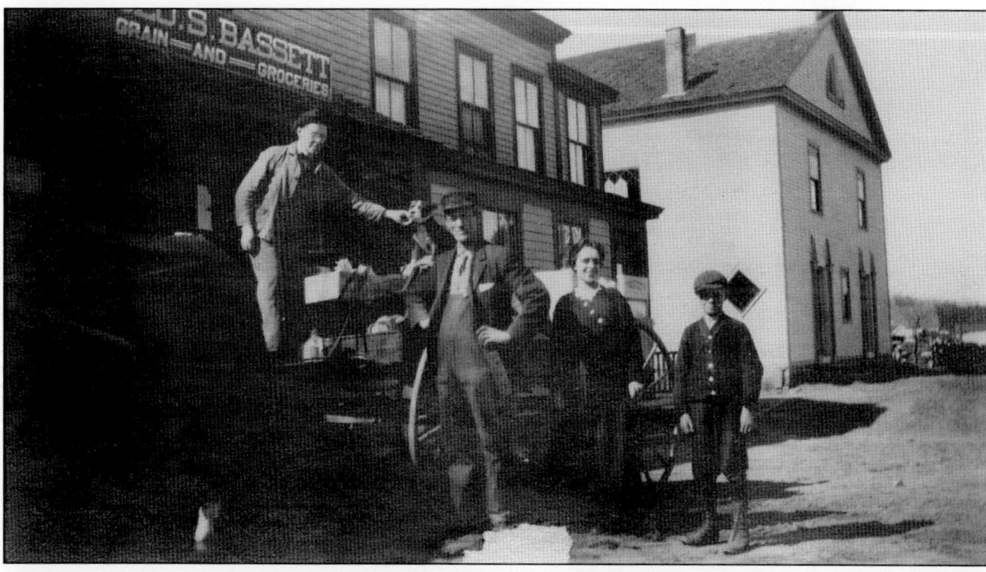

Proudly posing with their wagon loaded with supplies, this family was one of many who bought their grain and groceries at Bassett's store. George S. Bassett was one of 18 owners of the "Center Store" through the years. The Sanborn family owned and operated it for the longest stretch of time: 40 years, from 1863 to 1910. The store was in continuous operation from 1841 until a fire destroyed the structure in 1998. (Courtesy of Eleanor Bassett.)

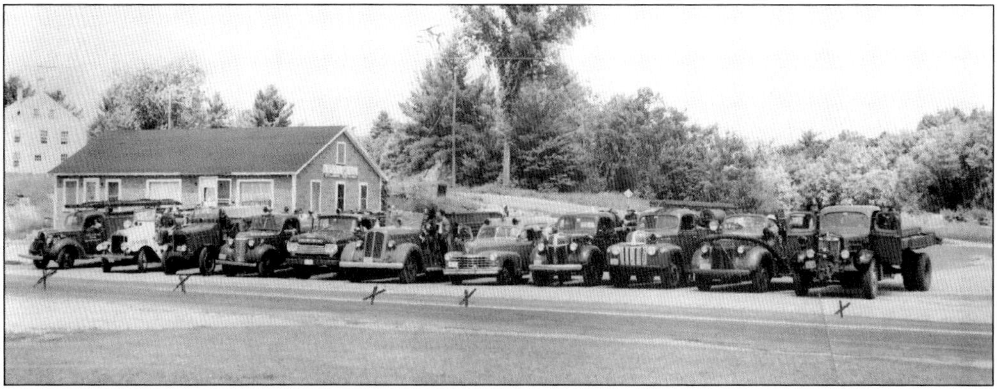

Fire trucks are lined up for a parade in front of Dinsmore's store on Main Street, near the depot. Willard and Mary Dinsmore owned the grocery store from 1943 to 1955. It continued as a market until 1968. After years as a rental property, the building was recently converted back into a store and is now the A&M Sandown Market. (Courtesy of the Sandown Fire Department.)

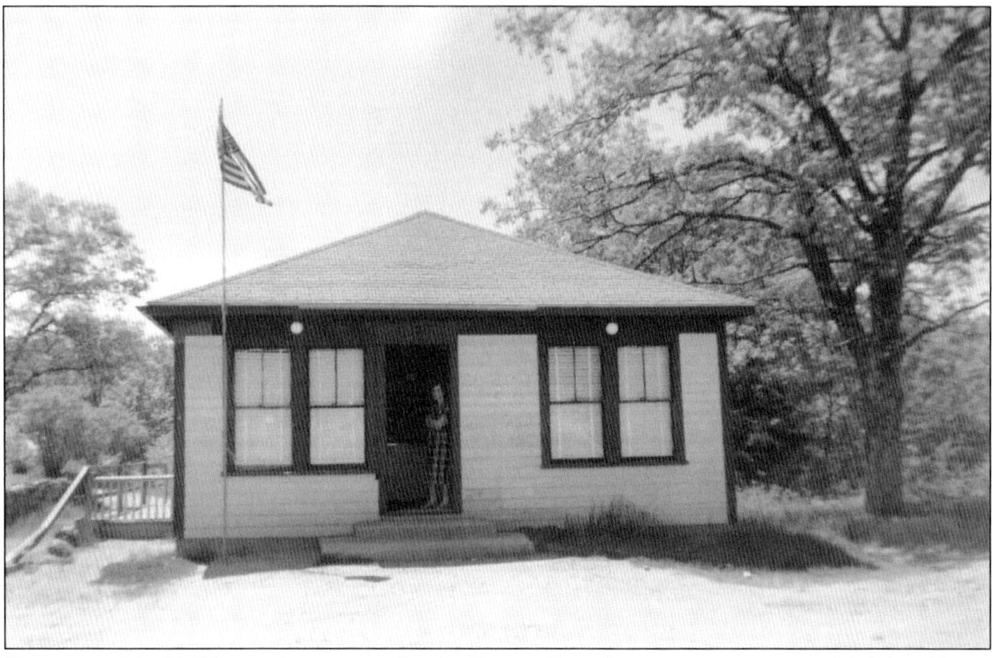

Constructed in 1926 by stationmaster Charles Burton French as a grocery store on his Main Street property, this small building served as the town's post office from 1926 to 1960. The post office was then moved farther north on Main Street to a carriage house near its current location. This building is now a private residence. (Courtesy of Eleanor Bassett.)

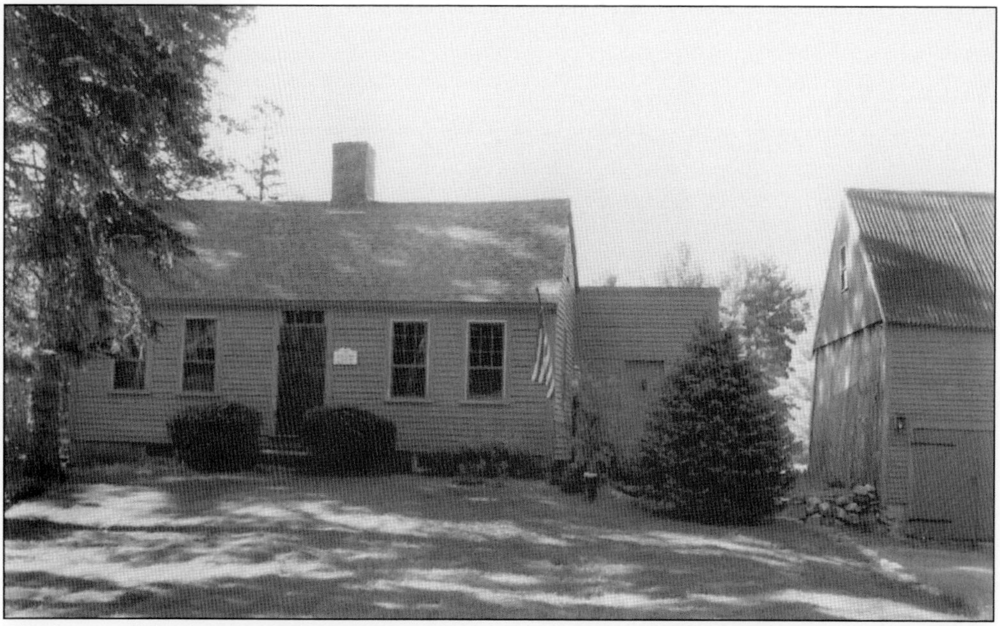

The home of the family of Theoliphilius Eaton, one of the founding families of Sandown, served as a tavern and as the area's first school in 1756. The home is on the corner of Odell Road and Main Street. Eaton had to apply for a license to operate a tavern in his home. (Courtesy of the Sandown Historical Society.)

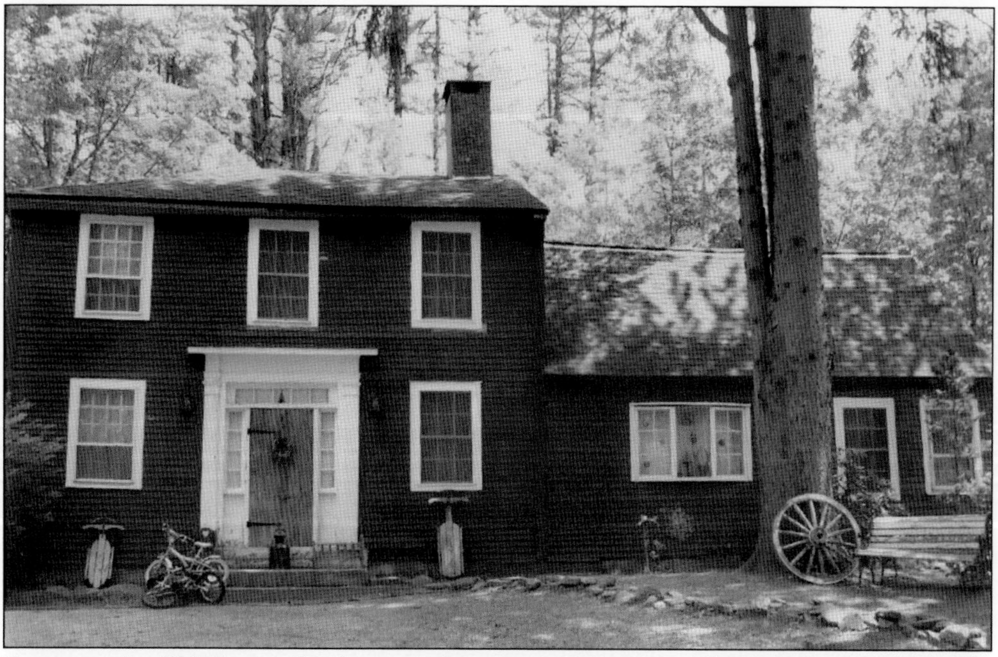

Known as the Old Tavern, this home at the corner of Fremont and North Roads was built by Jonathan Sanborn. It is one of the oldest buildings in Sandown and is believed to have served as a tavern in the 1700s, when the territory was still part of Kingston. The main route from Chester to Kingston passed by this property, making it a convenient resting place for travelers. (Courtesy of the Sandown Historical Society.)

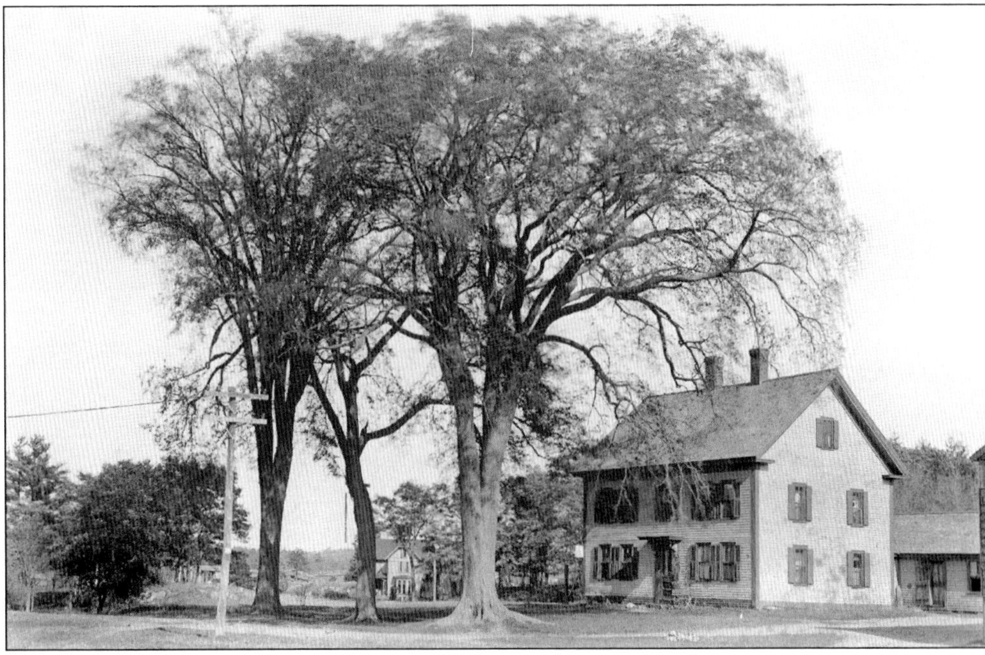

With three large elm trees in the front yard, the Triple Elms Hotel, on Main Street across from the Methodist church, was easy for guests to find. It was also a short walk from the railroad depot and close to Phillips Pond, making it a popular resort stop. The home is currently owned by Lisa Peterson. Two businesses are located on the property, Bruchetti's Restaurant and Little Patriots Daycare Center. (Courtesy of Eleanor Bassett.)

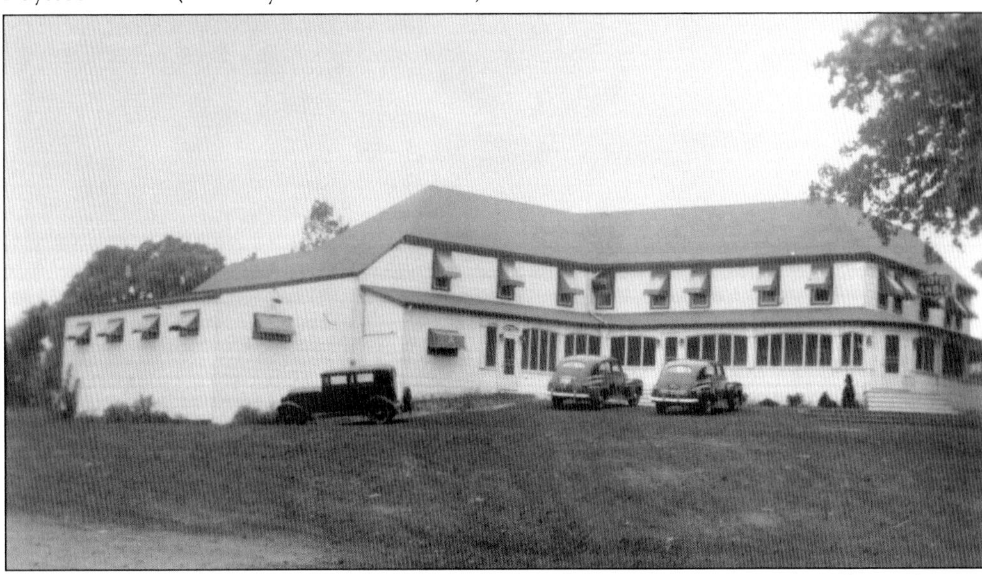

The Angle Pond Hotel was a popular tourist destination from 1948 to 1962. Brothers John and Francis Lagasse created the hotel and banquet hall by renovating the former Pillsbury home on South Main Street. By 1955, the business was known as Church's Holiday Inn and owners Frederick and Emily Church had added a restaurant and bar. Serving all-you-can-eat chicken dinners for $1 made the restaurant popular with area residents as well. A fire in 1962 destroyed the building. (Courtesy of the Sandown Historical Society.)

Three

Sandown Homes and Families

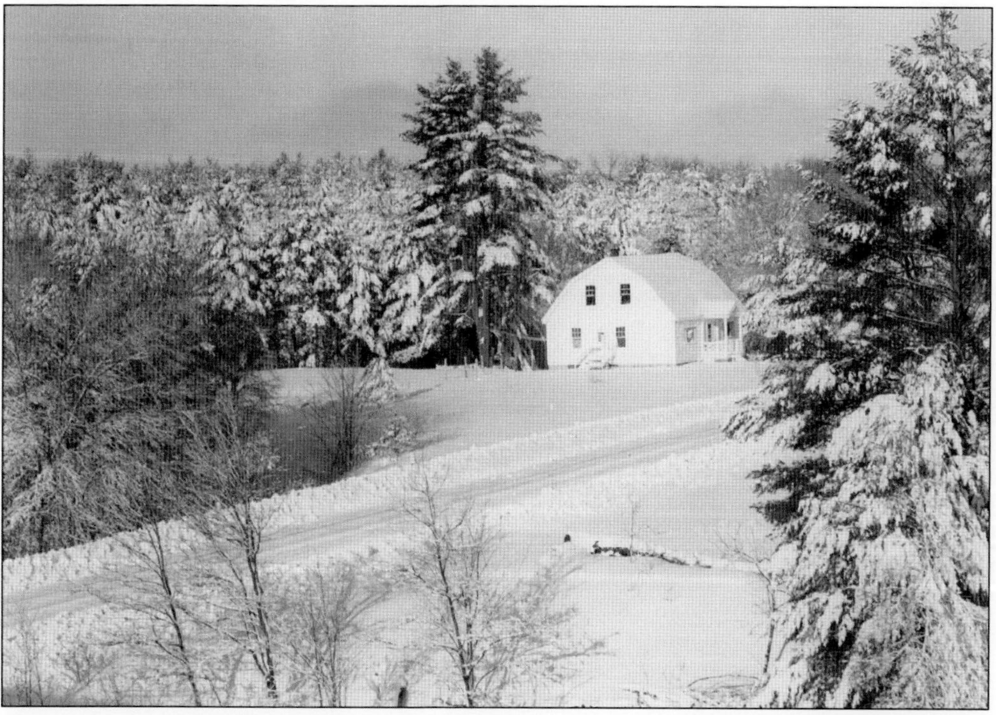

This is a lovely winter photograph of the home built by Steven Arnold Buckley, the son of general store owner Mary Dinsmore. Buckley refused to sell coffee ice cream to children. He believed it was not good for them and would simply say, "I think you had better choose another kind." This home, on Main Street across from the post office, is now the commercial office of Sue Padden Real Estate, LLC. (Photograph by Mal Cameron; courtesy of the Sandown Public Library.)

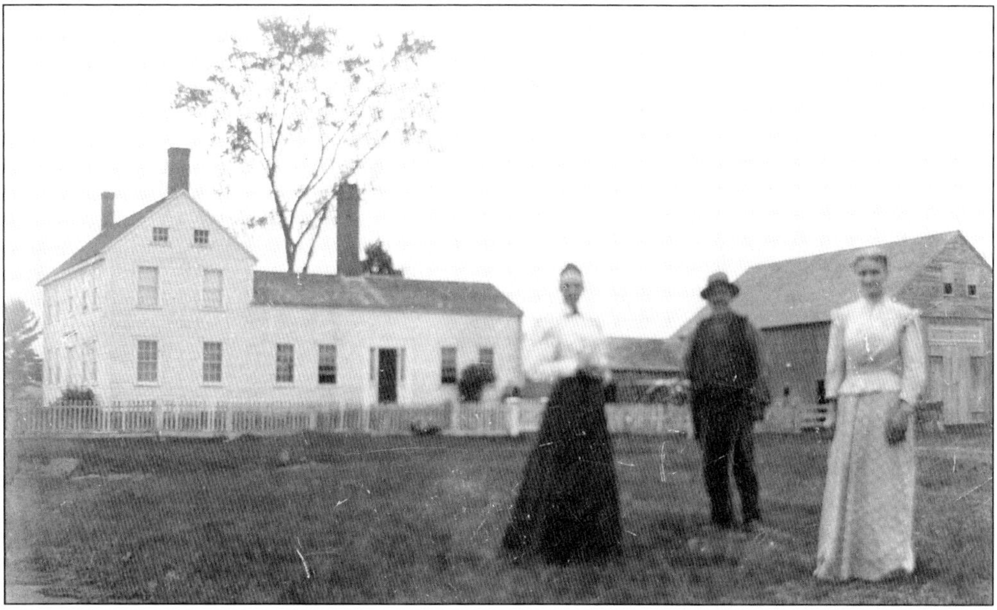

Across the street from the Old Meeting House stands the original Peter Colby home, built in the 1700s. Colby served as a church deacon and was active in town government. In the early 1900s, the home was owned by the Fitts family, seen here. They are, from left to right, Mary Jane, Edwin, and Helen Fitts. Although the barn is no longer standing, most of the original home remains today. The current owners are Brad and Carol Robie. (Courtesy of Eleanor Bassett.)

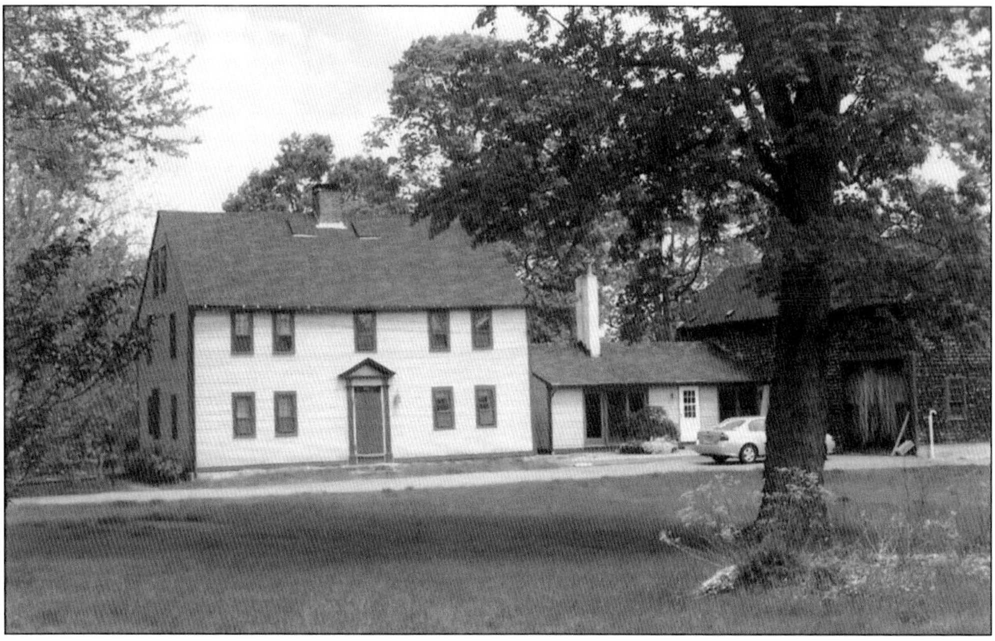

This home on Fremont Road dates from before 1756. It was owned by John Colby, who, in 1773, donated land to build a meetinghouse. The Sandown Public Library had its beginnings here under the direction of Celia Colby. Eventually, Thomas and Agnes Shaw purchased the home, leaving it to their son Adm. Howard R. Shaw, who lived here for many years when he was not on board a ship. (Courtesy of the Sandown Historical Society.)

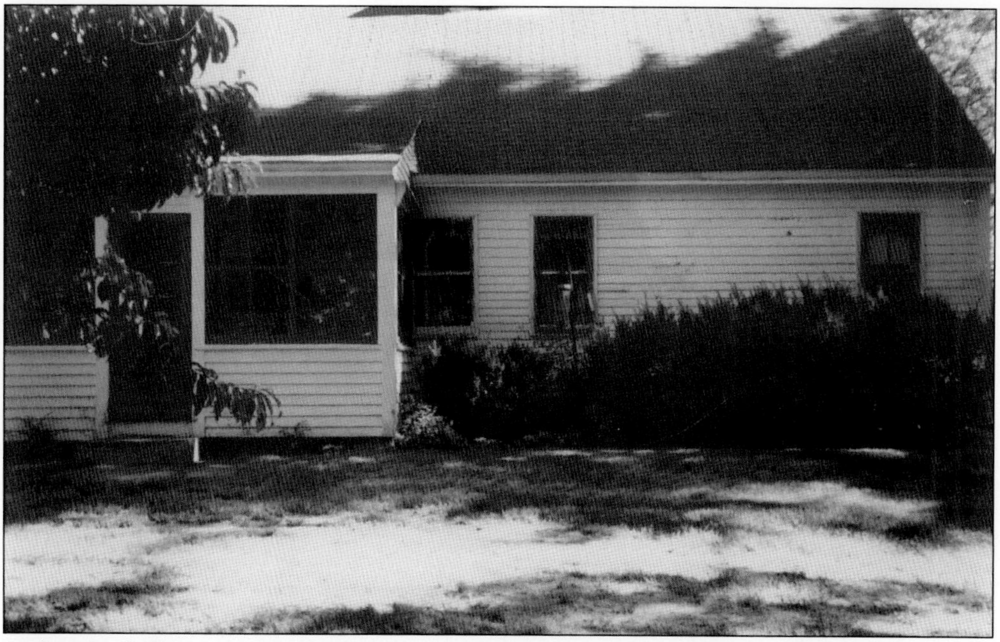

Built around 1740 on North Road, this is the oldest house still standing in Sandown. It was also the home of Sandown's first post office. Albert and Marguerite Drowne and their two daughters lived here for many years. Today, Allison and Keith Kellerman live here with their three sons. Allison is the granddaughter of Albert and Marguerite Drowne. (Courtesy of June McNally.)

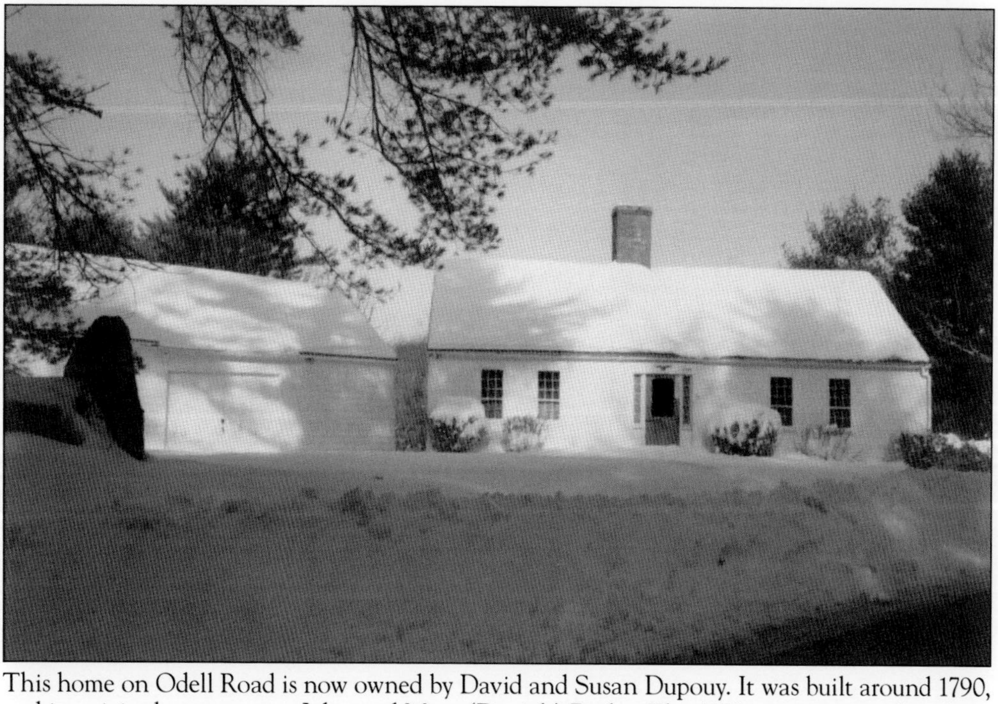

This home on Odell Road is now owned by David and Susan Dupouy. It was built around 1790, and its original owners were John and Mary (Daniels) Butler. The 1810 census states that there were eight people living in the home. Butler was born in Sandown in 1763. He died in 1811 and is buried in the Center Cemetery. (Courtesy of Susan Dupouy.)

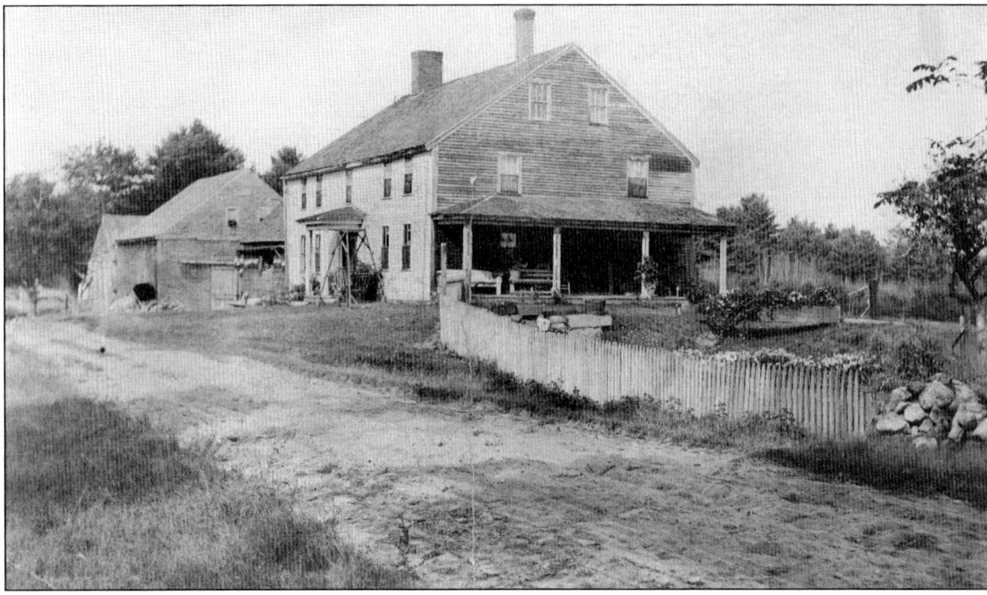

This home, known as Tilton Place, was built in 1744. The Tiltons made their living by making leather. Timothy Tilton helped build the meetinghouse in 1773 and served as a selectmen beginning in 1778. For many years, this was the home of F. Edward and Bertha Deveau and their five children. Bertha Deveau is now the curator of the Depot Museum, and their youngest daughter, Patricia Teague, still resides in Sandown. (Courtesy of the Sandown Historical Society.)

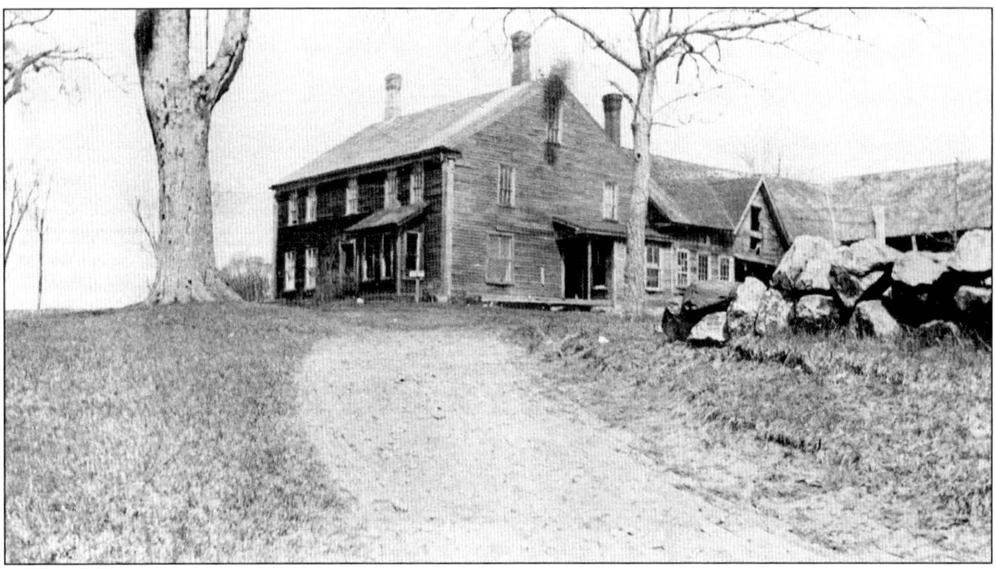

This house was built by Winslow Fogg in 1775 and used as a tavern. The frame was reportedly raised during the Battle of Bunker Hill. Joseph and Lucy Bingham lived here in the early 1900s. Later, Everett and Evelyn (Brown) Huckins raised their large family here. It is now the home of Edward Mencis and Linda Meehan and also the home of Playmates Preschool and Sandlot Sports. (Courtesy of Lillian Loring.)

An unidentified lady poses for a photograph on October 6, 1911. Considering the heavy clothing she had to wear, she must have been happy to see the hot summer days behind her. (Courtesy of Marion Jean.)

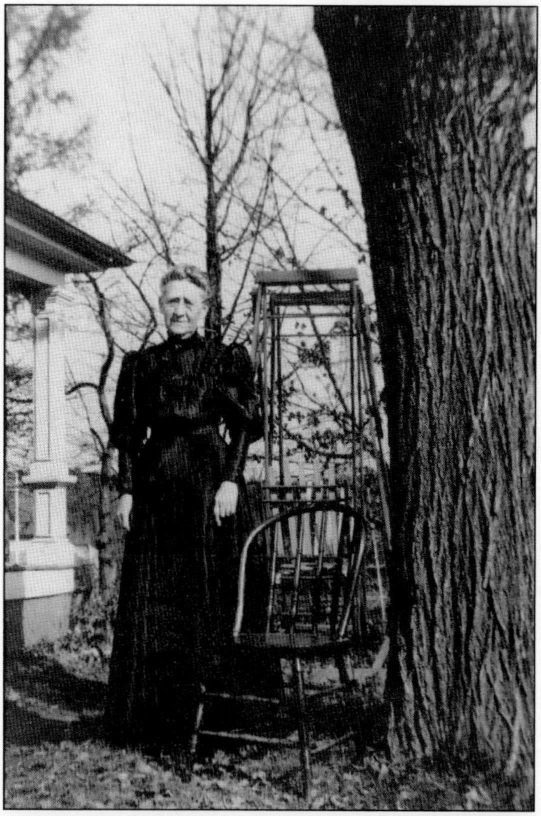

The back of the photograph below says, "To Aunt Flora from Charlie." It is not known who Charlie was, but Aunt Flora was Flora Kelley, the beloved matriarch of the well-known Kelley family. Charlie was obviously very proud of his team of oxen. (Courtesy of Marion Jean.)

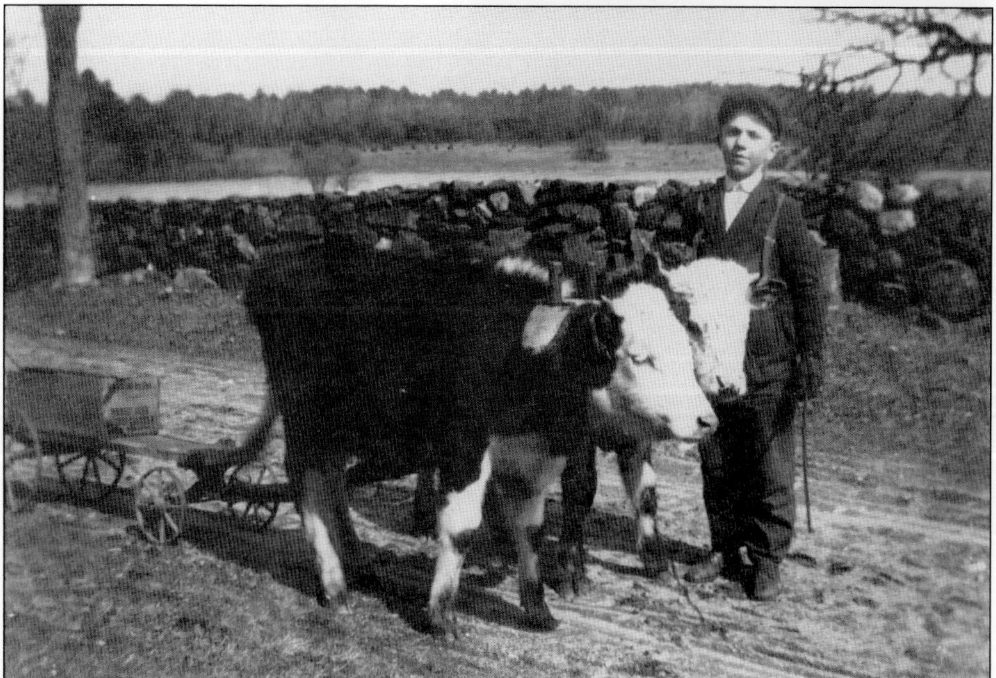

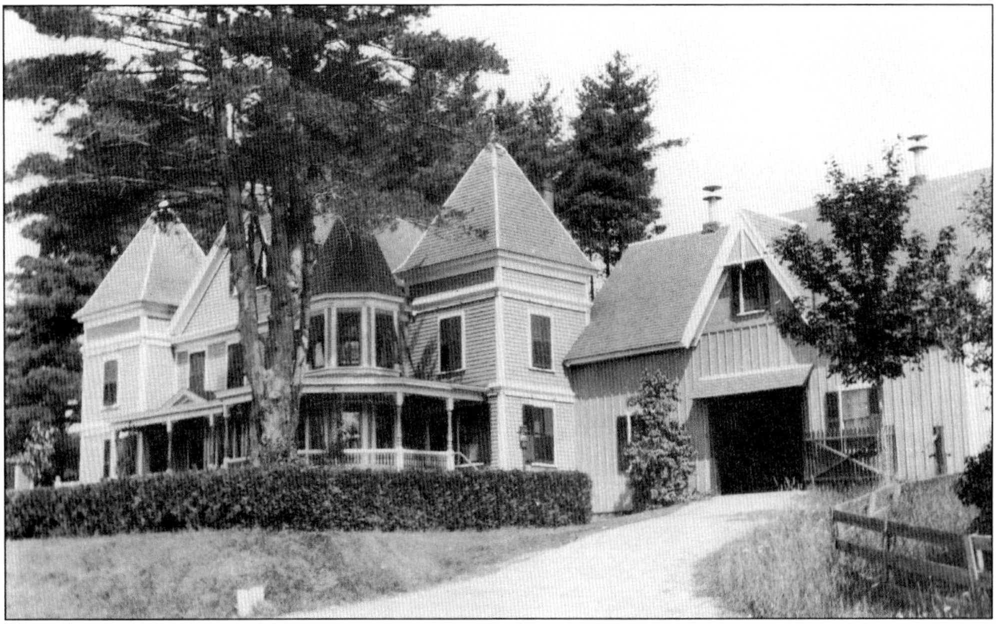

This home is known by most Sandown residents as "the Victorian on Main Street." Its most famous owner was John Lovering, who owned and operated the Lovering mill. Later, the home was willed to the Methodist Church and then sold to Ralph True, who operated a sawmill there. More photographs of this historic property are in chapter two. The Jarvis family lives there today. (Courtesy of Eleanor Bassett.)

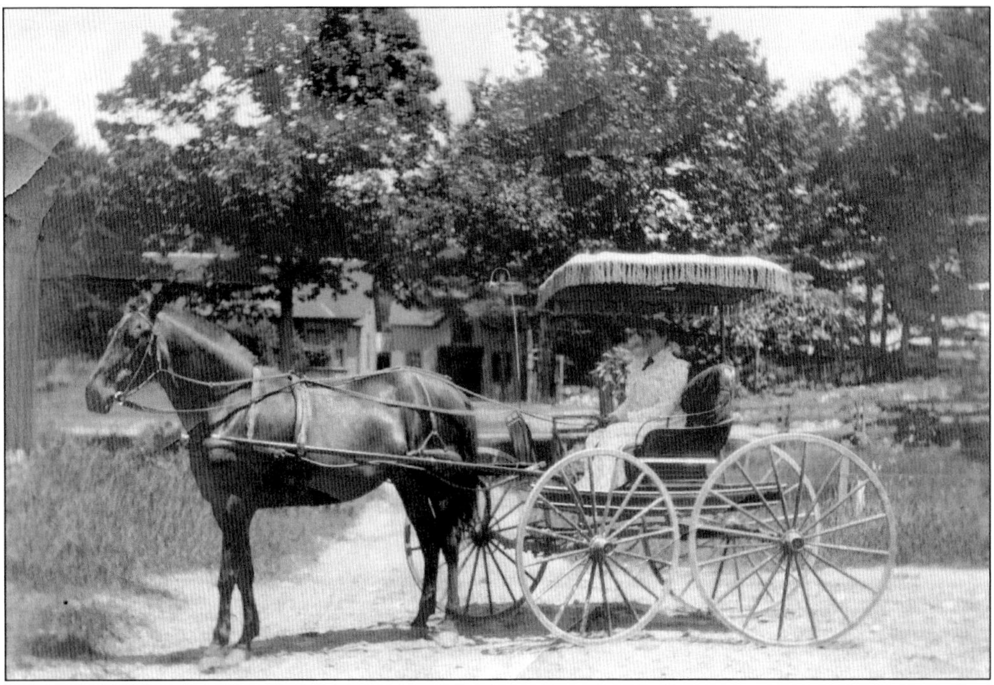

Even though the Lovering mill was prosperous enough for John W. Lovering to purchase the first automobile in Sandown in 1902, it looks as though Sarah Priscilla Lovering preferred to travel by horse and buggy. (Courtesy of Eleanor Bassett.)

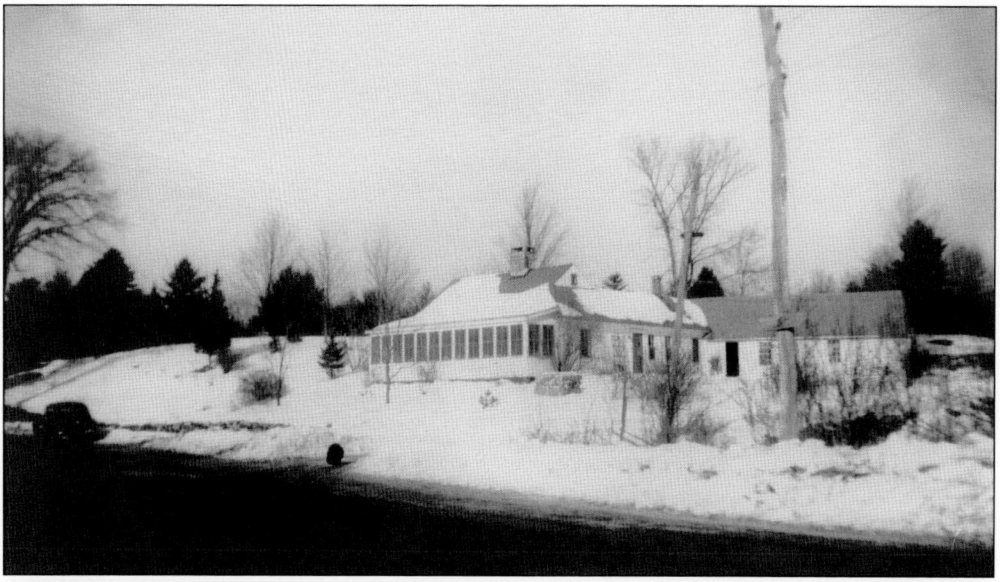

These two photographs show the Theoliphilius Eaton home, at the corner of Odell Road and Main Street. In 1756, it was both a tavern and a school—hardly an appropriate atmosphere for young minds. The photograph above was taken in 1947 when the Roy Miller family lived there. The recreation field across Main Street from the home is named after the family. In the 1980s, Miller's son, also named Roy, donated 15 acres of land to the town to be used for a park. There are very few Sandown children who have not visited the playground or played baseball in the Roy L. Miller Recreation Field. The home is seen below in the current day. (Above, courtesy of Juliana Ball; below, courtesy of the Sandown Historical Society.)

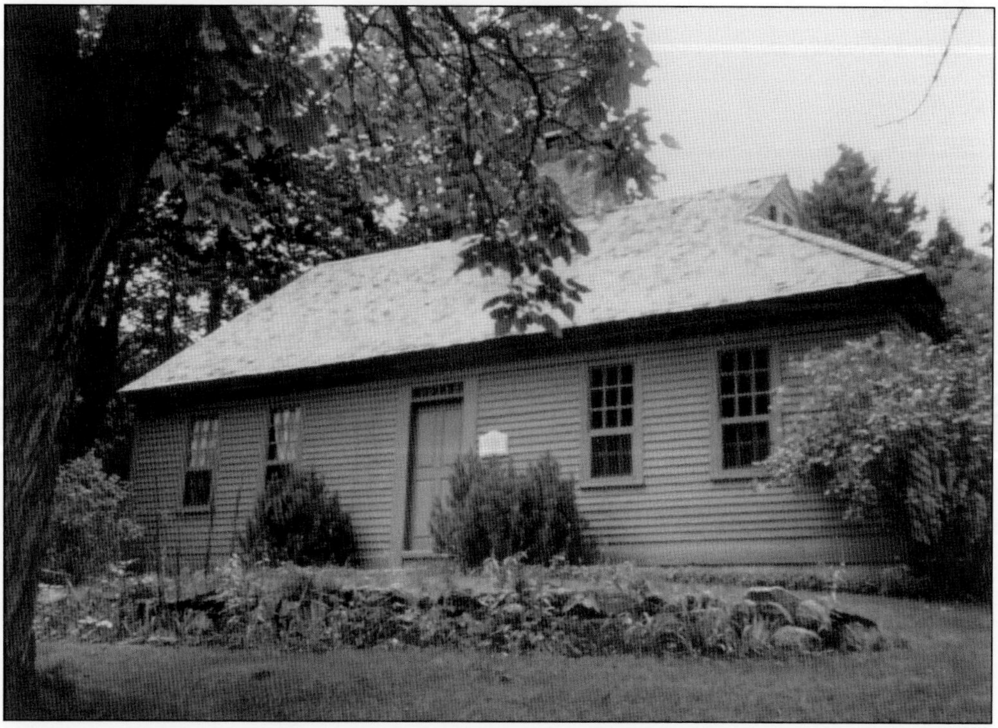

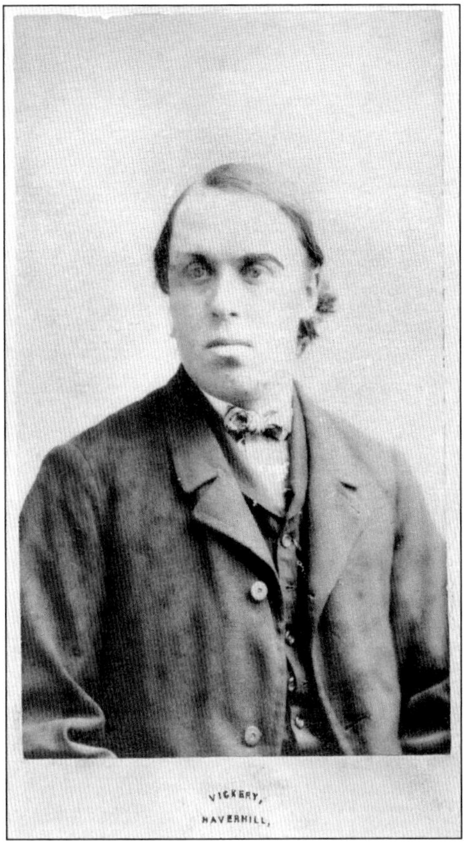

Alden Eaton Pillsbury and his wife, Lizzie Sargent Pillsbury, are seen here. The Pillsbury family had its beginnings in Sandown around 1770, when Benjamin Pillsbury married Anne Plummer of Sandown. Alden Pillsbury, Benjamin's great-grandson, was born in 1837, attended Sandown district schools, completed his education in Andover, Massachusetts, and was a prosperous farmer in Sandown until his death in 1911. He served as a selectman, a tax collector, and a school board member. He inherited the homestead property, the Pillsbury estate, which consisted of 150 acres in the south end of town, near Angle Pond, and married Lizzie Sargent in 1871. They had two children, Frank Newton Pillsbury and Gertrude Sargent Pillsbury. Both children, as well as some of their children, remained in Sandown as adults and carried on the family tradition of serving their community. (Both, courtesy of Linda Torre.)

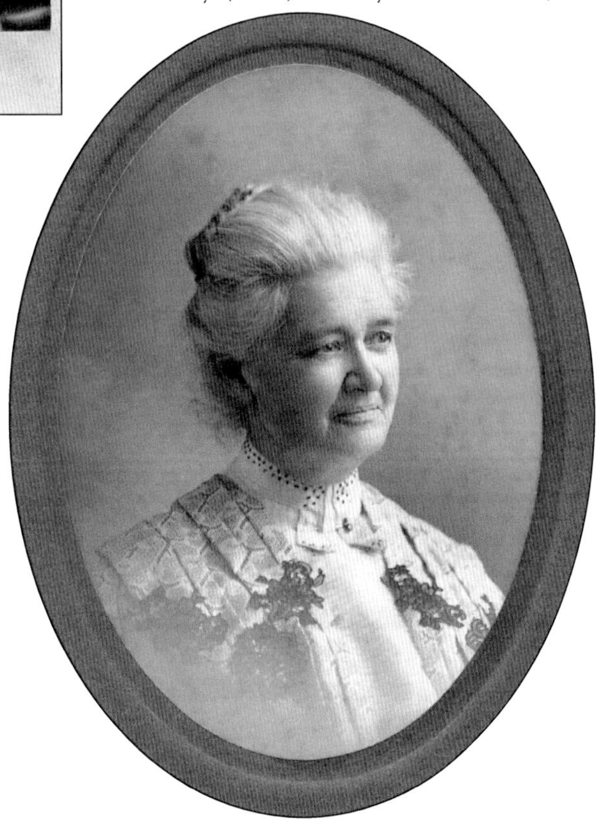

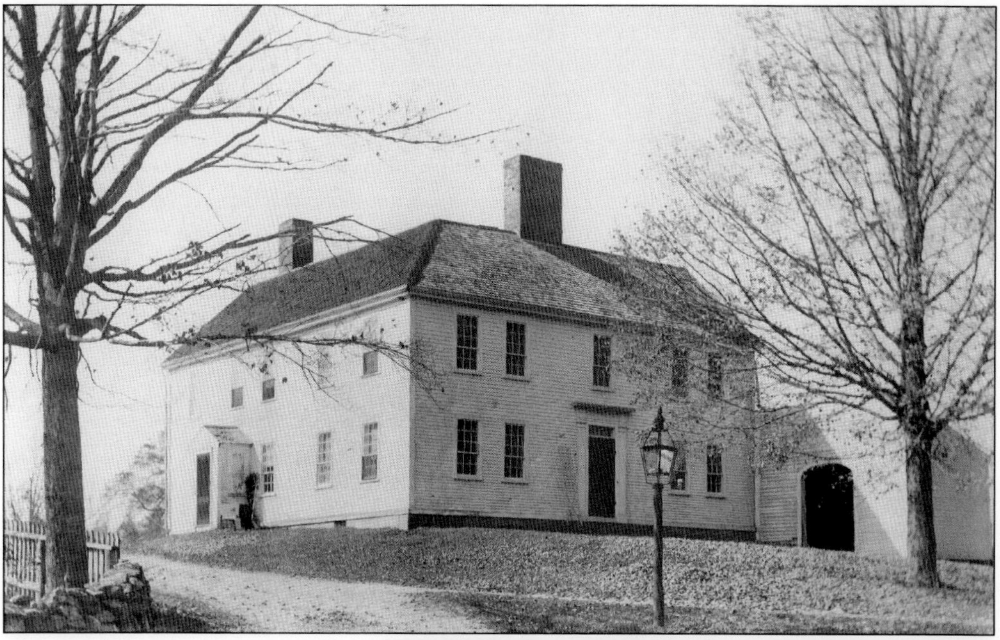

The stately farm above, originally belonging to the Pillsbury family, stood in a field near the corner of Main Street and Pillsbury Road. When Gertrude Pillsbury married Herbert True, it became known as the True farm. In 1948, the property was purchased by brothers John and Francis Lagasse, who renovated it to create the Angle Pond Hotel. (Courtesy of the Sandown Public Library.)

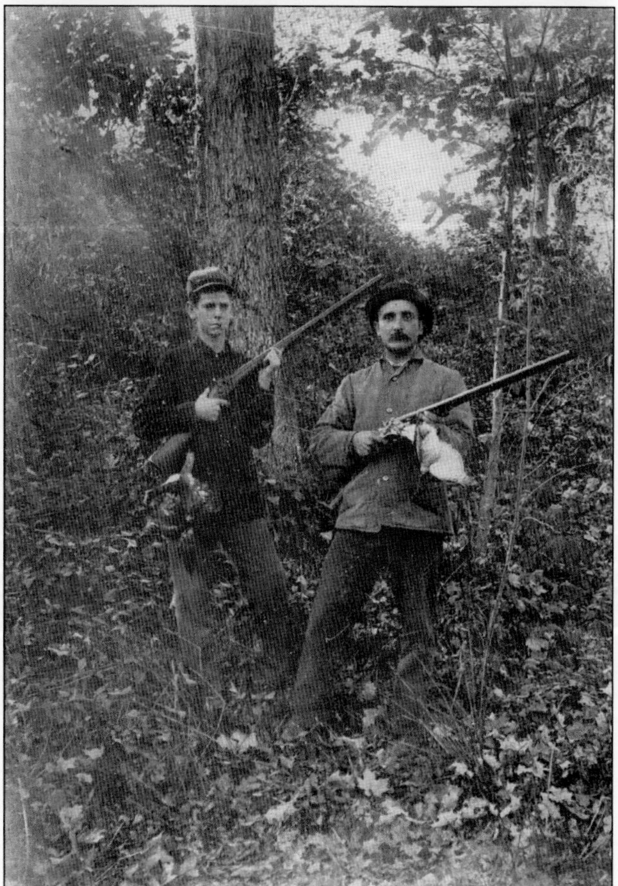

A young Herbert True is seen here with his father, Alden True. In those days, meat was not as readily available as it is today, so hunting was necessary in order to put food on the family table. The woman of the house was usually able to prepare delicious fare with whatever the men brought home. (Courtesy of Alden True.)

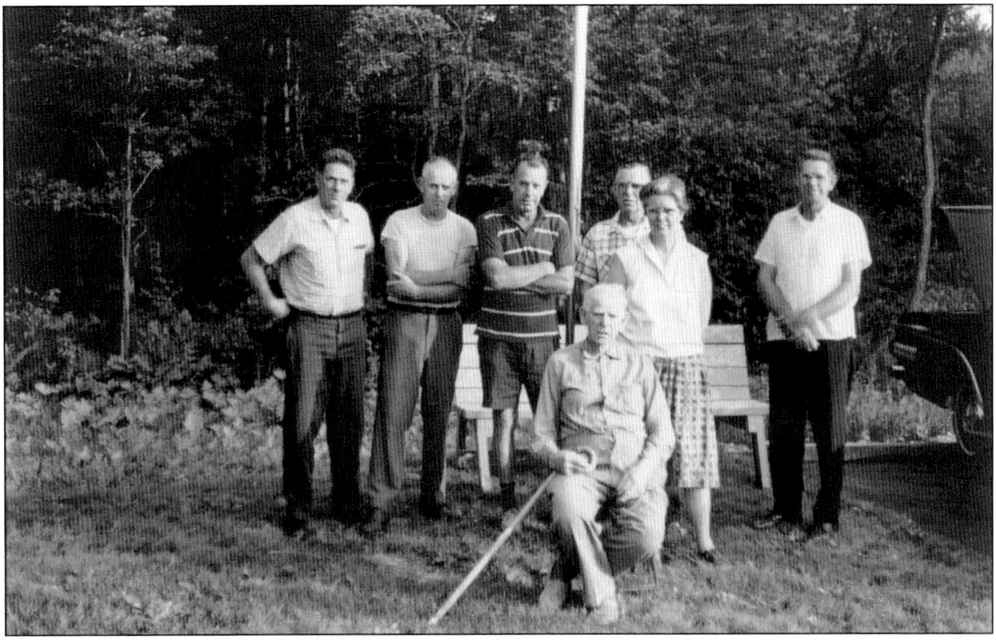

The Herbert True family was well known in Sandown. They believed in serving their community, and it was a common sight to see at least one member of the True family volunteering in every Sandown activity or committee. Herbert is seen here with some of his many children standing behind him. From left to right are Edwin, Rudolph, Zeke, Roland, Hazel, and Richard. (Courtesy of Alden True.)

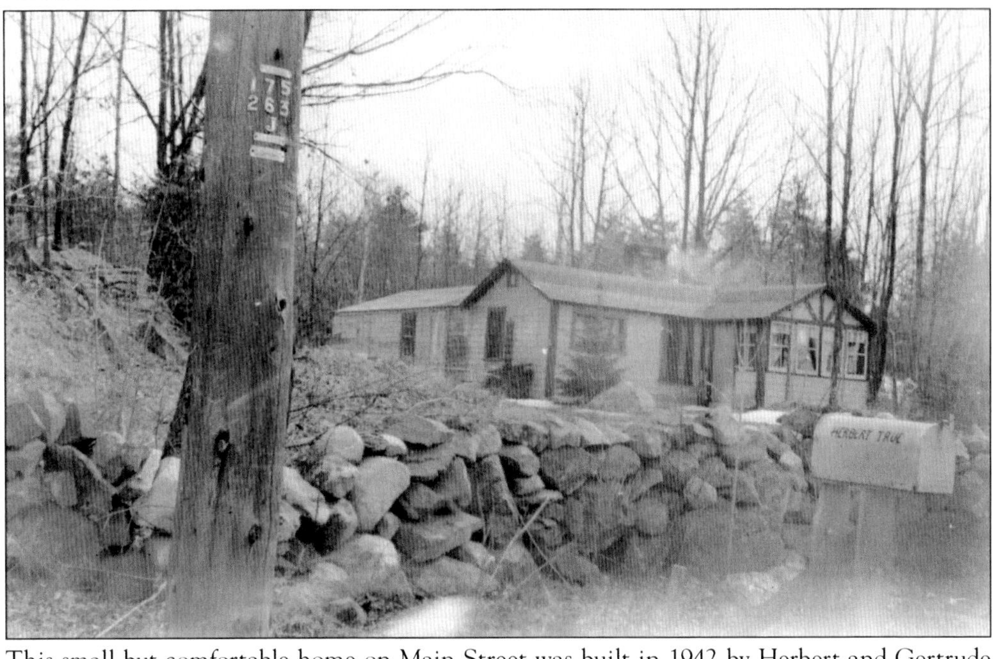

This small but comfortable home on Main Street was built in 1942 by Herbert and Gertrude (Pillsbury) True. It no longer stands today, but two of the Trues' sons, Clifton and Rudolph "Rudy," lived here until their deaths. Clifton True passed away in 2003 and Rudy in 2006. The reading area of the Sandown Public Library is dedicated to the True family. (Courtesy of Linda Torre.)

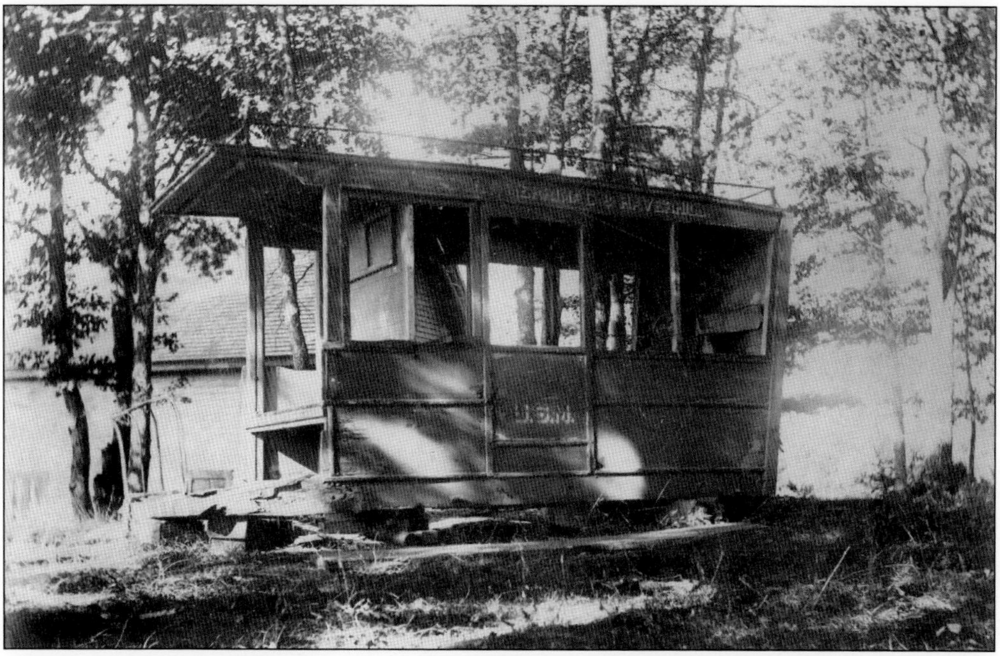

After the railroad arrived in town, the stagecoach line became obsolete. This stagecoach, originally part of the Haverhill, Merrimac & Amesbury line, was placed in the Sandown woods to be a children's playhouse around 1900. (Courtesy of Robert and Lois MacKinnon.)

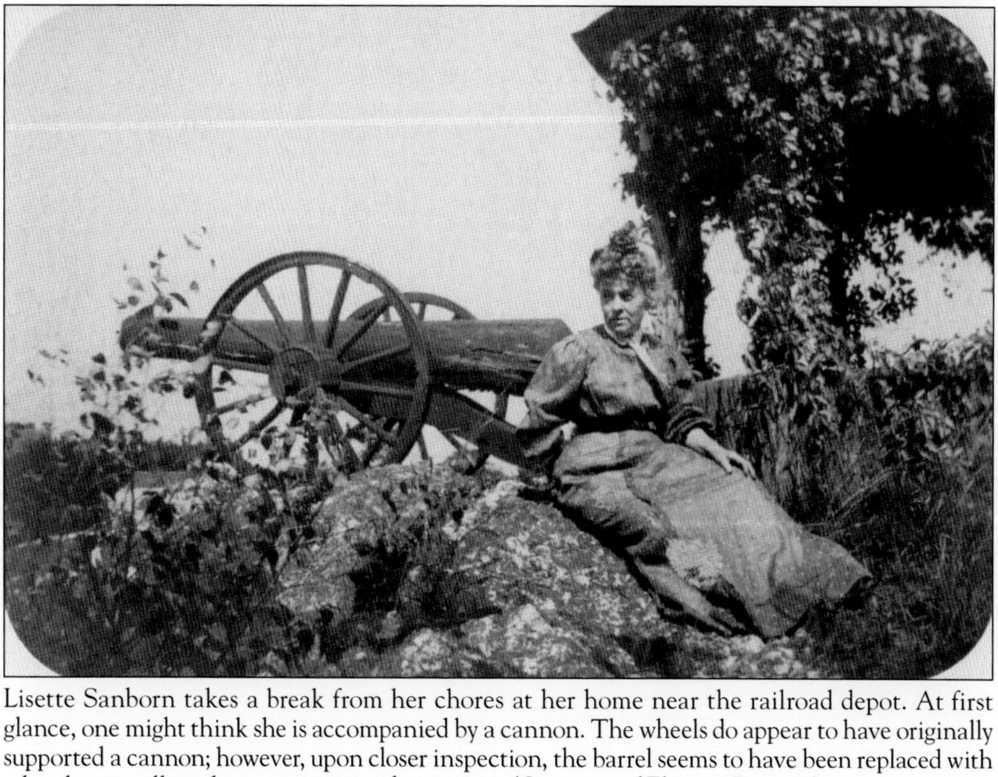

Lisette Sanborn takes a break from her chores at her home near the railroad depot. At first glance, one might think she is accompanied by a cannon. The wheels do appear to have originally supported a cannon; however, upon closer inspection, the barrel seems to have been replaced with a log, but it still made an interesting decoration. (Courtesy of Eleanor Bassett.)

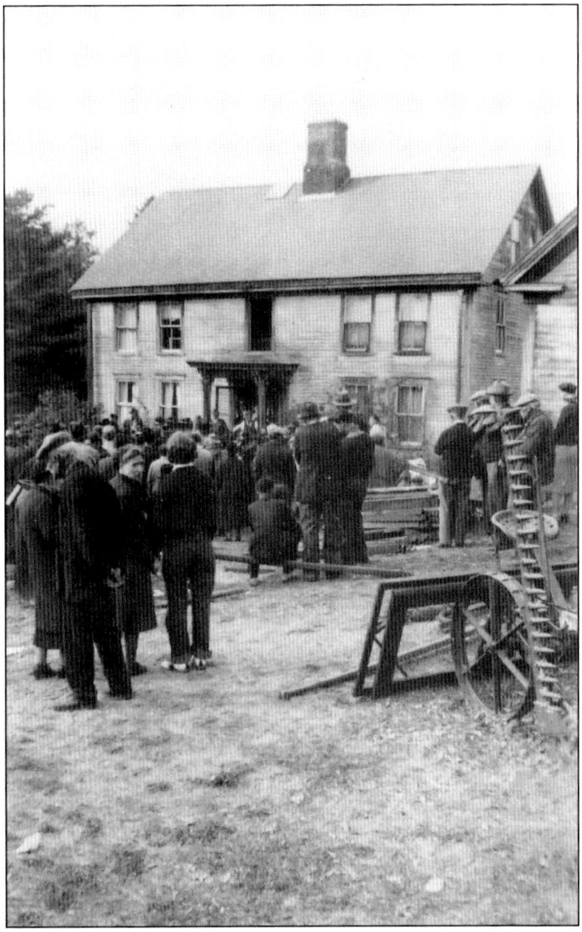

This home still sits at the end of Fremont Road. This photograph was taken at an auction in 1940, when the Burt Lovering family lived here. Longtime Sandown residents call the house the Chapman place because Rev. John Rae Chapman and his wife, Deana Jo, lived there for many years. The home has been beautifully restored and is currently owned by the Minton family. (Courtesy of Richard Holmes.)

The beautiful winter scene below looks up Fremont Road at the Chapman place. The photograph was taken by the bridge over the Exeter River, near the intersection with Sargent Road. This was originally the Clark homestead and is also where Clark's mill stood. (Courtesy of June McNally.)

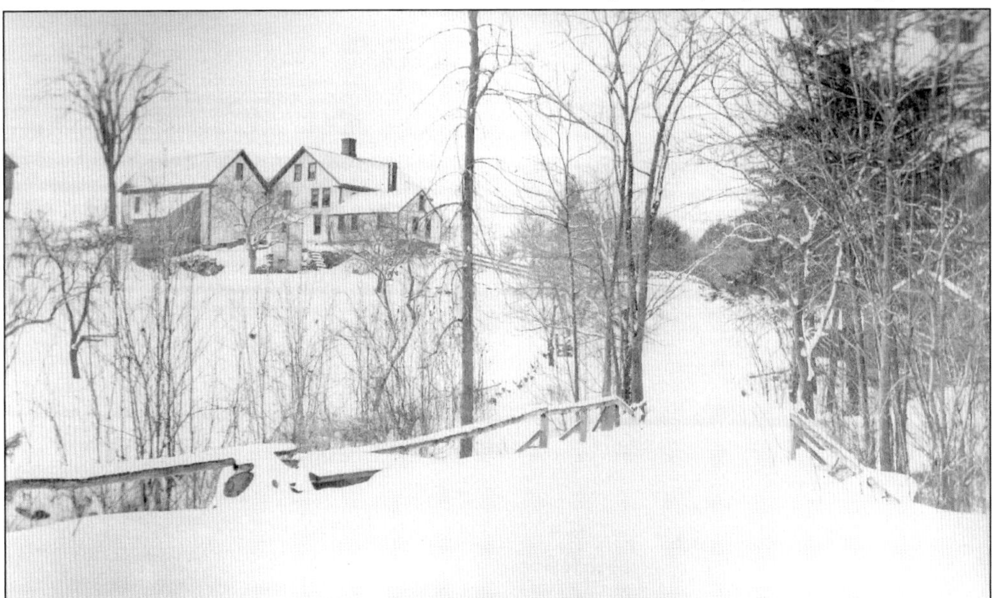

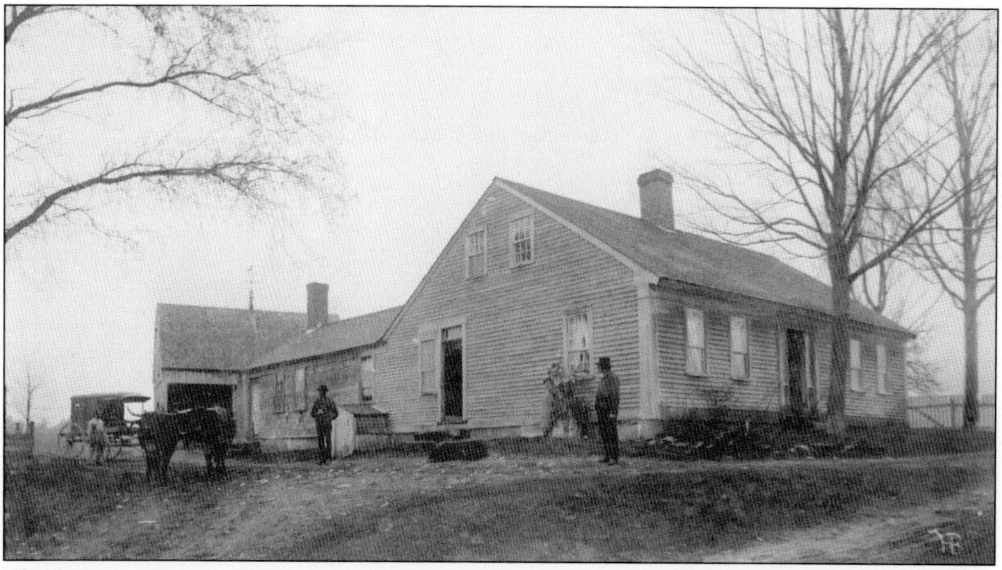

This home on Fremont Road was completely destroyed by fire on Christmas Eve 1945. It was built by Sherburne Sanborn, one of Sandown's first settlers. At the time of the fire, Priscilla Knights Bassett, a direct descendant of the original Sanborn family, still lived there. She and her husband, Raymond K. Bassett, and their 16 children were left homeless. The family rebuilt on the same foundation and still owns the property today. (Courtesy of Eleanor Bassett.)

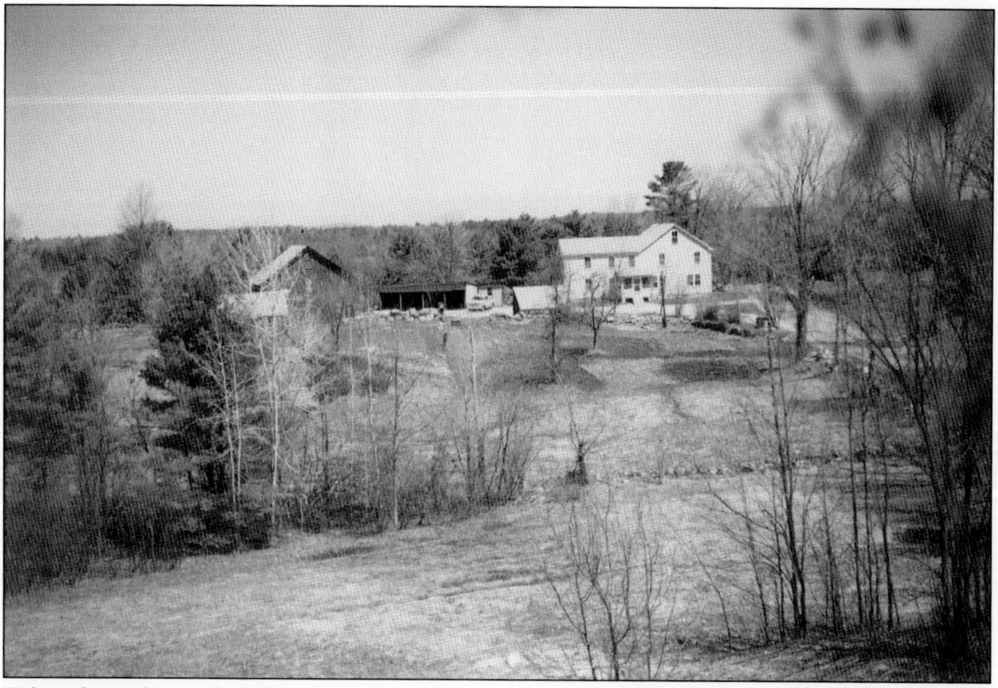

Taken from the roof of the barn at the adjacent Gerard and Barbara Lachance property, this photograph shows a wonderful view of the Bassett farm. It shows the home after it was rebuilt following the devastating Christmas Eve fire. (Courtesy of Gerard Lachance.)

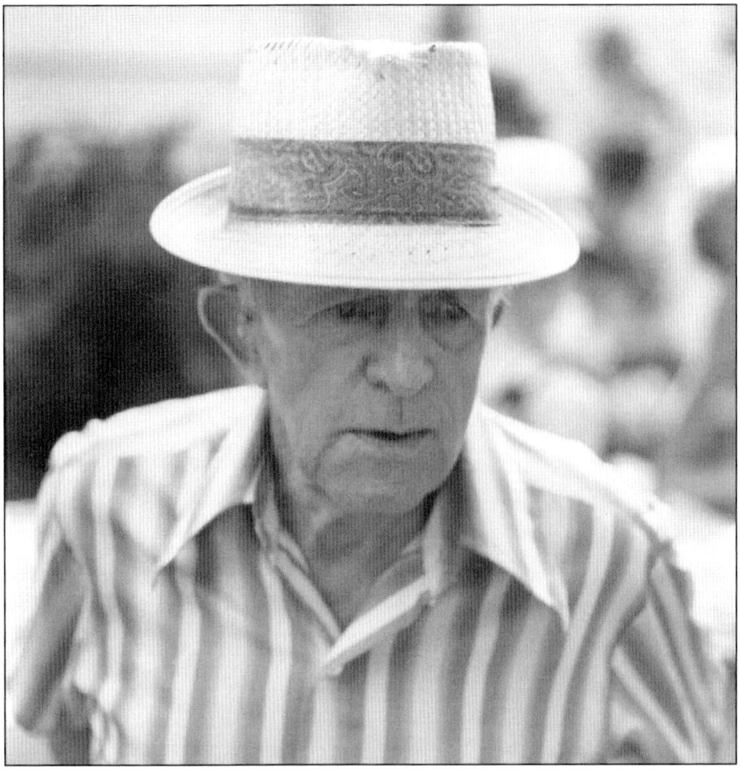

Raymond K. "Papa" Bassett was a well-known presence in Sandown. Not only was he the father of 16 children, but he also found time to serve his community. He was active at St. Matthews United Methodist Church and was a cemetery sexton, a school board member, the town treasurer, a Grange member, and a state forest fire warden. He was a also a charter member of the Old Meeting House Historical Association and the "Keeper of the Key." (Courtesy of Carroll Bassett.)

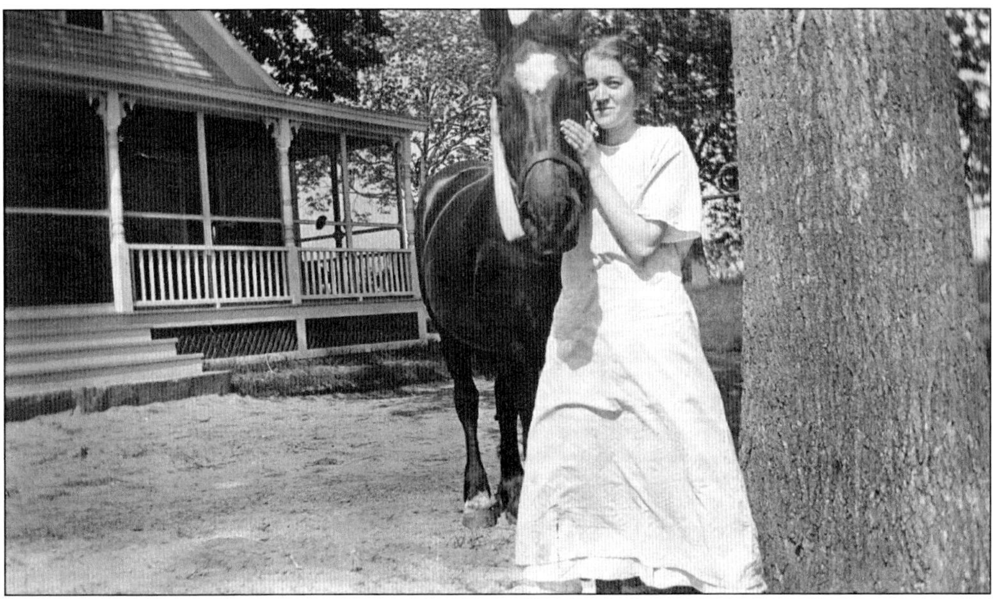

Priscilla (Knights) Bassett is seen here with her horse. Besides being the mother of 16 children, she was active in her community. She was a charter member of the Old Meeting House Historical Association, serving as treasurer. She was also Sandown's town treasurer, a Grange member, a Sunday school treasurer, a newspaper correspondent, a member of the 200th anniversary planning committee, and the coauthor of the 200th anniversary commemorative book. (Courtesy of Carroll Bassett.)

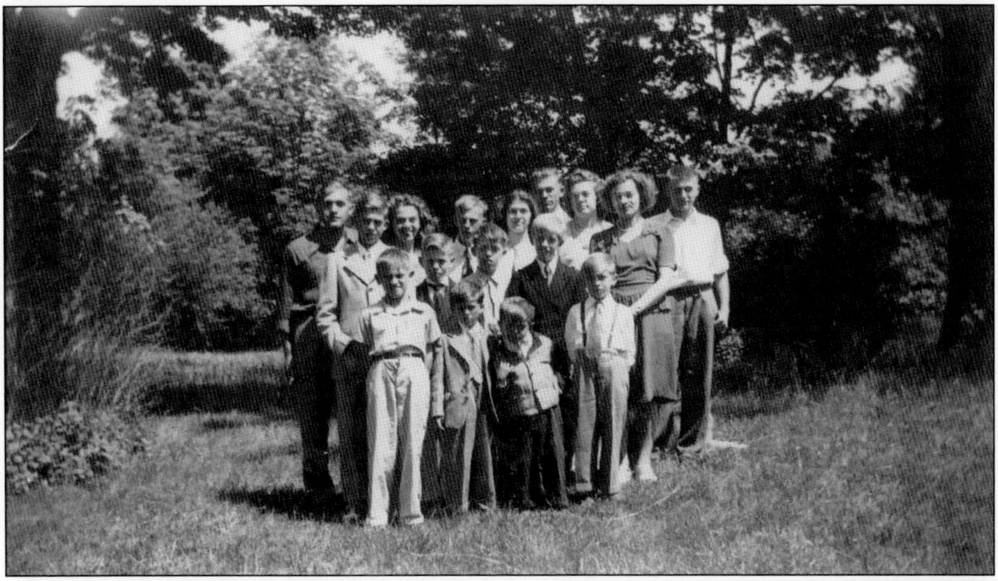

The 16 Bassett children posed for this photograph in 1947. They were all born between 1921 and 1941. The Bassetts tied with the Harrison Kelley family for the title of Sandown's largest family. There were also 16 Kelley children, born between 1890 and 1917. (Courtesy of Carroll Bassett.)

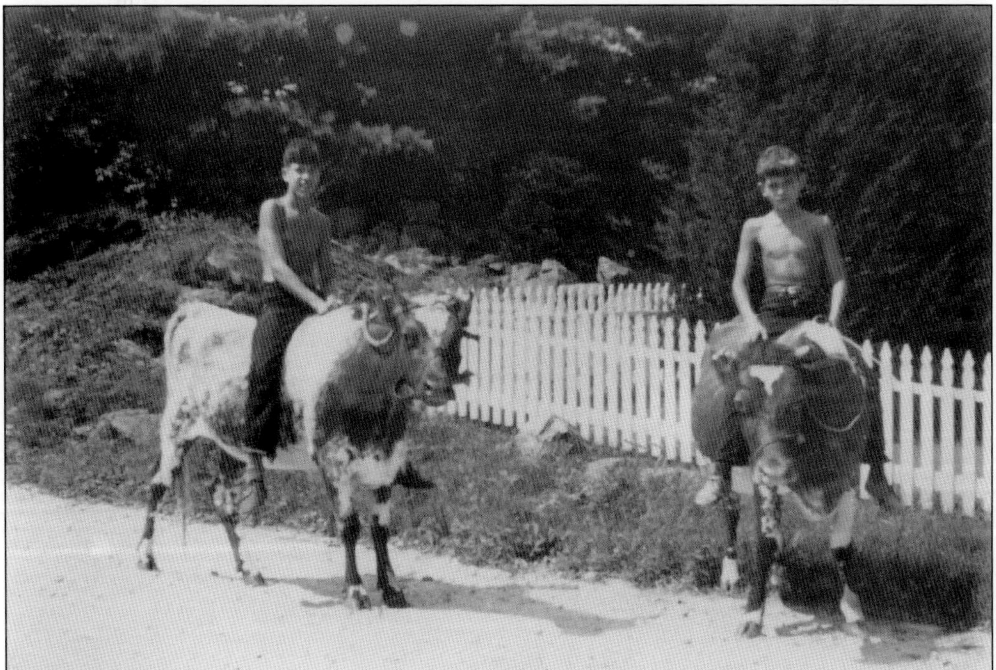

These two young "cowboys," brothers Carroll (left) and Irving Bassett, discovered the fastest way to get the cattle back to the barn after a summer of grazing in the pasture. It was likely not the safest way, however. (Courtesy of Eleanor Bassett.)

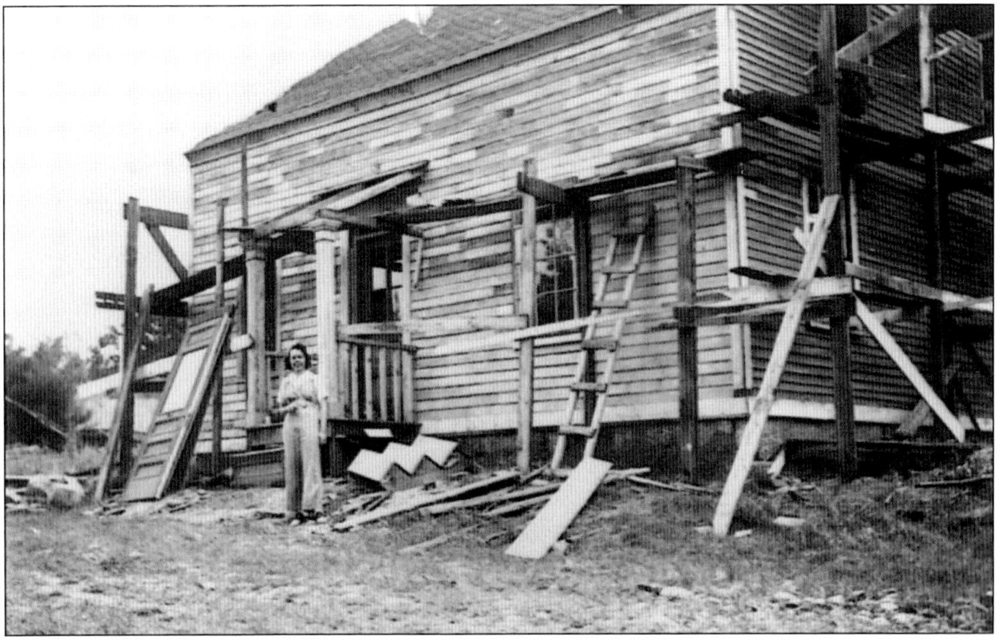

In 1940, this house was purchased by John and Marjorie Holmes. Fortunately, John was a carpenter and turned it into the lovely Cape Cod–style home that can be seen today at the corner of Holmeswood Drive and Main Street. Richard Holmes, the author of *A View From Meeting House Hill: A History of Sandown, New Hampshire*, grew up in the home. (Courtesy of Arlene Bassett.)

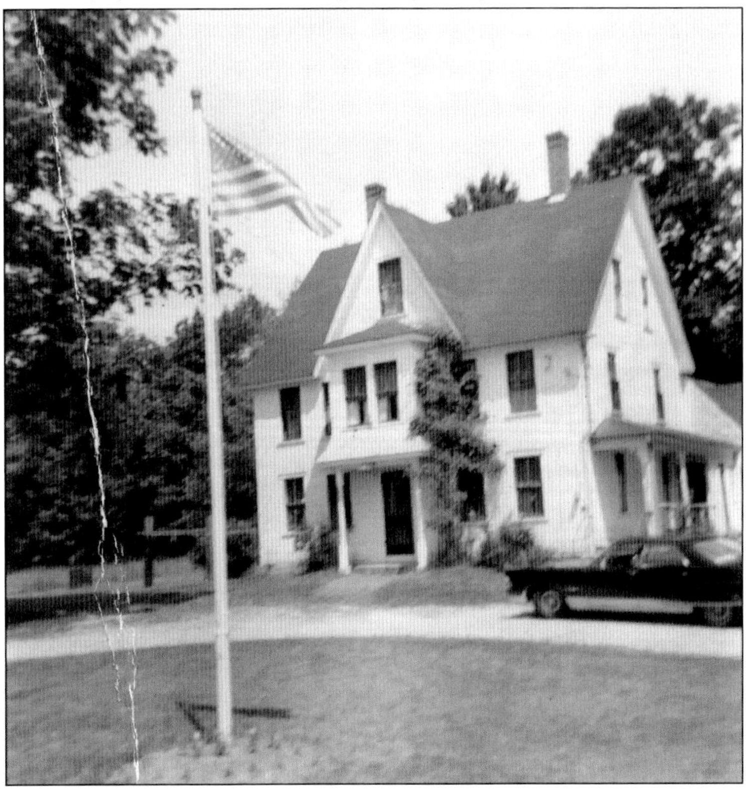

This home on Main Street is known as the Hunt place. Although he was not the first resident, Eliphalet Hunt lived here in the 1790s with his wife and nine children. Until 2012, the home was owned by Everett "Bud" and Ruth Holmes. They have both passed away, and the house is now owned by Daniel and Rebecca Fournier. (Courtesy of Arlene Bassett.)

Ralph Drowne and his pet raccoon share a tree while brother Fred and his dog stand guard at the bottom. Perhaps the dog is the reason the raccoon climbed the tree. (Courtesy of June McNally.)

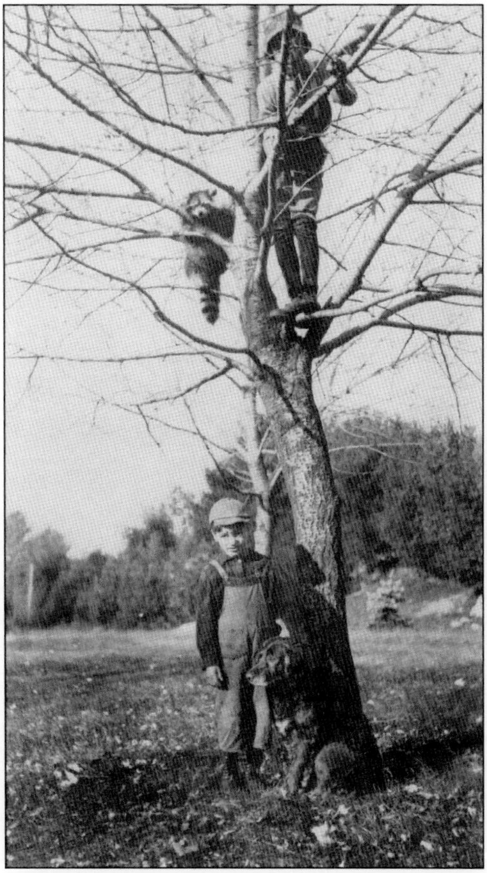

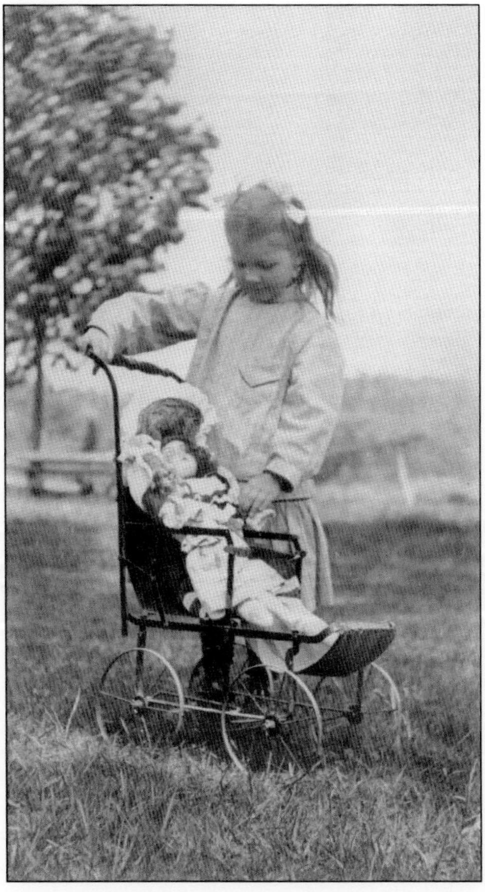

Seven-year-old Frances Smith gives her doll a ride in her stroller in 1916. While it may be less likely to see a little girl playing outside in a dress today, dolls never seem to lose their popularity. (Courtesy of Lillian Loring.)

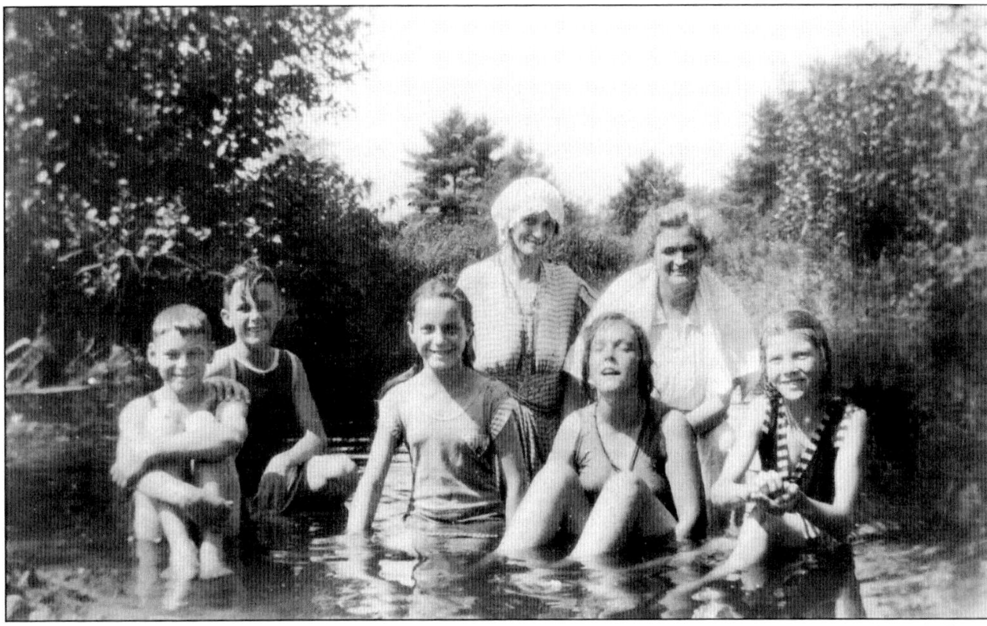

This photograph, taken in the early 1920s, is titled "Ole Swimmin' Hole." It was taken behind the Bingham property, which is now home to Playmates Preschool on North Road. The back of the photograph identifies the people as "Back row, Benning Sanborn, Aunt Belle, and Ma Smith; front row; unidentified, Norma Sanborn, Cousin Esther and Frances Smith." There is now a private beach club, Sandlot Beach Club, near this location. (Courtesy of Lillian Loring.)

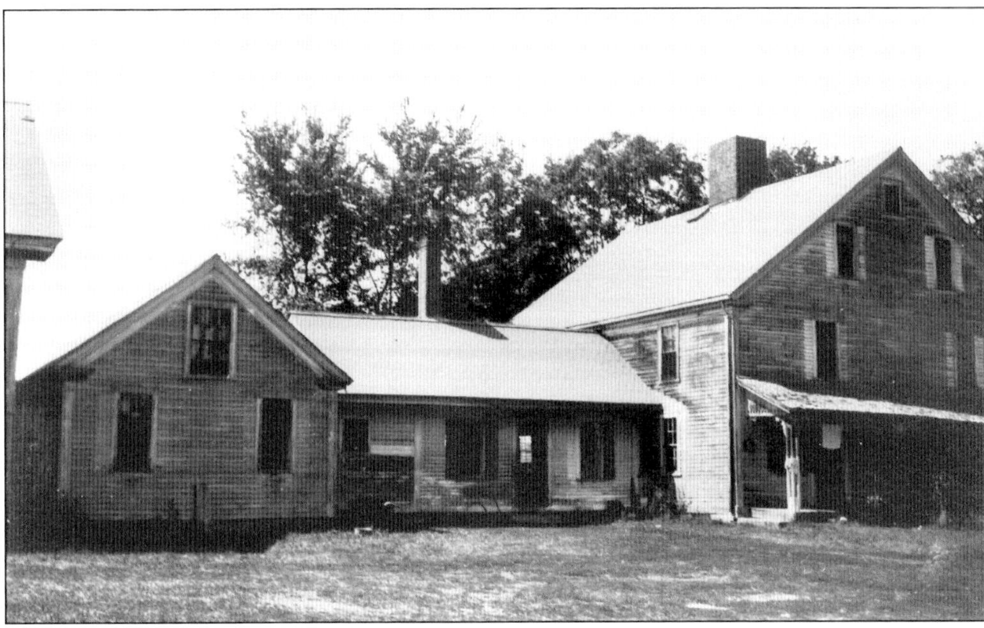

A long line of families have called this lovely old farmhouse on Sargent Road home. Living here at one time or another, but not in any particular order, were: John and Fred Lovering; Frank and Emma Brown; Nelson R. Lovering; James Sleeper; the Crawford family, who built the barn in 1858; and Fred and Dorothy (Love) Drowne and their sons Richard and David. Today, the property is owned by David Drowne and his wife, Kathy. (Courtesy of Alden True.)

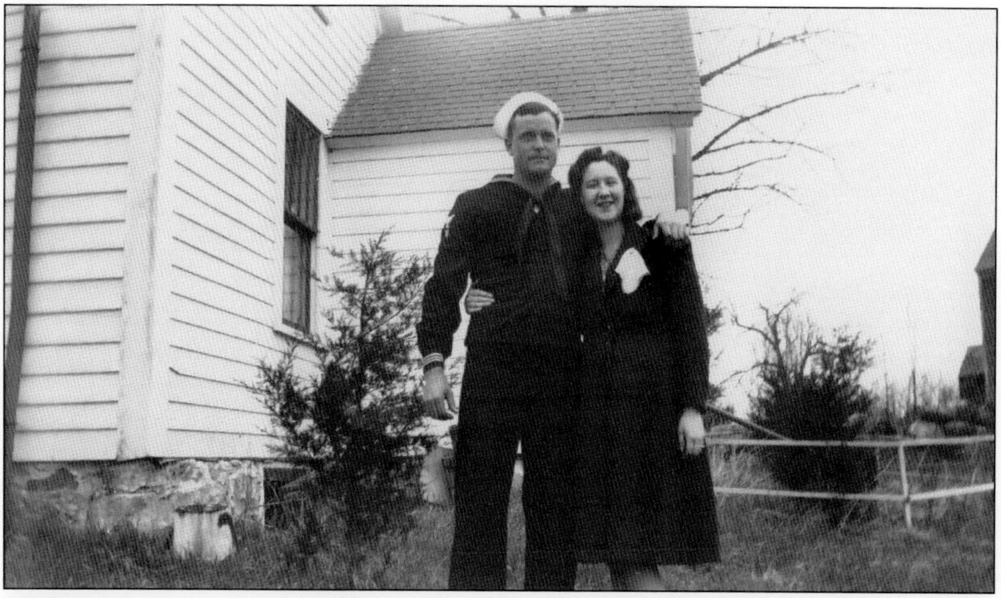

Ralph Drowne Sr. served in the Navy in the 1940s. He is seen above with his wife, Pearl Taylor Drowne, beside their home on Main Street. (Courtesy of Suzanne Anderson.)

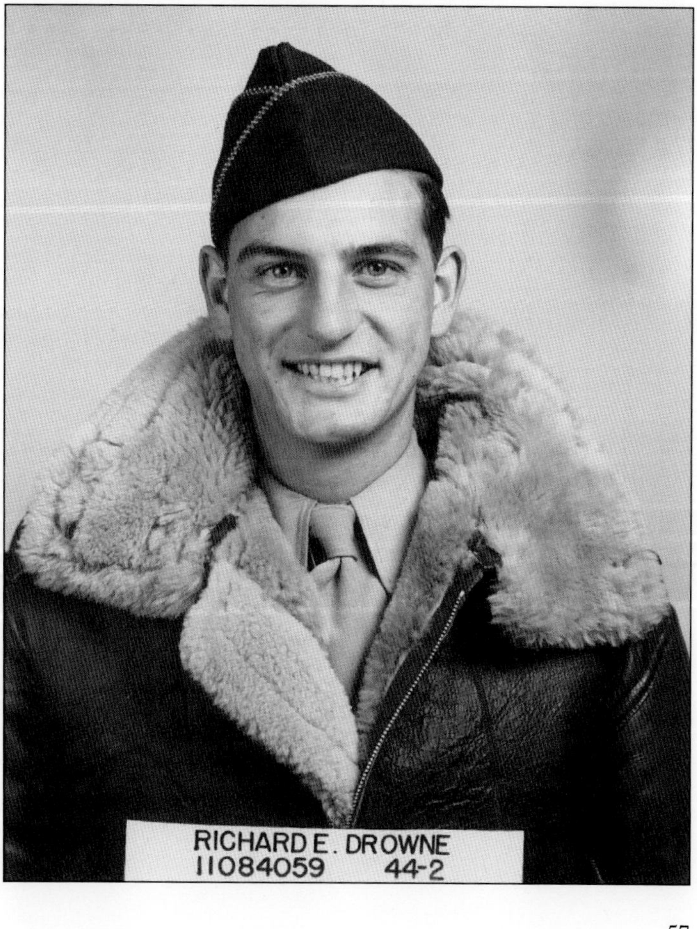

2nd Lt. Richard E. Drowne served in the US Army Air Corps. He was a bombardier and a navigator. He lost his life when he was shot down over Germany on November 22, 1944. He was the son of Clarence and Marion Merrick Drowne. Many of Richard's nieces and nephews still live in Sandown, and one nephew is proud to be his namesake. (Courtesy of June McNally.)

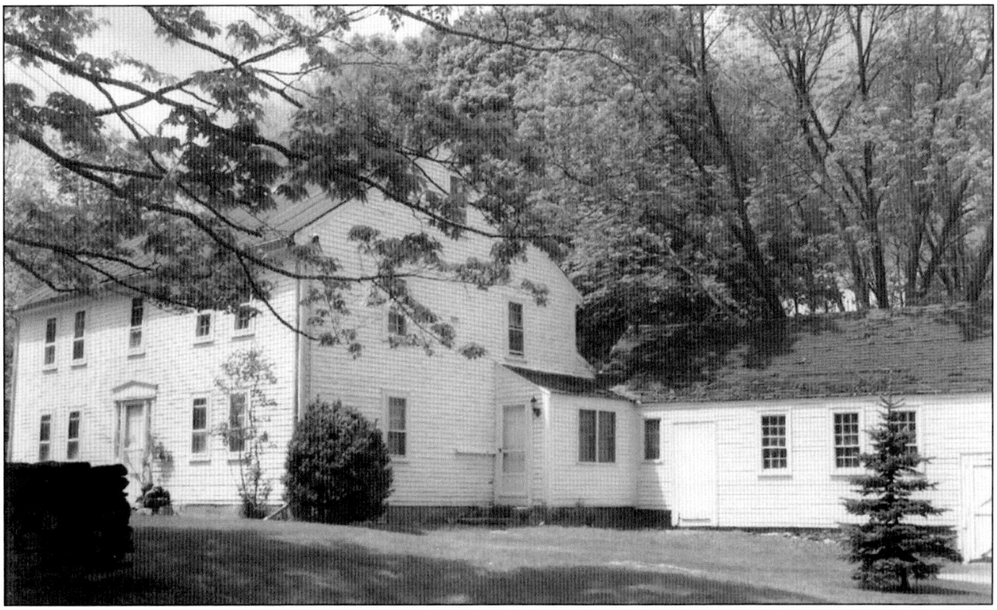

Rev. William French built The Laurels (above) on Odell Road in 1830. Reverend French's son, also named William, was a justice of the peace, a school superintendent, a Sandown selectman, and a representative to the state legislature. When well-known pastor Dr. Willis P. Odell married Mary French, The Laurels became their summer home. Odell Road was named for Dr. Odell. He later remarried, to Eva Beede, whose poetry was published under the name Eva B. Odell. The Odells willed the property to the Methodist Conference, and it became a home for retired pastors. The MacGregor family bought the property at auction in 1953. The poem below was written by Eva B. Odell and published in one of her books, *Winnipesauke: and Other Poems*, around 1912. Note that the poem was autographed by the author. (Above, courtesy of the Sandown Historical Society; below, courtesy of Marion Jean.)

THE BERMUDAS

Eva Beede Odell

FAR out at sea the fair Bermudas lie,
  A chain of emeralds on ocean floor,
  In diamond setting of spray-dashed shore,
All guarded safe by reefs of coral high,
Where purple sea-fans wave the surface nigh.
  There turquoise waters glint the white sands
    o'er,
  While sunbeams all the shades of opal pour,
Then tint with amethyst the twilight sky.
The garden of the rose, the lily's home,
  With white-roofed houses gleaming midst
    the green
  Of oleander, palm and cedar trees,
Delight of those who from the snow-lands roam
  Are these blest isles, bedight in summer sheen,
    By breezes ever fanned from sapphire seas.

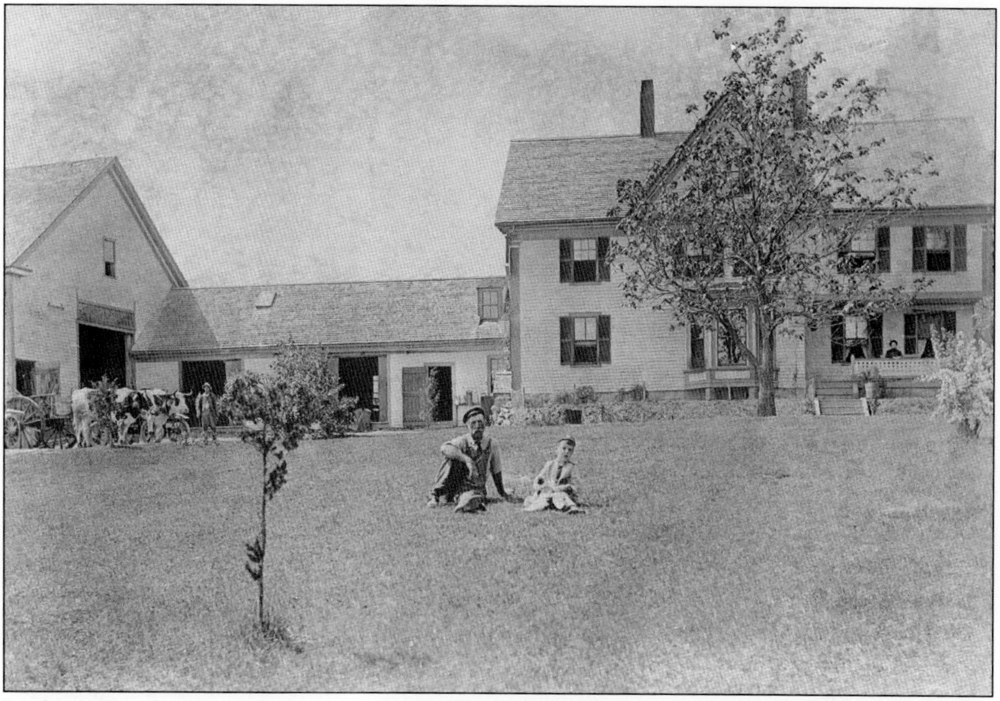

In the 1870s, the home above on Main Street was owned by Elwin and Sarah Mills. Elwin Mills was a prominent citizen, serving as a tax collector, a road agent, a selectman, and a school board member. He manufactured shoes here, employing some 60 workers. The Sawyer family lives in the house today. (Courtesy of the Sandown Historical Society.)

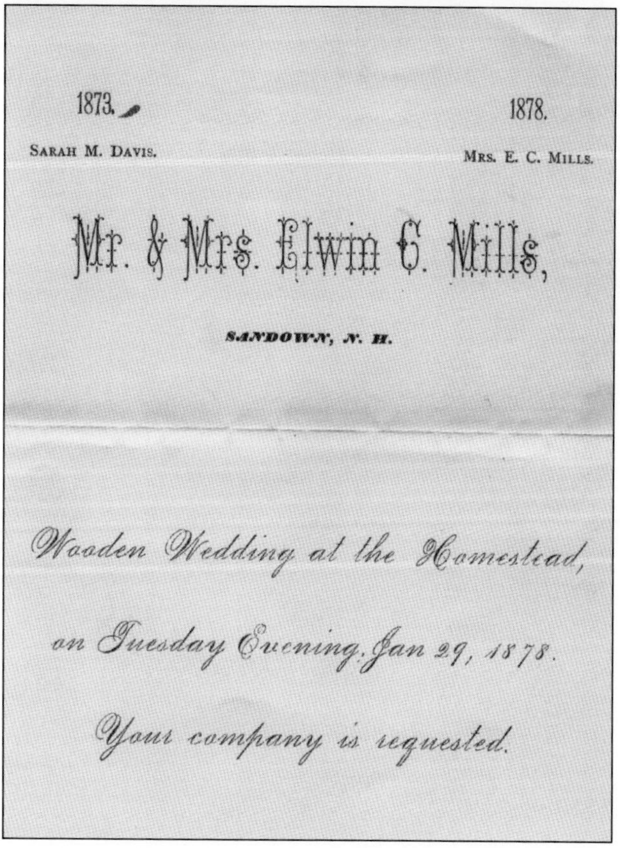

1873. 1878.

SARAH M. DAVIS. MRS. E. C. MILLS.

Mr. & Mrs. Elwin C. Mills,

SANDOWN, N. H.

Wooden Wedding at the Homestead,

on Tuesday Evening, Jan 29, 1878.

Your company is requested.

This invitation to a "Wooden Wedding" was a mystery at first. However, note that the upper left corner reads, "Sarah M. Davis 1873," and the upper right corner reads, "Mrs. E.C. Mills 1878." In 1873, Sarah Davis had married Elwin C. Mills, making Mrs. E.C. Mills her married name. Because the fifth wedding anniversary is known as the wooden anniversary and 1878 was five years after her wedding, this is an invitation to a fifth wedding anniversary. (Courtesy of the Sandown Historical Society.)

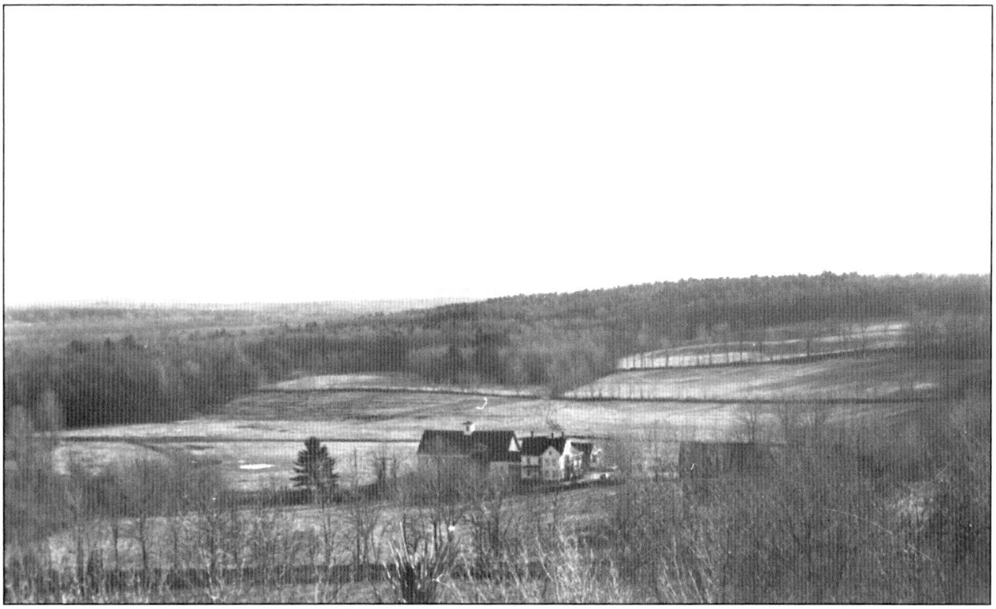

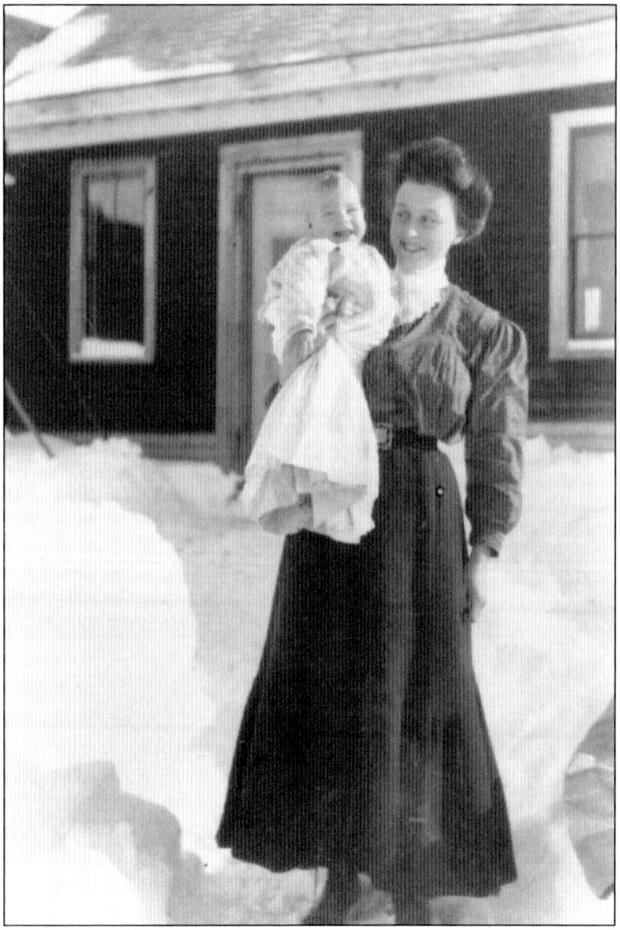

Seen above is the Rowell farm, appropriately located on Rowell Road. Helen Rowell grew up on the farm and continued to live in the family home with her husband, John James Pinard, and their four children. Today, these fields have all been subdivided and developed. One of the Pinard children, Dorothy Batchelder, lives in a home on a portion of the land with her husband, Gary, and one of the Pinard granddaughters, Christina Hubley, lives in one of the developments with her husband, Richard. (Courtesy of Dorothy Batchelder.)

Marion Merrick Drowne holds baby Albert, the oldest of her five children, in front of her home on North Road around 1910. At the time, it was customary for boys to wear dresses for their first few years. Marion's dress was also very stylish for the day. (Courtesy of Suzanne Anderson.)

This photograph shows sisters Marion Merrick Drowne (left, with baby Eleanor) and Harriet Merrick Seeley. Harriet was the grandmother of Stephen Merrill, the governor of New Hampshire from 1993 to 1997. Marion and her husband, Clarence Drowne, were the owners and operators of the apple and peach orchard on North Road. (Courtesy of Suzanne Anderson.)

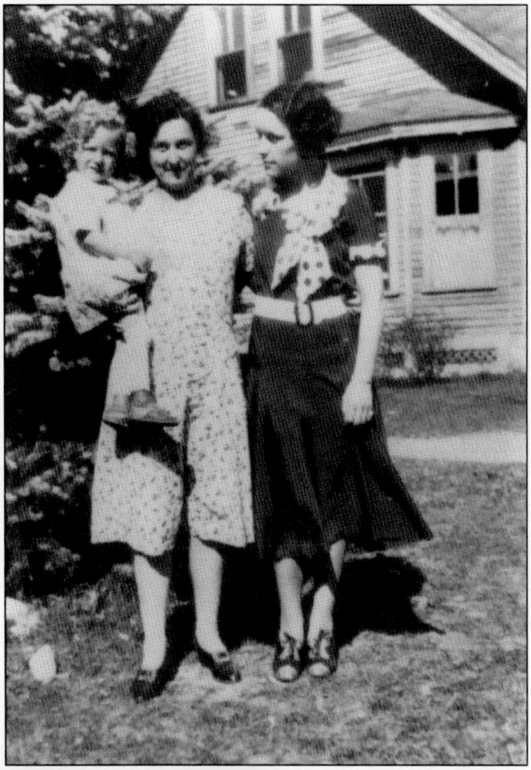

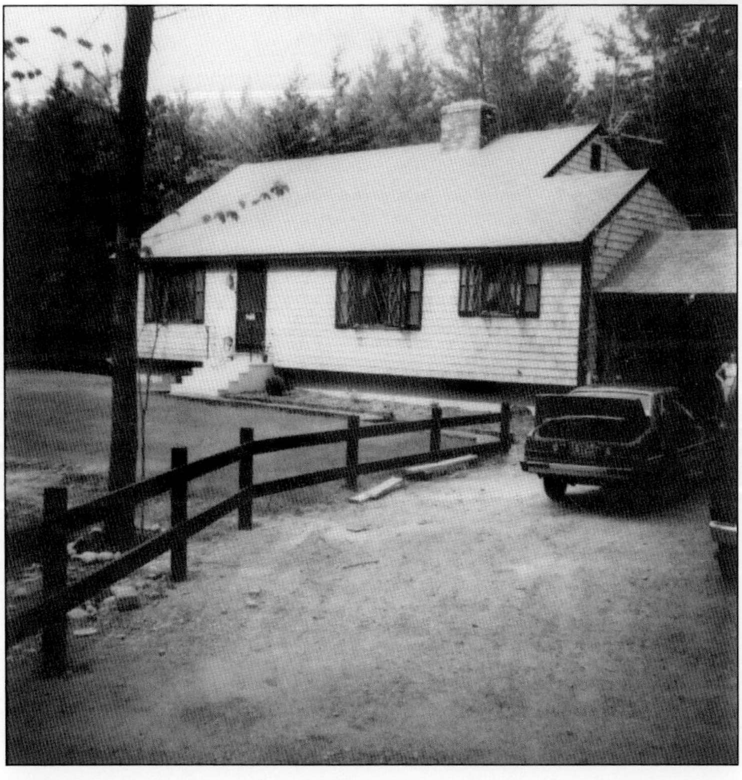

The housing boom in Sandown began in the 1970s with the construction of homes in Kings Range Estates, which was developed on tracts of land owned by John B. Holmes Jr., Everett Holmes, and Allen Love. The first houses built were similar in design and size. Holmeswood Road was the first road developed in the subdivision, followed by Royal Range Road. Current town clerk Michelle Short grew up in this house on Royal Range Road. (Courtesy of Michelle Short.)

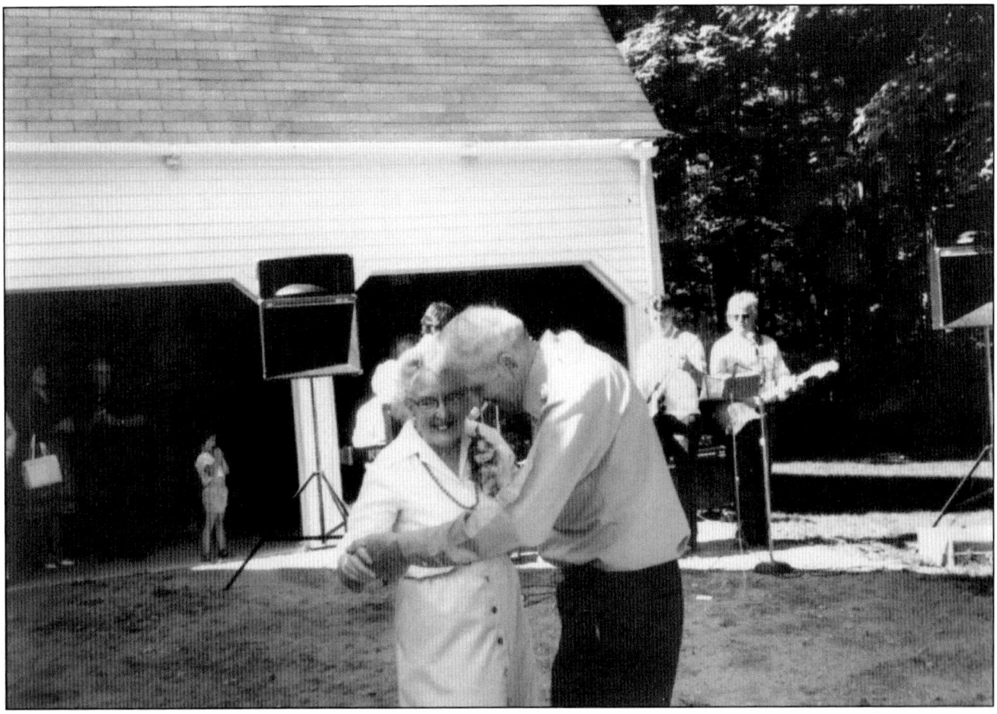

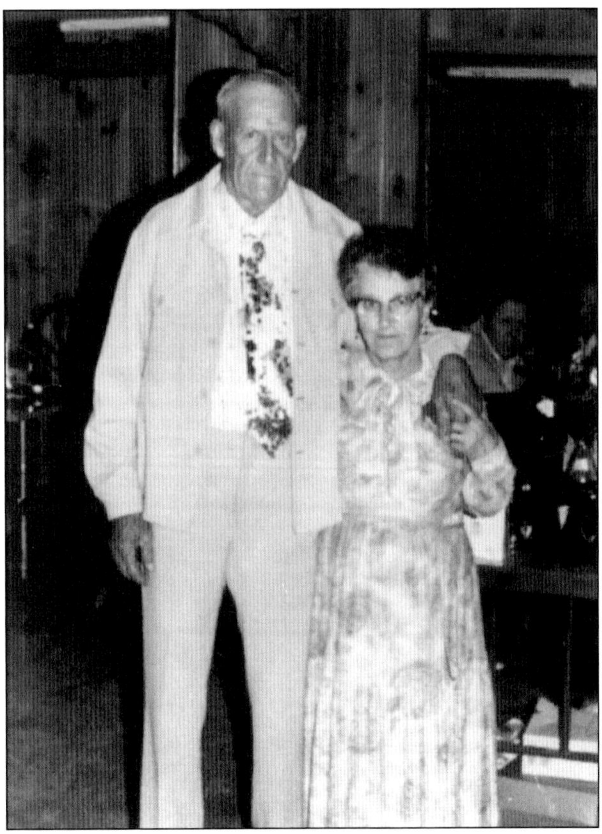

Above, Harold and Nellie Lovering dance at their 50th wedding anniversary party, held at the home of Everett and Ruth Holmes. The entire town came together to give the couple a day to remember. Harold was a storyteller, and one had no choice but to listen to his thick New England twang. Nellie was meek and gentle, staying in Harold's six-foot-plus shadow. They were well liked by all who knew them. (Courtesy of Arlene Bassett.)

This photograph shows another well-known Sandown couple celebrating their 50th wedding anniversary. Everett "Bill" and Evelyn Huckins lived on North Road in the house that is now home to Playmates Preschool and Sandlot Sports. Evelyn was known for her piano-playing skill, although she could not read a note of music. Every dance at the town hall found Evelyn at the keyboard. (Courtesy of Suzanne Anderson.)

Four

Educating Our Children

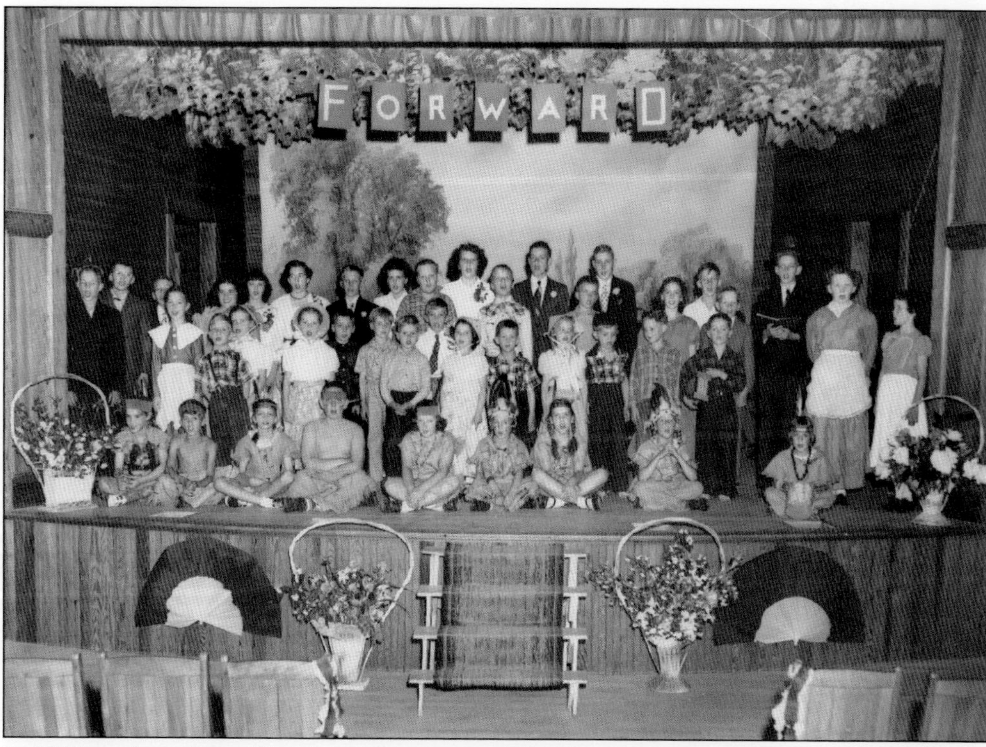

In 1948, students from all eight grades came together from both one-room schools to present a play at graduation. It was a historical presentation, as seen by the Native American and pilgrim costumes. Only a handful of these students are actually the eighth-grade graduates. The graduating girls are wearing corsages and the boys are sporting neckties. (Courtesy of Richard Holmes.)

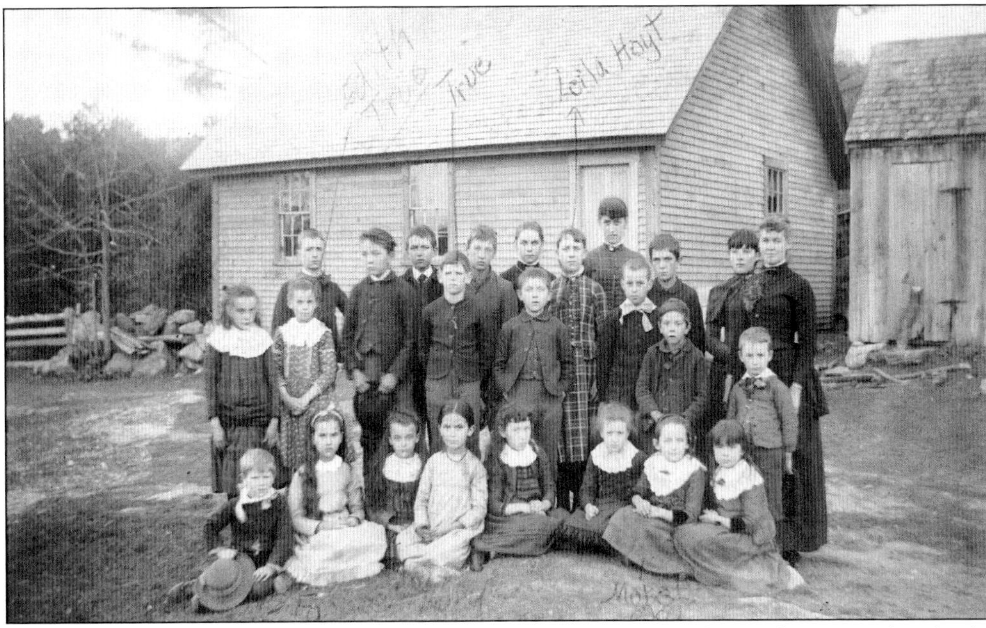

Immediately after the Town of Sandown was established in 1756, the residents voted to fund a school. The nearest school was 10 miles away in Kingston, so it was logistically impossible for most Sandown children to attend. This photograph shows students at the Pine Grove School around 1890. (Courtesy of Dorothy Batchelder.)

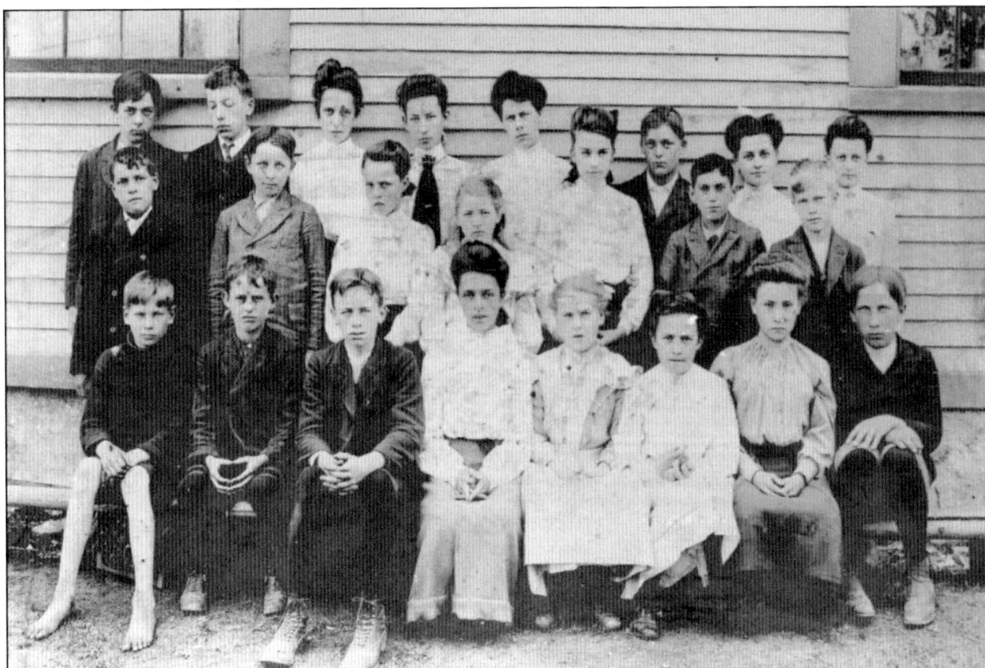

This photograph shows grades one through eight at one of the four district schools in 1905. As all of the schools were constructed in the same manner, it is unknown which of the four schools it is. Note the hairstyles on the girls, which would be unusual by today's standards. (Courtesy of David Drowne.)

This six-year-old Sandown youth shows off his fine clothes around 1906. It is hard to imagine any first-grader today wearing such an outfit to school. (Courtesy of the Sandown Public Library.)

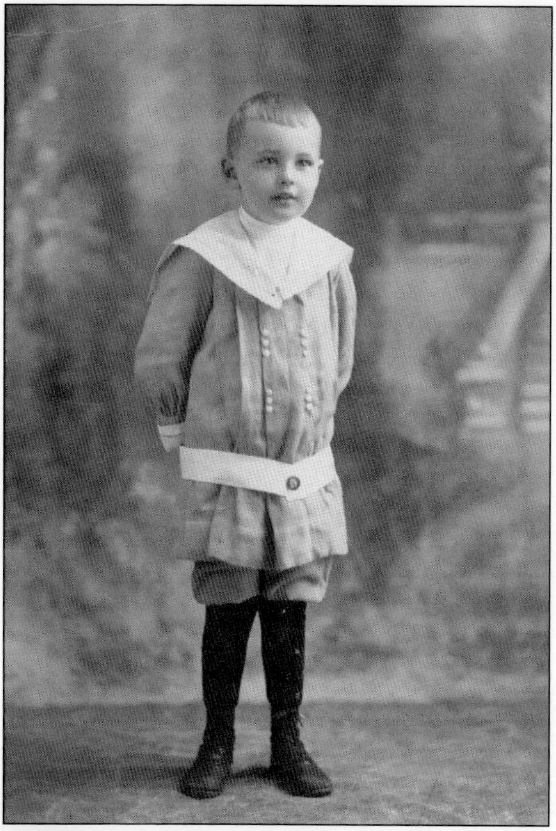

The first Sandown schools were in private homes, with rooms rented to double as classrooms. In 1794, residents voted to build three schoolhouses. They were District One: Chestnut Hill School; District Two: Pine Grove/Black Hole School; and District Three: Clark School. All eight grades at one of them is seen below in 1915. (Courtesy of Robert and Lois MacKinnon.)

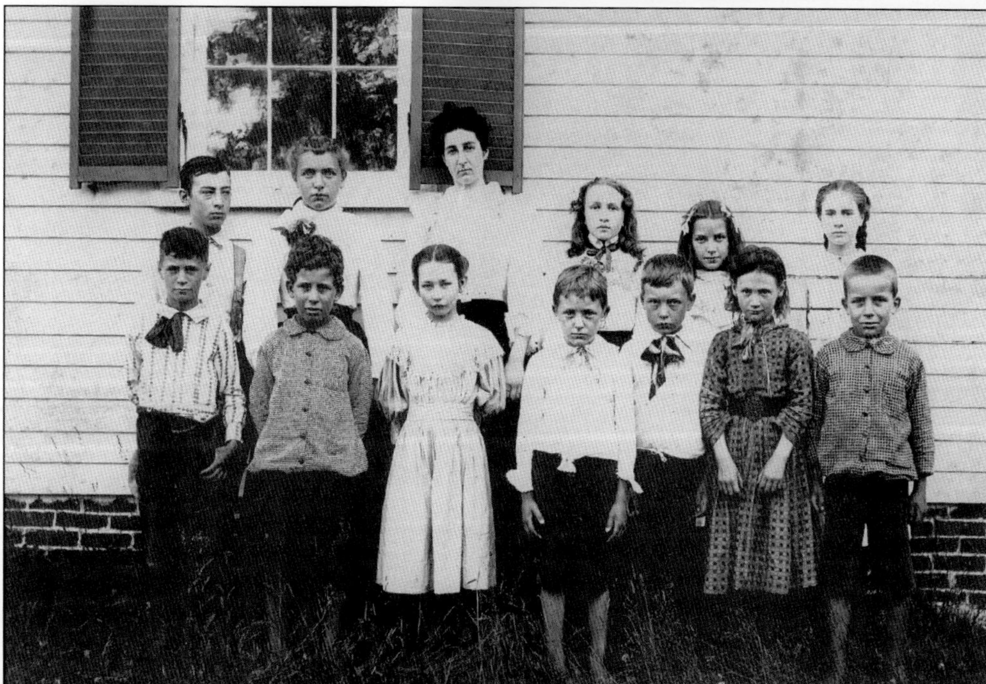

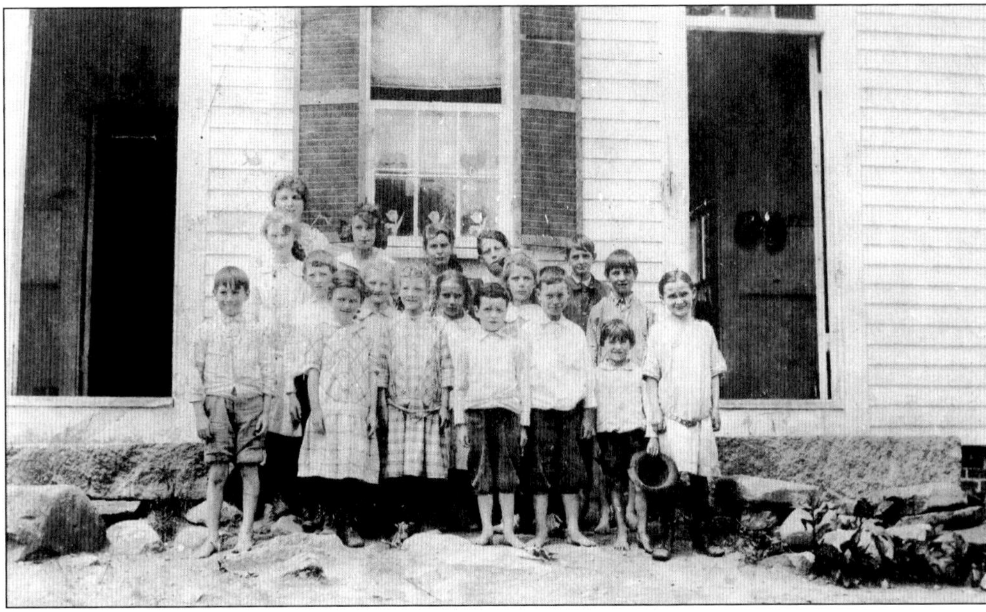

In 1830, the three school districts were divided to create a fourth district, which was known as Tilton School. The only difference in the four buildings was that the Tilton School had light-blue shutters. Although this identification is not positive, these two photographs are both likely of Tilton School. It was located at the corner of North Road, Hale True Road, and Main Street. (Both, courtesy of June McNally.)

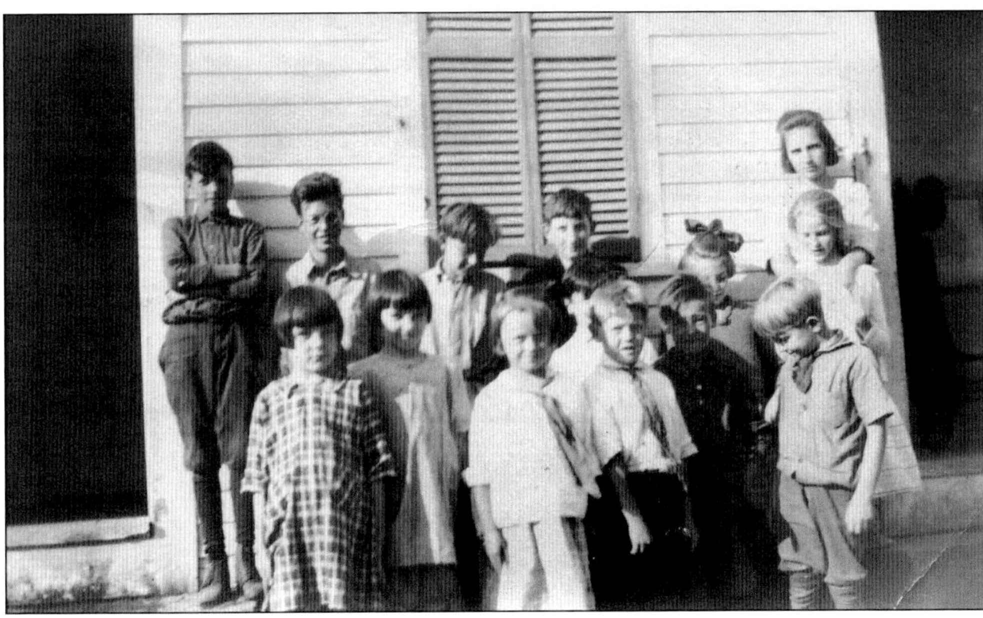

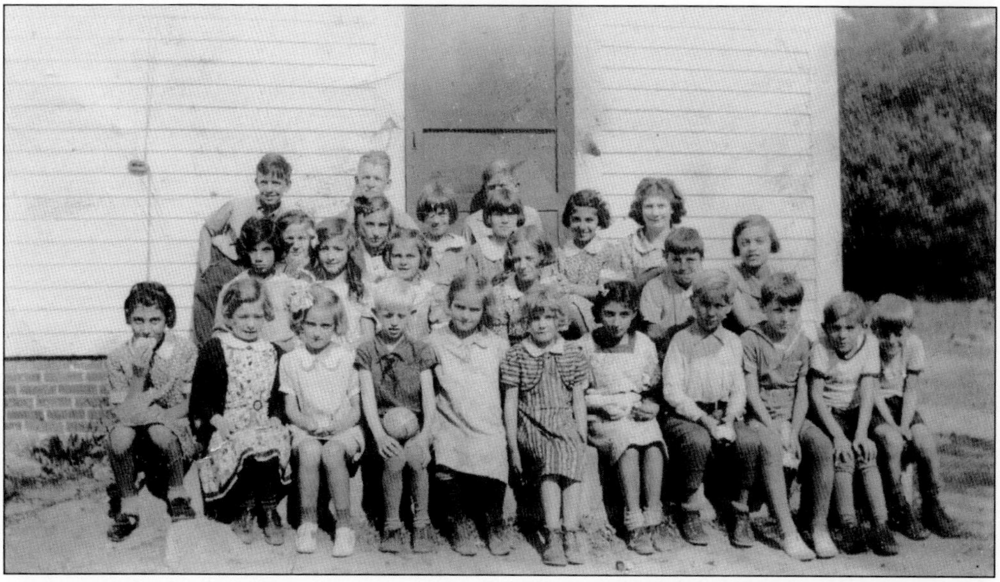

Two of the four district schools are seen here. All of the schools had one story and one chimney, with the interiors measuring approximately 18 feet by 22 feet. The exterior walls were clapboard, and there were windows on two sides. The buildings were heated with wood-burning box stoves. The photograph above shows an unusually large student population in 1938. The photograph below was taken around 1940. (Above, photograph by Bicknell Photograph Service; both, courtesy of June McNally.)

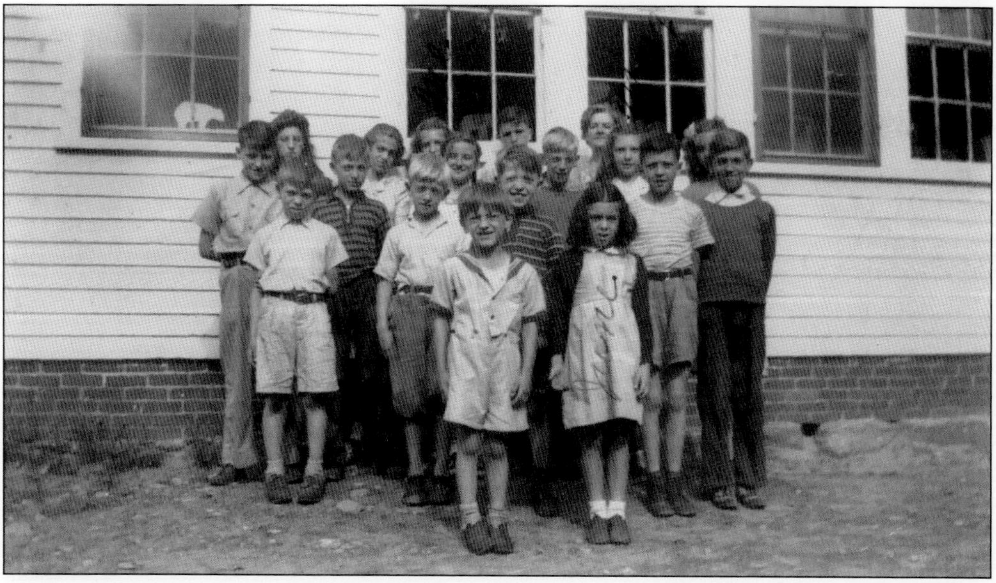

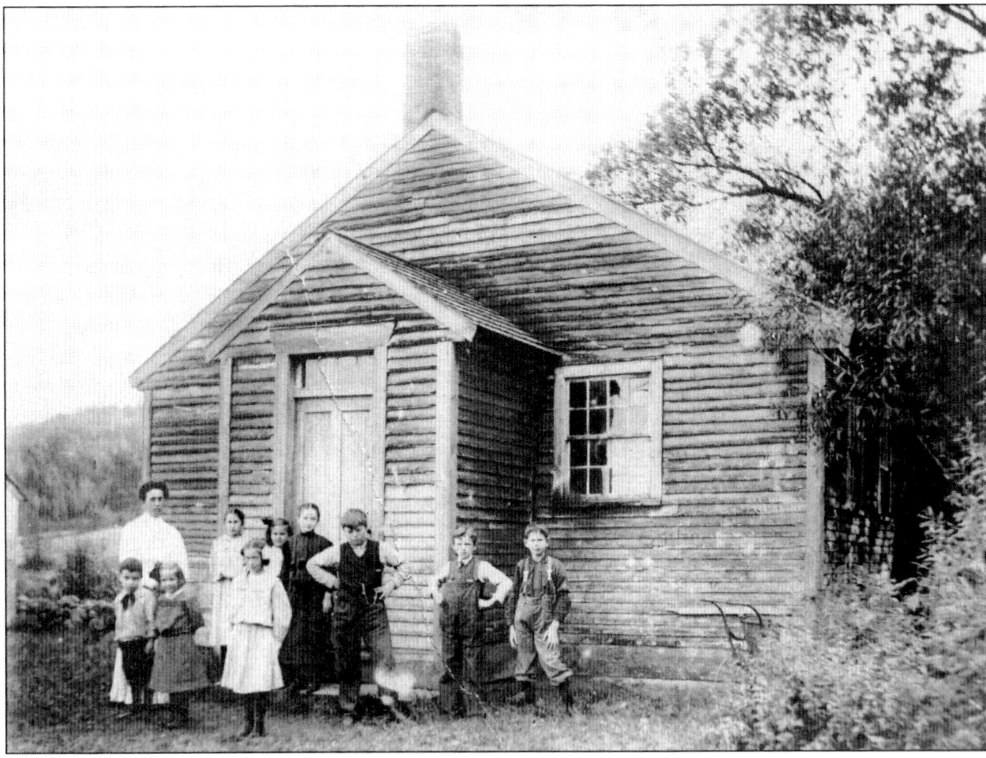

The District One school, also known as Chestnut Hill School, is seen in these two photographs. It is now a private home on the south end of Main Street, diagonally across from Michael Circle. Schools were referred to as either "master's schools" or "mistress' schools," depending on whether they were taught by a man or a woman. Female teachers were rare in the early days, usually only teaching summer sessions to other women. (Above, courtesy of Robert and Lois MacKinnon; below, courtesy of David Drowne.)

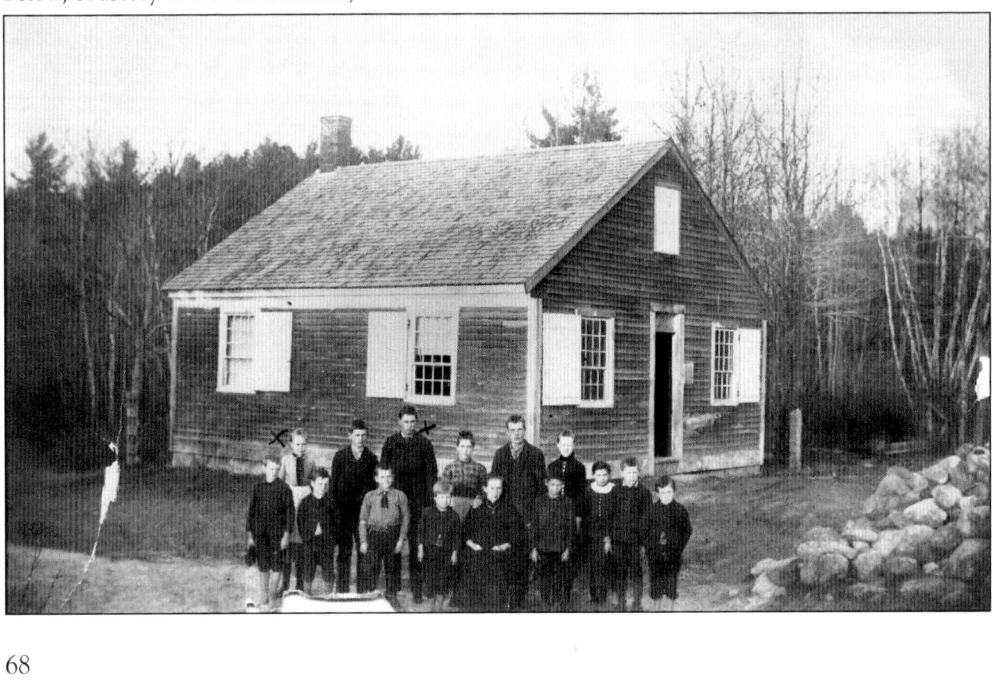

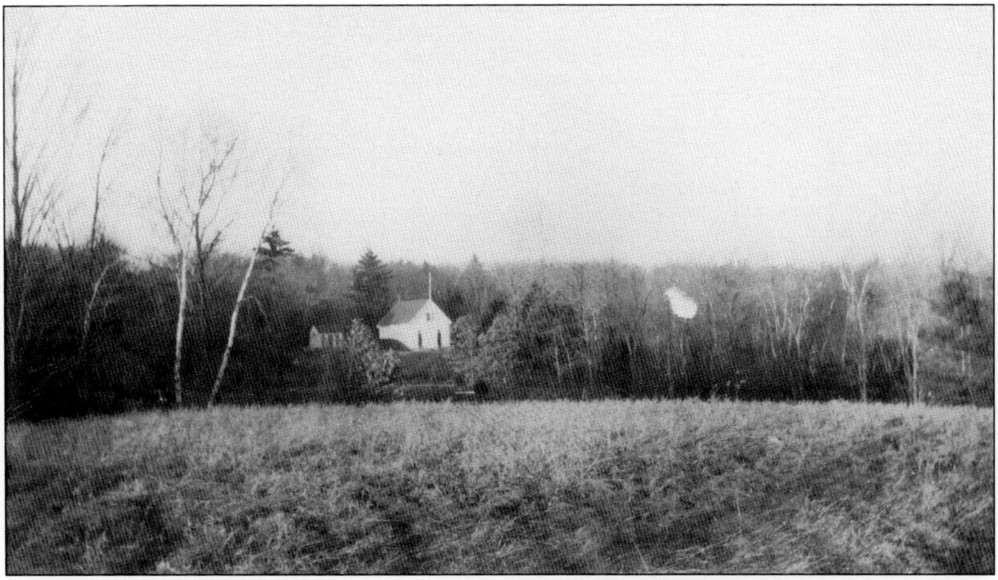

In 1922, the four district schools were condensed into two districts. Seen above is Pine Grove School, also known as Black Hole School, which was on Schoolhouse Road and taught grades one through four. Below is Clark School, on Fremont Road, which taught grades five through eight. Today, both are private homes. Note the small buildings to the right of Pine Grove School and to the left of Clark School. They were used as woodsheds and outhouses. (Both, courtesy of Eleanor Bassett.)

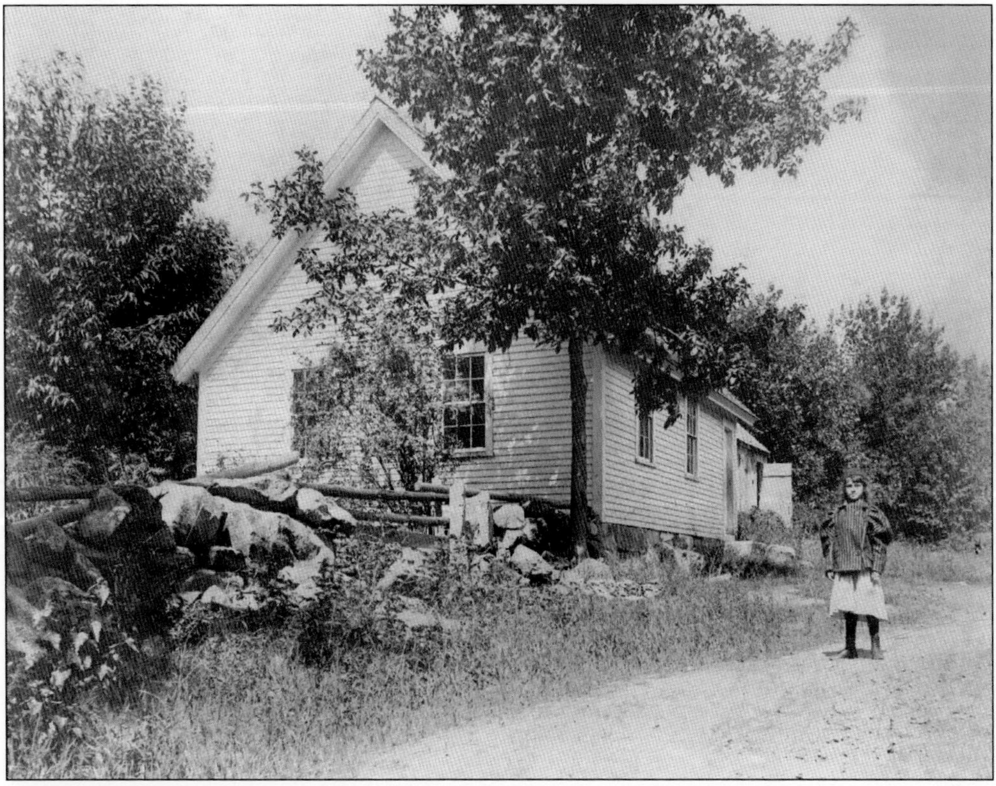

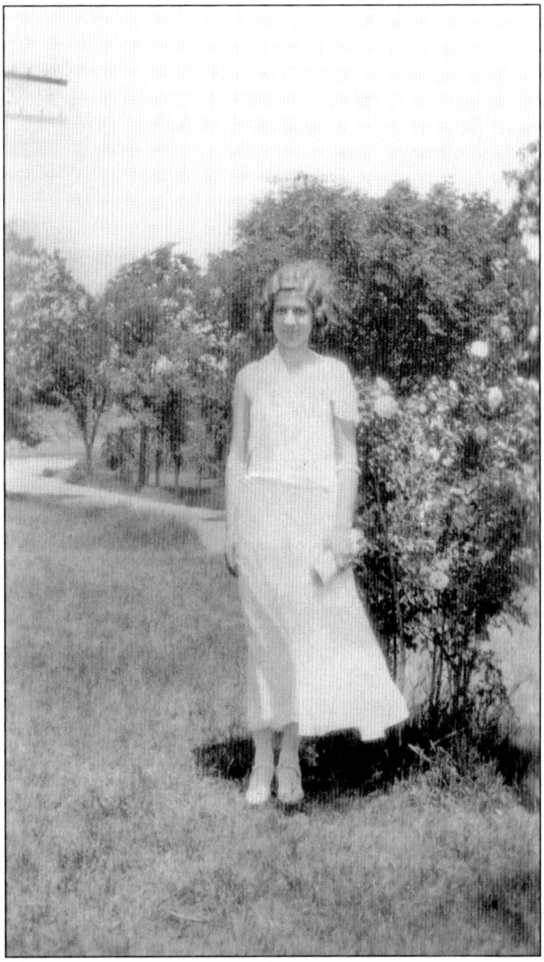

Helen Rowell proudly poses on the day of her graduation. The diploma in her hand proves that she has completed eight years at the one-room school known as Pine Grove or Black Hole. She went on to become a teacher in Derry and was a school board member in Sandown for many years. (Courtesy of Dorothy Batchelder.)

There was no playground equipment at the Clark School around 1950, leaving the students on their own to entertain themselves. For many years, the rock below was known as the "Indian mortar" because it was said that Indians had used the rock to grind corn. True or not, it made for a perfect place to sit during recess. Seen here from left to right are Eleanor Drowne, Martha Bassett, Olive Huckins, and William Hutchinson. (Courtesy of Richard Holmes.)

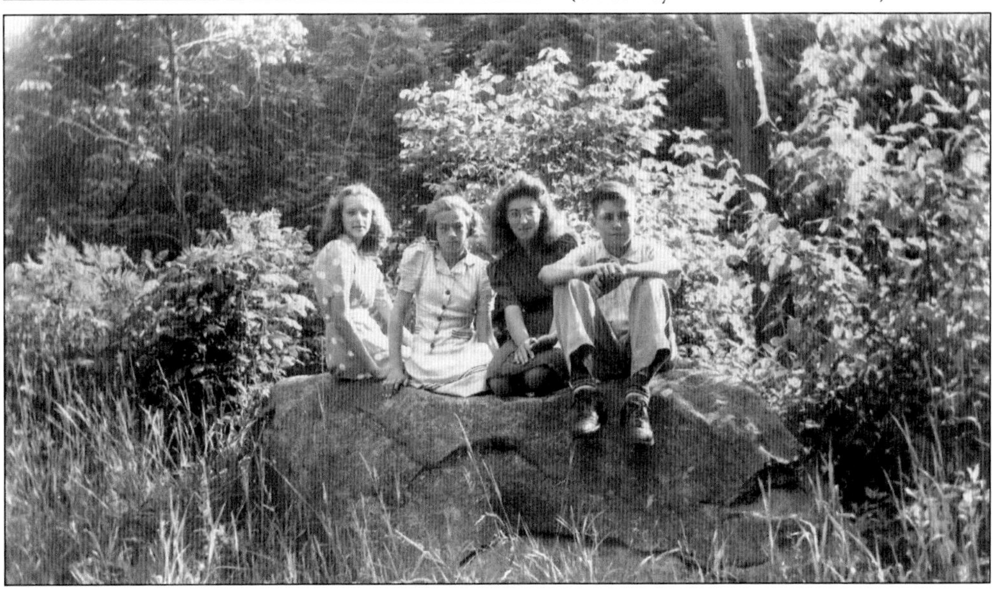

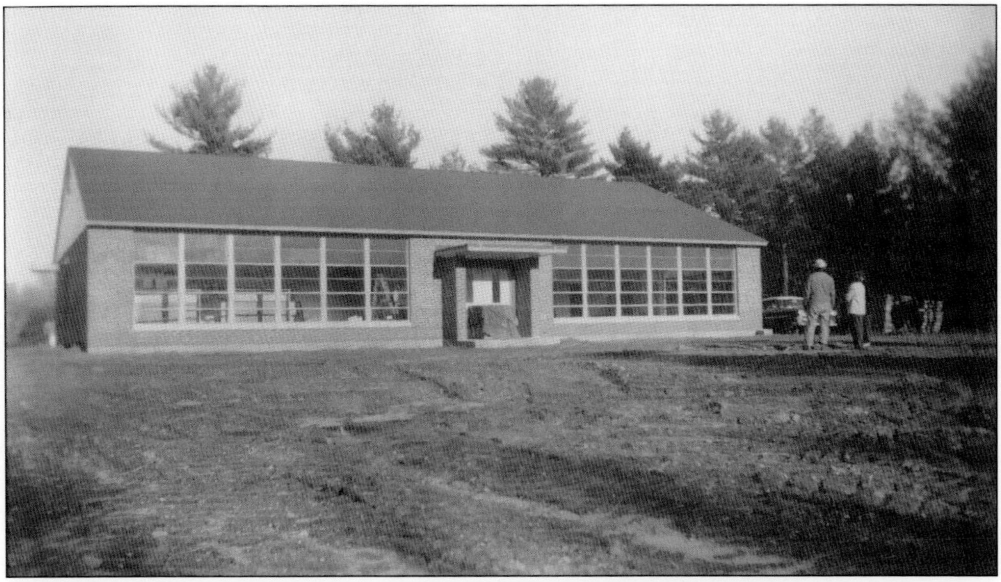

The Sandown Central School, seen here, was built in 1954. It housed all eight grades in two classrooms. The children reported that the very best feature of the new school was the "real" bathrooms. This school still stands in the same location today, but it has been swallowed up by subsequent additions. Today, only grades four and five attend school here. (Photograph by Mal Cameron; courtesy of John Cameron.)

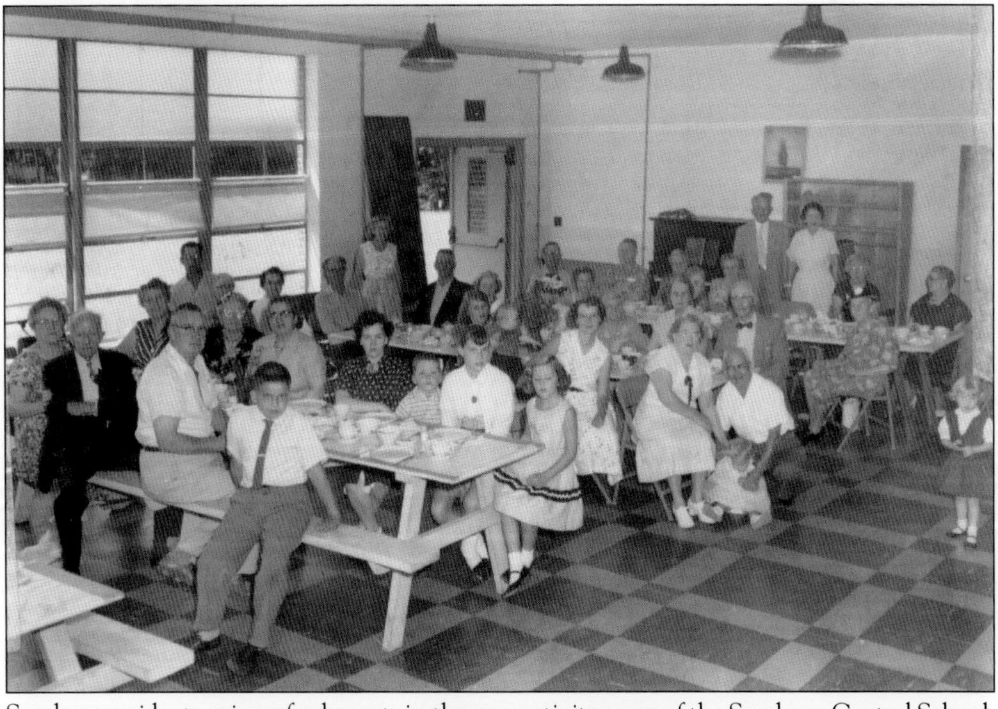

Sandown residents enjoy refreshments in the new activity room of the Sandown Central School. The building had two classrooms, the activity room, two bathrooms, a utility room, and a kitchen. The activity room served as the cafeteria at lunchtime as well as a music room and a space for afternoon dances. (Courtesy of the Sandown Historical Society.)

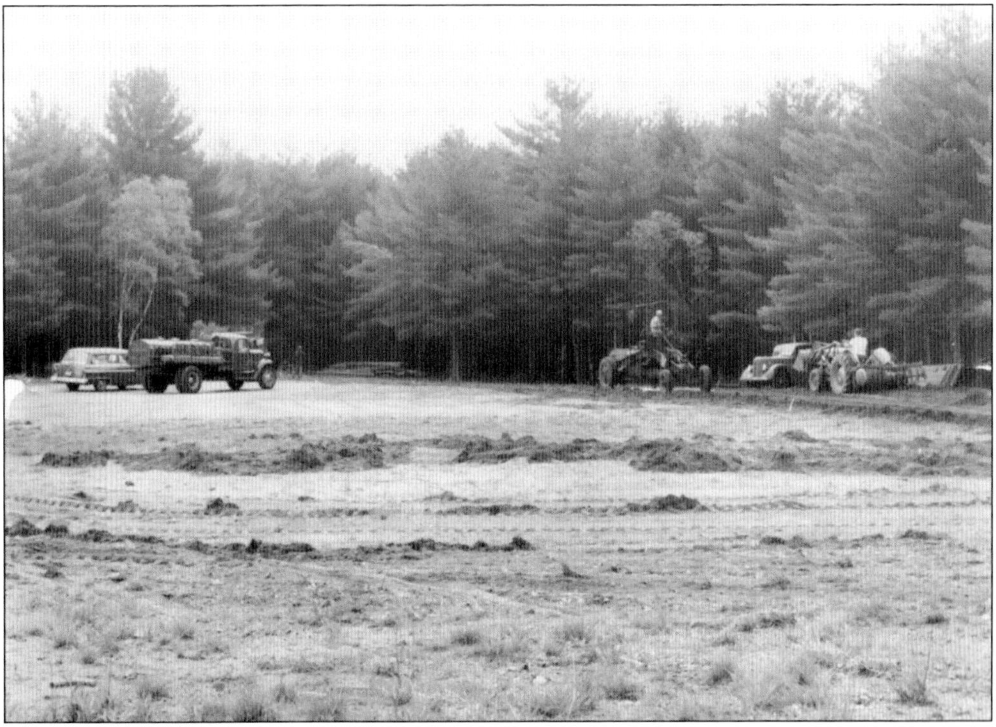

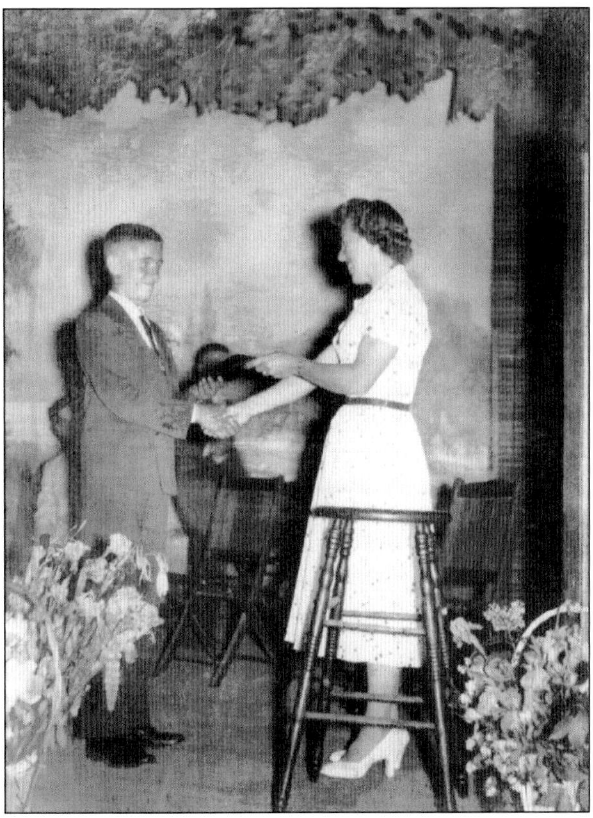

Once Sandown built the Central School, there needed to be a place for the students to play. Preparing the ball field and playground (above) took several pieces of equipment and many volunteer hands. (Courtesy of the Sandown Fire Department.)

Eighth-grade graduations took place at Sandown Town Hall until Timberlane Middle School was built in 1966. Here, in 1955, eighth-grader Robert Holmes receives his diploma from school board chairman Marguerite Drowne. Holmes was a member of the first Central School graduating class. (Courtesy of Richard Holmes.)

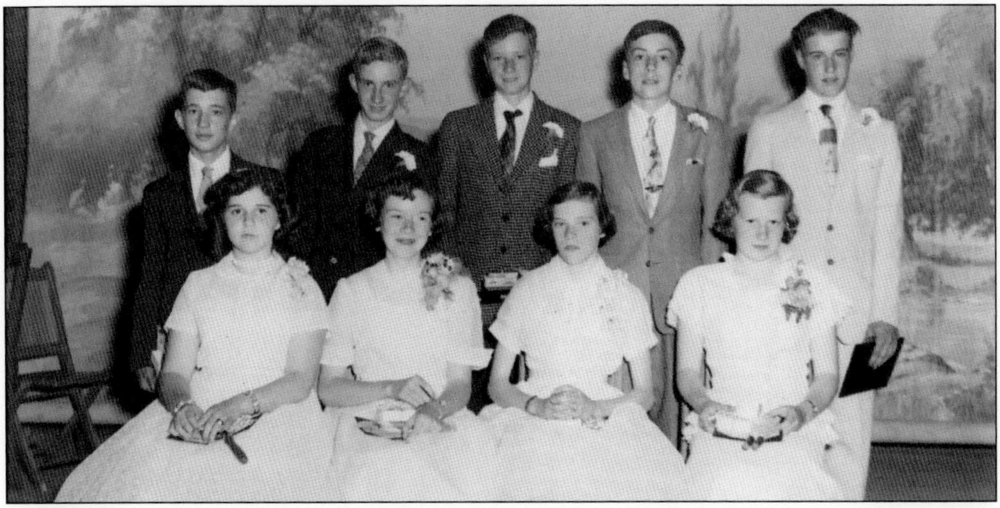

Graduations were a formal event held at the town hall, with most residents attending. This 1956 eighth-grade graduation was no exception, as seen by the corsages and boutonnieres on the graduates. The students are, from left to right (first row) Dorothy Pinard, Jean Spencer, Joan Follansbee, and Barbara Rayner; (second row) Carl Geisser, Everett "Bill" Huckins, Paul Newton, Richard Shepard, and David Ray. (Courtesy of the Sandown Public Library.)

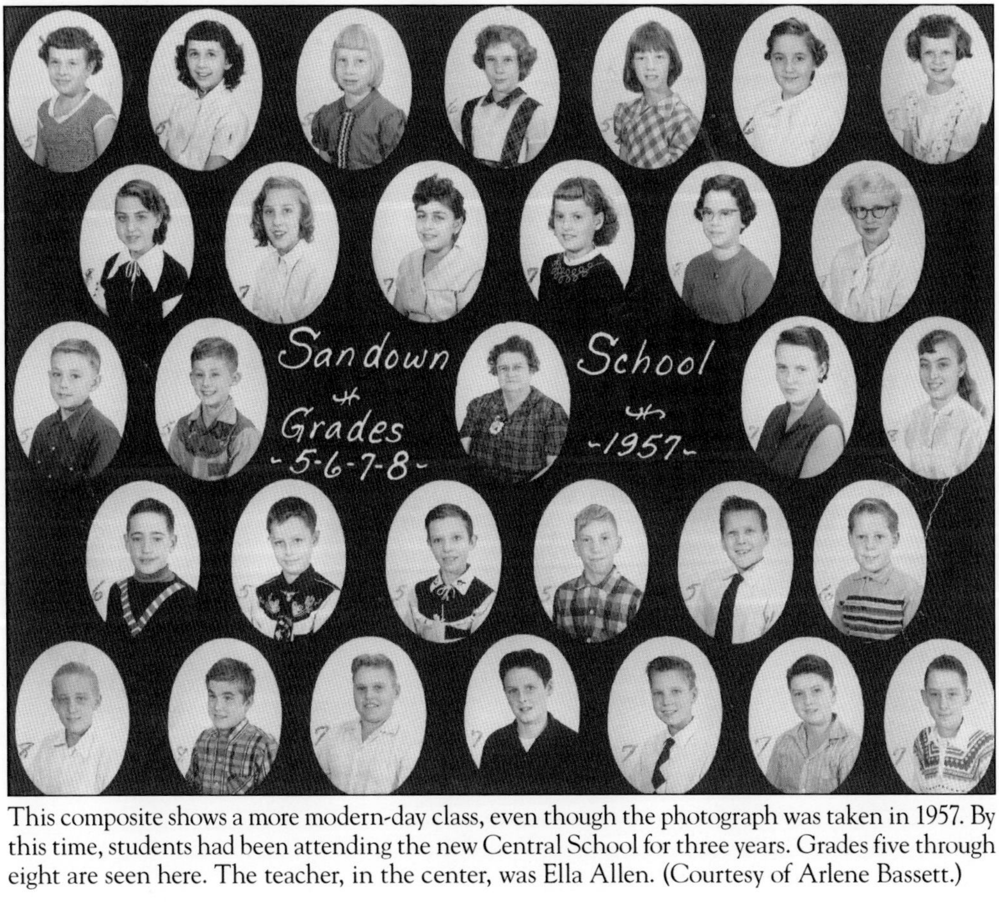

This composite shows a more modern-day class, even though the photograph was taken in 1957. By this time, students had been attending the new Central School for three years. Grades five through eight are seen here. The teacher, in the center, was Ella Allen. (Courtesy of Arlene Bassett.)

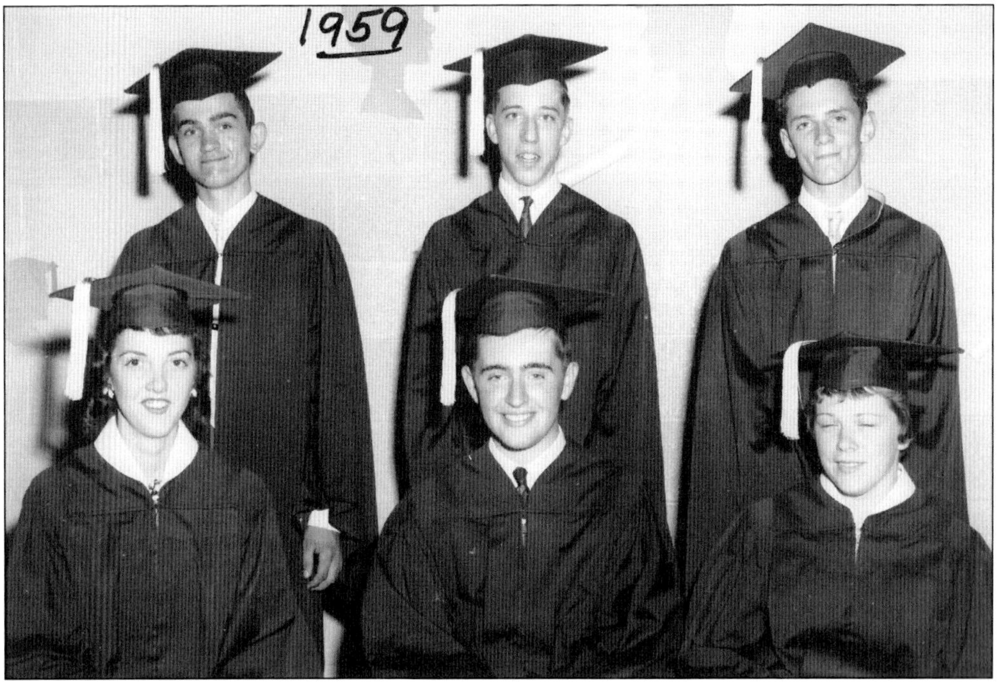

Seen here are the members of Sandown's senior class that graduated from Sanborn Seminary in 1959. They were joined by the seniors from eight other surrounding towns who also attended Sanborn. They are, from left to right, (first row) Patricia Bauer, Robert Holmes, and Judy Follansbee; (second row) Irving Bassett, Mal Cameron Jr., and Robert Pratt. (Photograph by Mal Cameron; courtesy of Richard Holmes.)

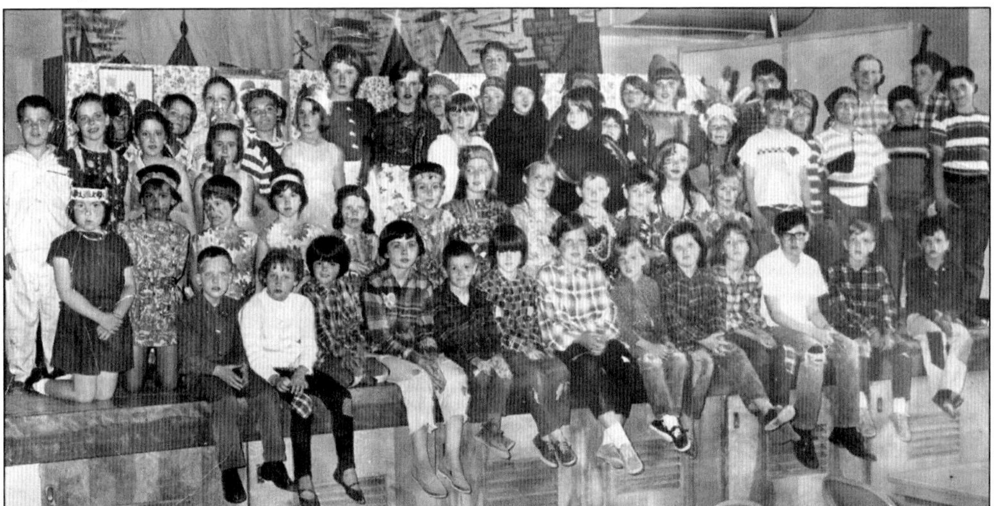

In 1968, the entire student body of Sandown Central, which numbered a little over 50, performed a school play for the three other elementary schools in the Timberlane Regional School District. The district was formed in 1964 by the towns of Sandown, Danville, Plaistow, and Atkinson. Today, there are over 550 students in Sandown's elementary grades, which are divided into two schools, with Sandown North teaching kindergarten through third grade and the Central School teaching fourth and fifth grades. (Courtesy of Jacqueline Burke.)

Five

Serving the Community

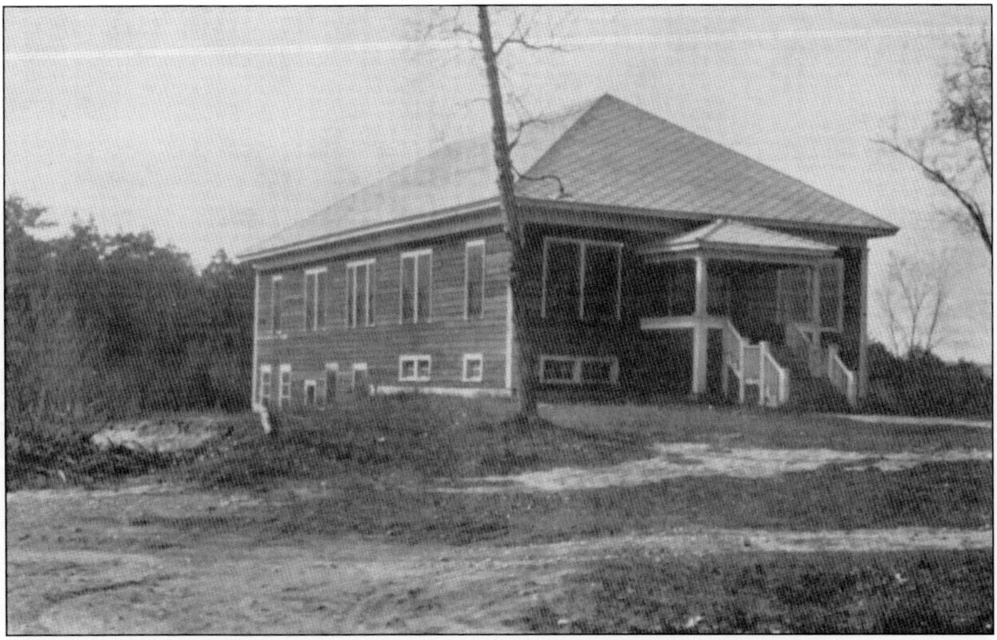

The Sandown Community Hall was built in 1921. It officially became Sandown Town Hall when the new designation was accepted at a town meeting on March 11, 1930. (Courtesy of Eleanor Bassett.)

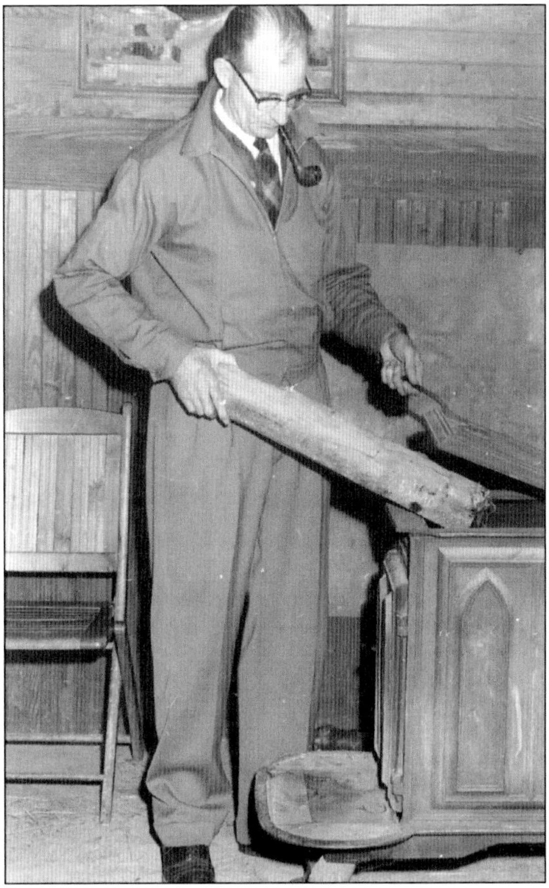

Selectman John B. Holmes Jr. feeds the wood stove at Sandown Town Hall. It was one of two wood stoves in the building, both of which were on the ground floor. In addition, there was a wood furnace that heated the upstairs. A central heating system was installed in 1957. (Courtesy of Richard Holmes.)

Below, members of the Old Meeting House Association enjoy an event at the town hall around 1955. From left to right are Angela "Nell" Cameron, Mildred Patten Wood, Hazel T. Rogan, and Eleanor Bassett. (Courtesy of Linda Torre.)

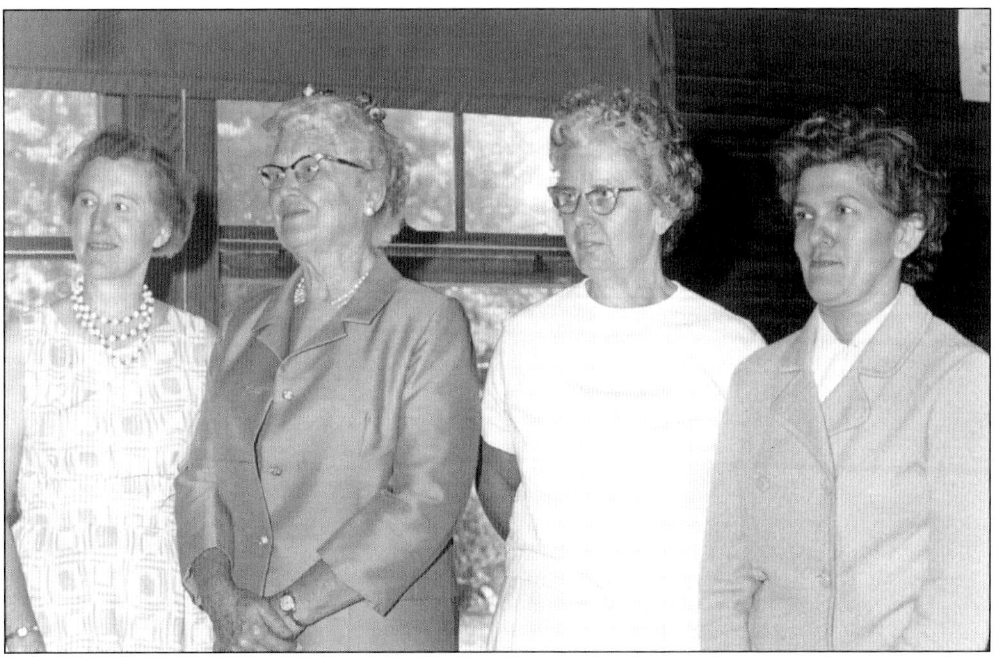

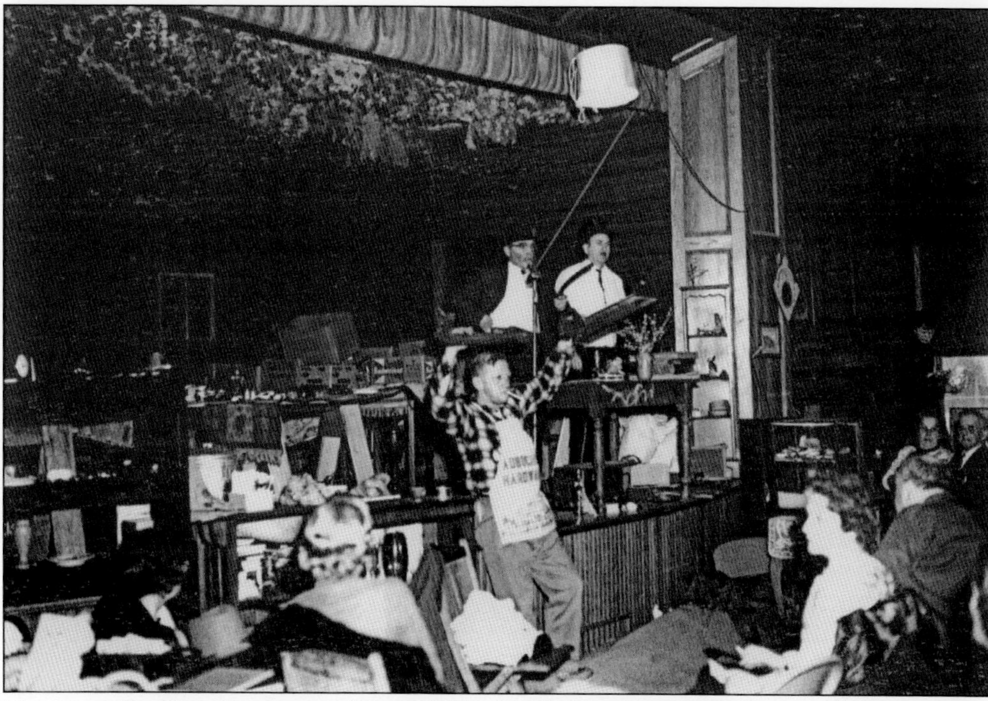

Most Saturdays found auctioneer "Topper" Hamblet holding an auction at Sandown Town Hall. Local young folks were hired to act as "runners," taking purchased treasures to patrons and collecting their money. Everyone thoroughly enjoyed these events and looked forward to them with much anticipation. (Photograph by Mal Cameron; courtesy of John Cameron.)

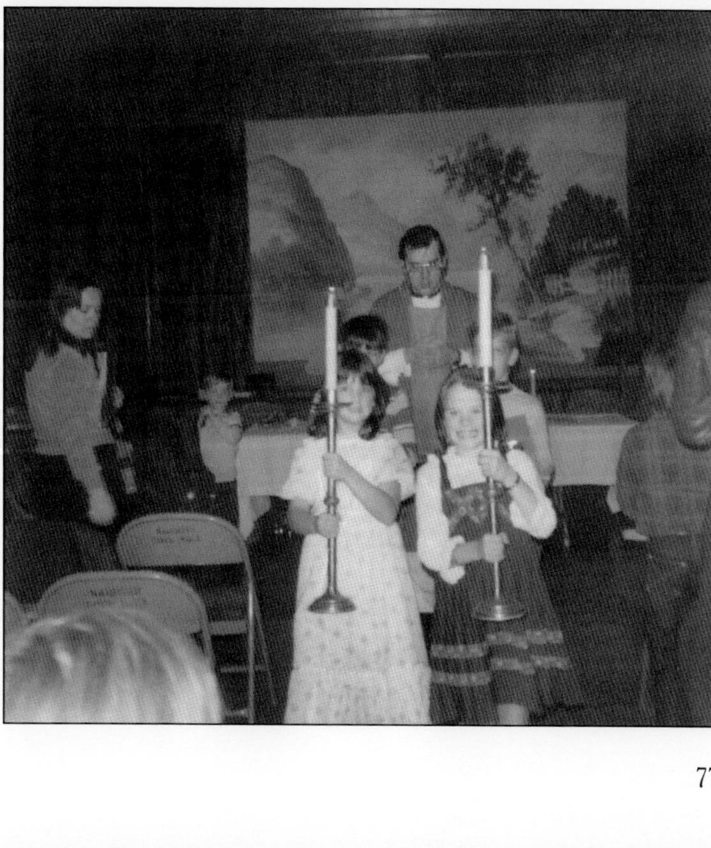

In the fall of 1977, the town hall took on a new role every Sunday morning as a place of worship for the growing Catholic population of Sandown. For the next 23 years, members of St. Michael's Catholic community gathered at the building, which was affectionately referred to as "St. Town Hall." Leading the procession after mass with Fr. Paul Daneault are altar servers Jennifer Cabral (left) and Cheryl Reynolds. (Courtesy of Ann Cabral.)

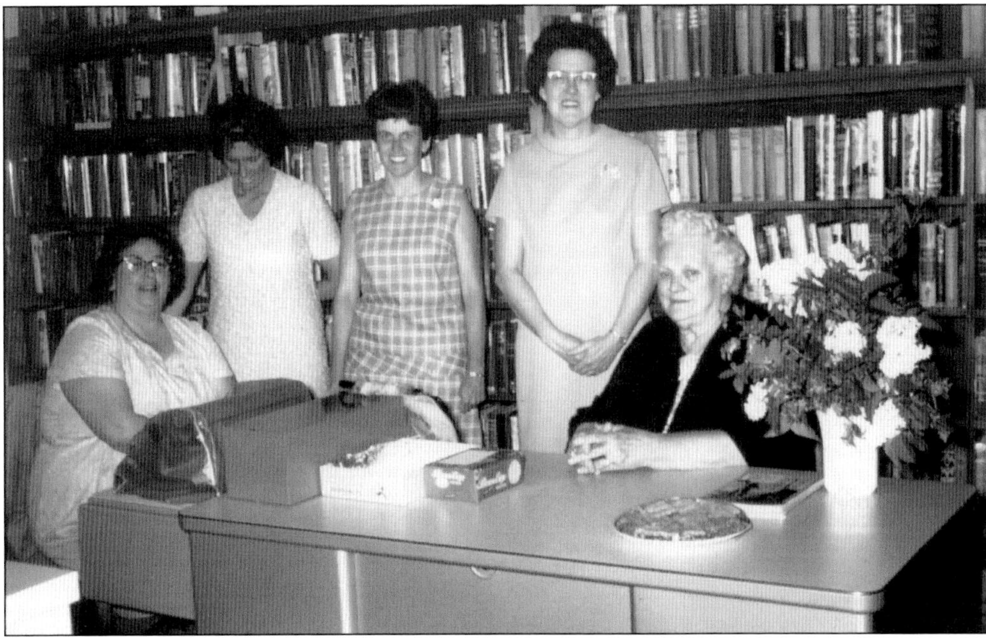

From 1936 until 1975, the public library was housed in a small room in the town hall. By the 1960s, books and shelves filled the room, allowing no space for people to sit, read, or study. As seen here, trustees and staff worked closely together to provide services for the residents. From left to right are trustee Virginia Lessard, two unidentified staff members, trustee Eleanor C. Bassett, and trustee Edith Love. (Courtesy of the Sandown Public Library.)

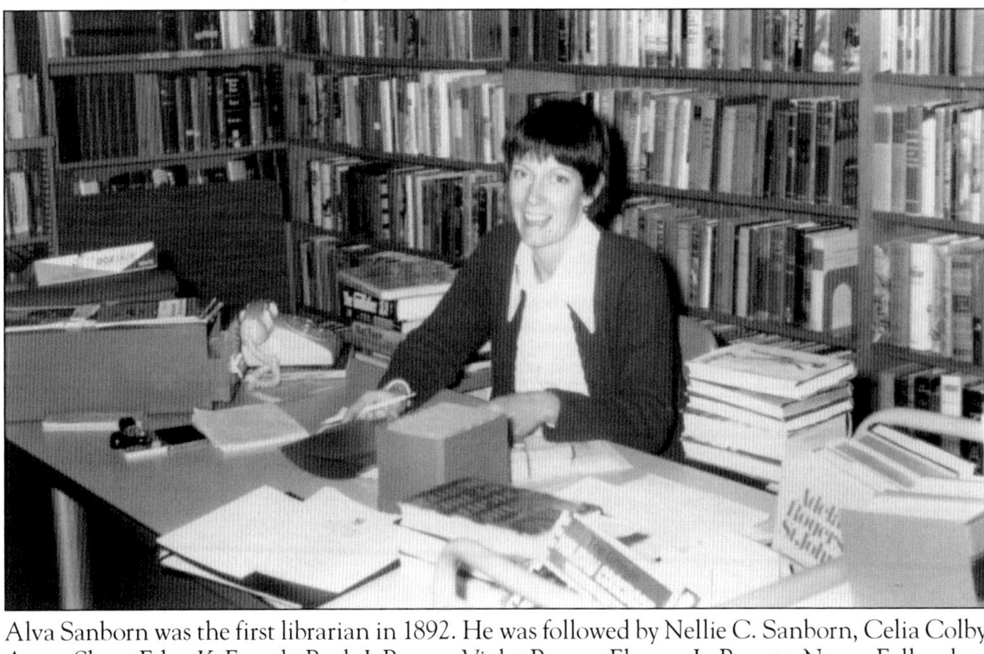

Alva Sanborn was the first librarian in 1892. He was followed by Nellie C. Sanborn, Celia Colby, Agnes Shaw, Edna K. French, Ruth I. Brown, Violet Brown, Eleanor L. Bassett, Nancy Follansbee, Mary Deamon, Virginia A. Spencer, and Alice J. Tarbox. In 1971, professional librarian Susan Mast of East Derry was hired. Mast, seen here in the town hall, helped move the library to its new building. (Courtesy of the Sandown Public Library.)

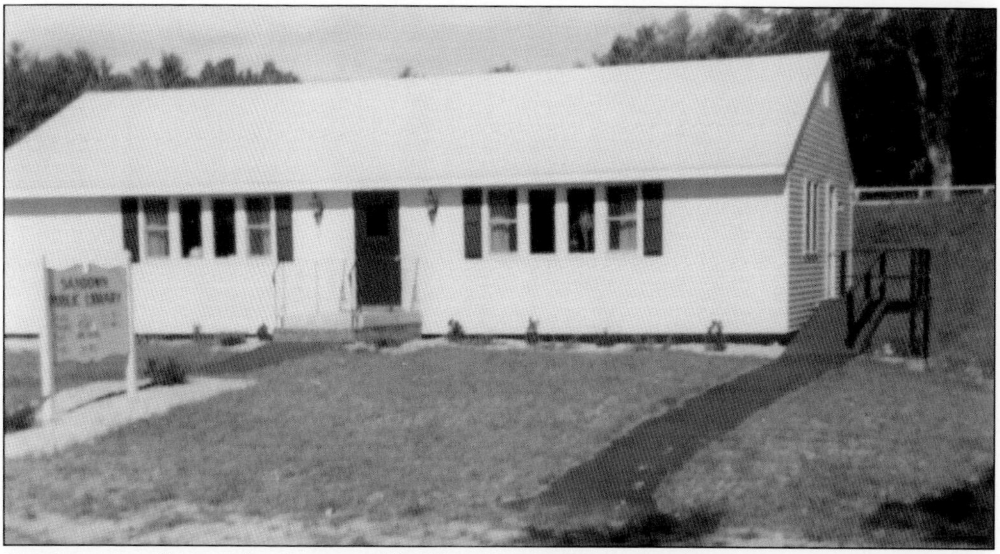

Sandown proudly voted to have a public library in 1892. However, books were originally housed in private homes before being moved to the town hall in 1936. In 1974, the town approved $30,000 to construct a library building (above) on Main Street in the former sandpit that was commonly known as the "bonfire site." The main floor featured a children's area, a magazine section, shelves for fiction and nonfiction, and tables for studying. The lower level was for storage and utilities. In later years, the police department was housed in the basement. Below, selectman Patrick Castonguay hands over the keys to the new building to library trustee Edith Love at the open house in March 1975. In the foreground are, from left to right, selectmen John B. Holmes and Richard Drowne and building designer Steven Twombly. (Both, courtesy of the Sandown Public Library.)

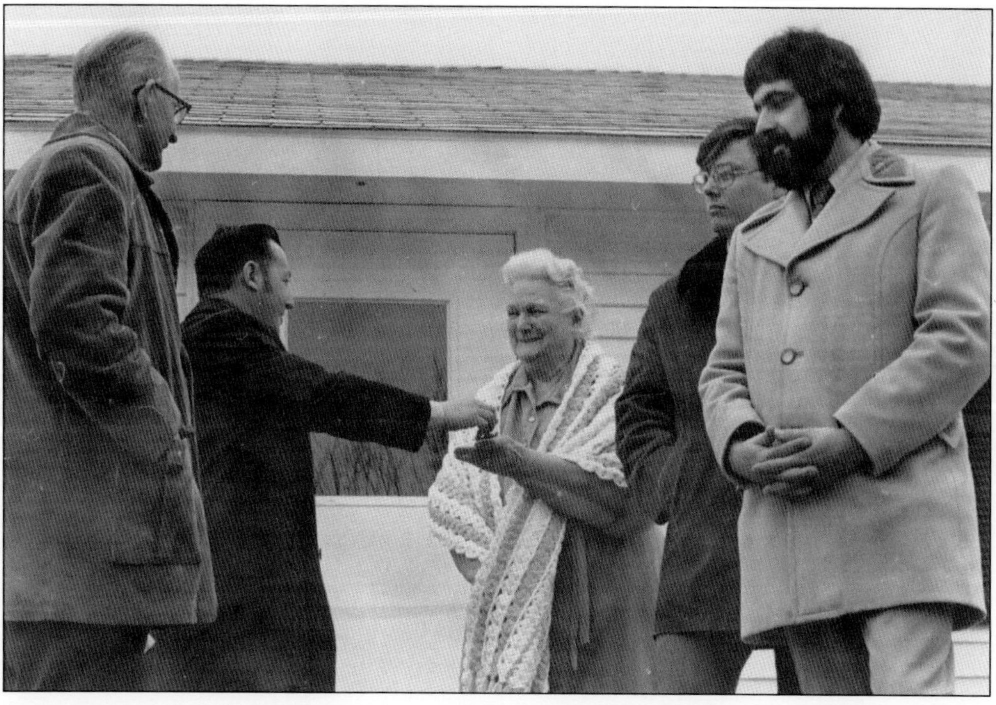

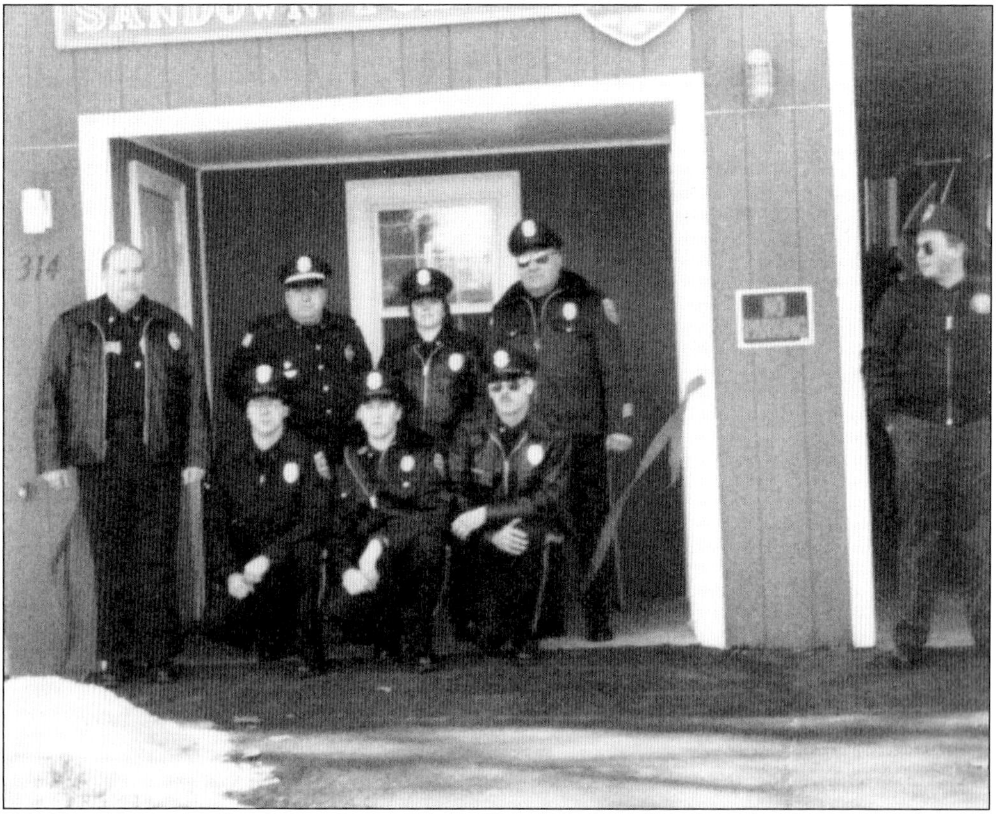

Sandown police chief James Comerford (far left) and members of his police department proudly stand for a group photograph. For most of the town's history, Sandown residents were appointed as special police. It was not until the mid-1900s that the town felt the need to have a year-round police force. (Courtesy of the Sandown Police Department.)

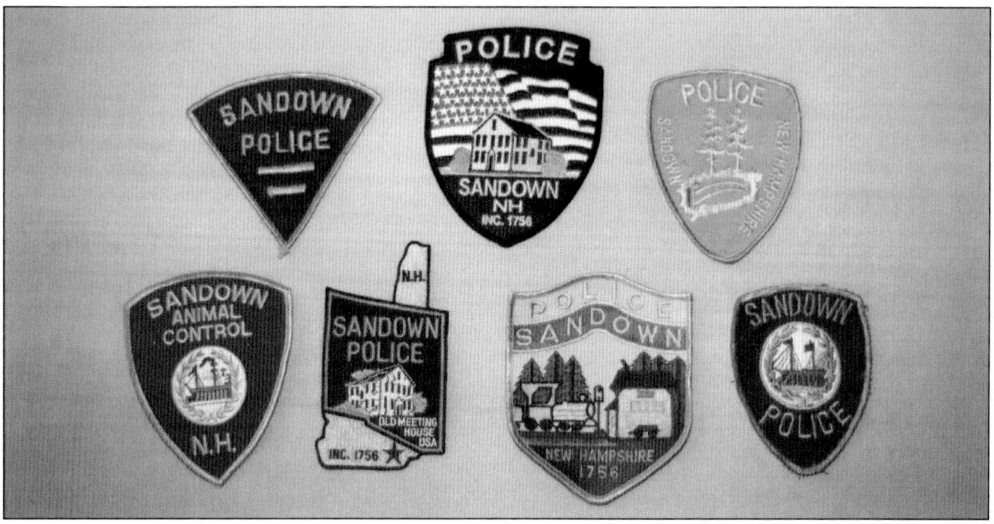

From their simple beginnings, the badges of the Sandown police department have proudly displayed the sense of community that officers protect day in and day out. The badge in the top middle is the new design currently in use. (Courtesy of the Sandown Police Department.)

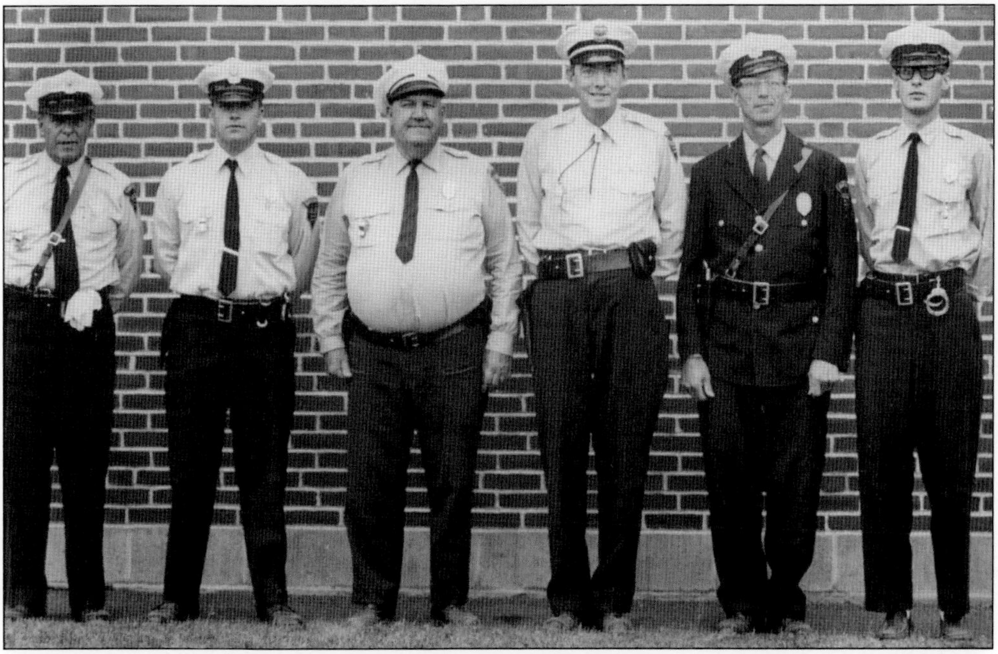

Lined up and ready for duty in 1964 are, from left to right, Sandown police officers Carroll Bassett, Richard Haggett, Ralph Millard, Chester Tarbox (chief), William Dombroski, and Patrick Burke. According to the 1964 annual report, the total budget for the police department was $950. With this modest budget, police officers used their own vehicles to answer calls and go on random patrols. (Courtesy of the Sandown Police Department.)

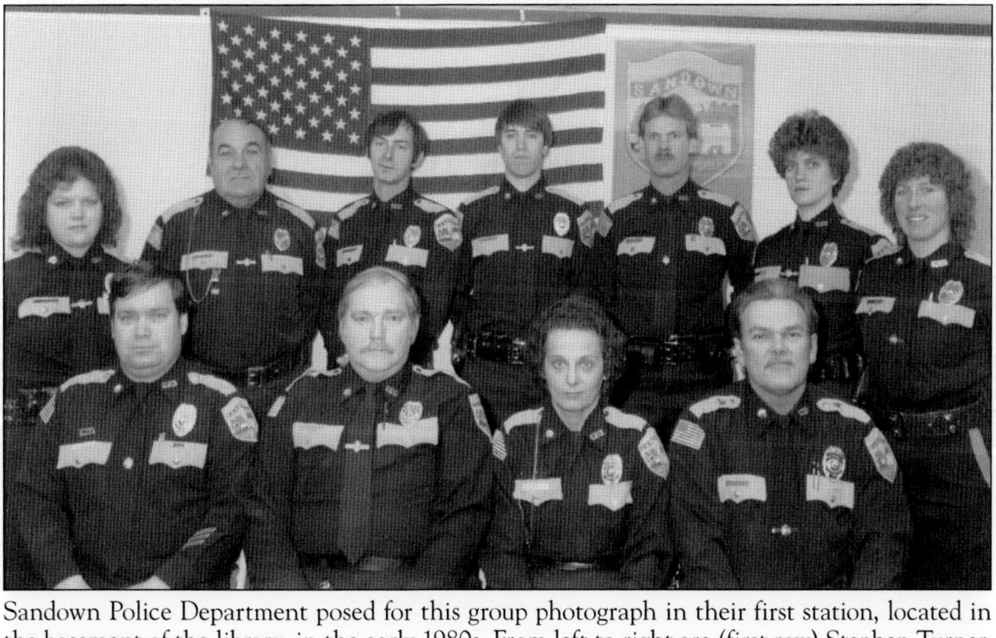

Sandown Police Department posed for this group photograph in their first station, located in the basement of the library, in the early 1980s. From left to right are (first row) Stephen Turner, James Comerford (chief), Mary Comerford, and Scott Ashley; (second row) Monique Vermette, Anthony Lopez, Vern Mowry, Joseph Woodbury, Al Cullen, Lisa Sturdavan, and Lauren Vlack. (Courtesy of the Sandown Police Department.)

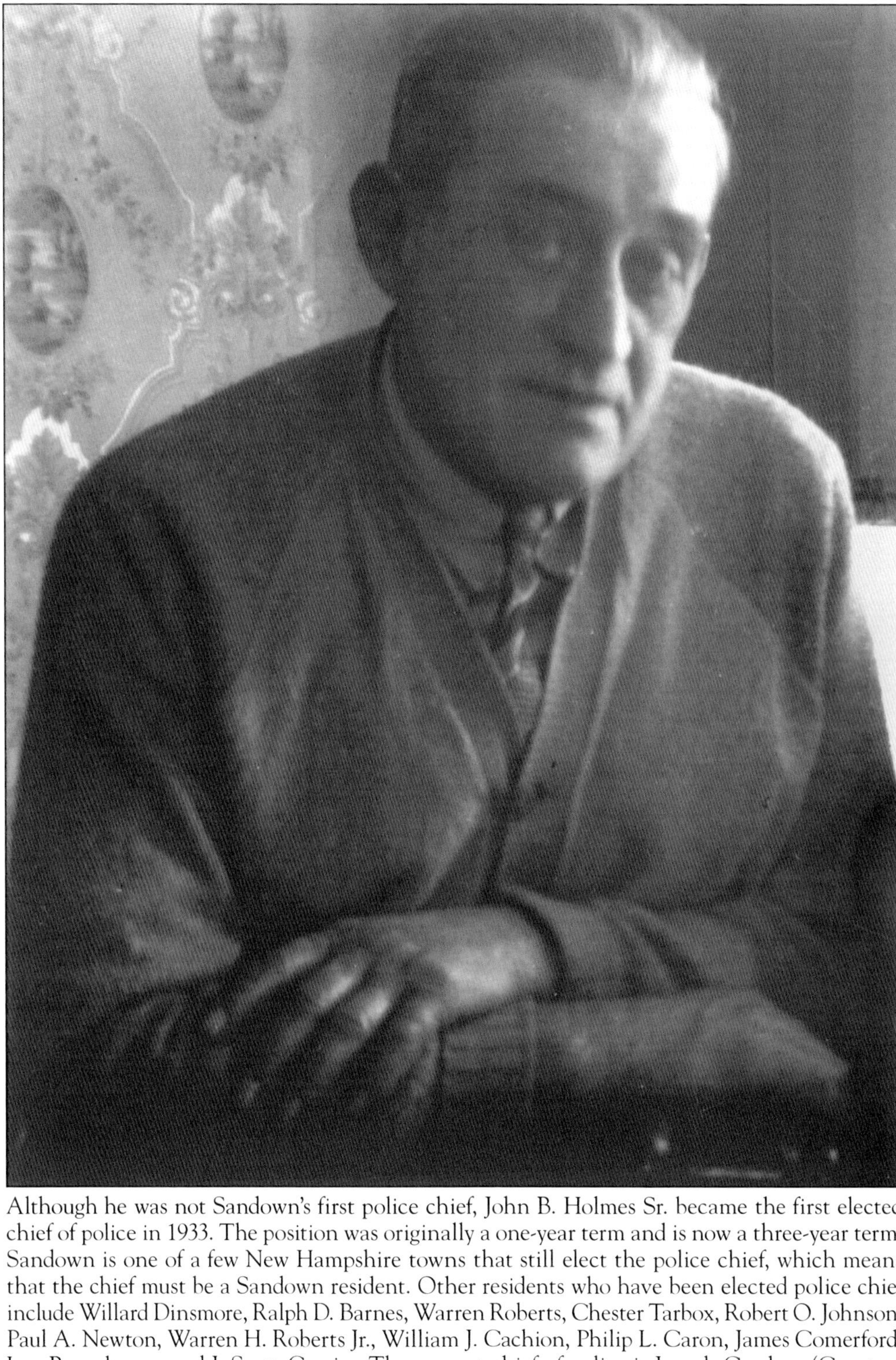

Although he was not Sandown's first police chief, John B. Holmes Sr. became the first elected chief of police in 1933. The position was originally a one-year term and is now a three-year term. Sandown is one of a few New Hampshire towns that still elect the police chief, which means that the chief must be a Sandown resident. Other residents who have been elected police chief include Willard Dinsmore, Ralph D. Barnes, Warren Roberts, Chester Tarbox, Robert O. Johnson, Paul A. Newton, Warren H. Roberts Jr., William J. Cachion, Philip L. Caron, James Comerford, Leo Beauchamp, and J. Scott Currier. The current chief of police is Joseph Gordon. (Courtesy of Arlene Bassett.)

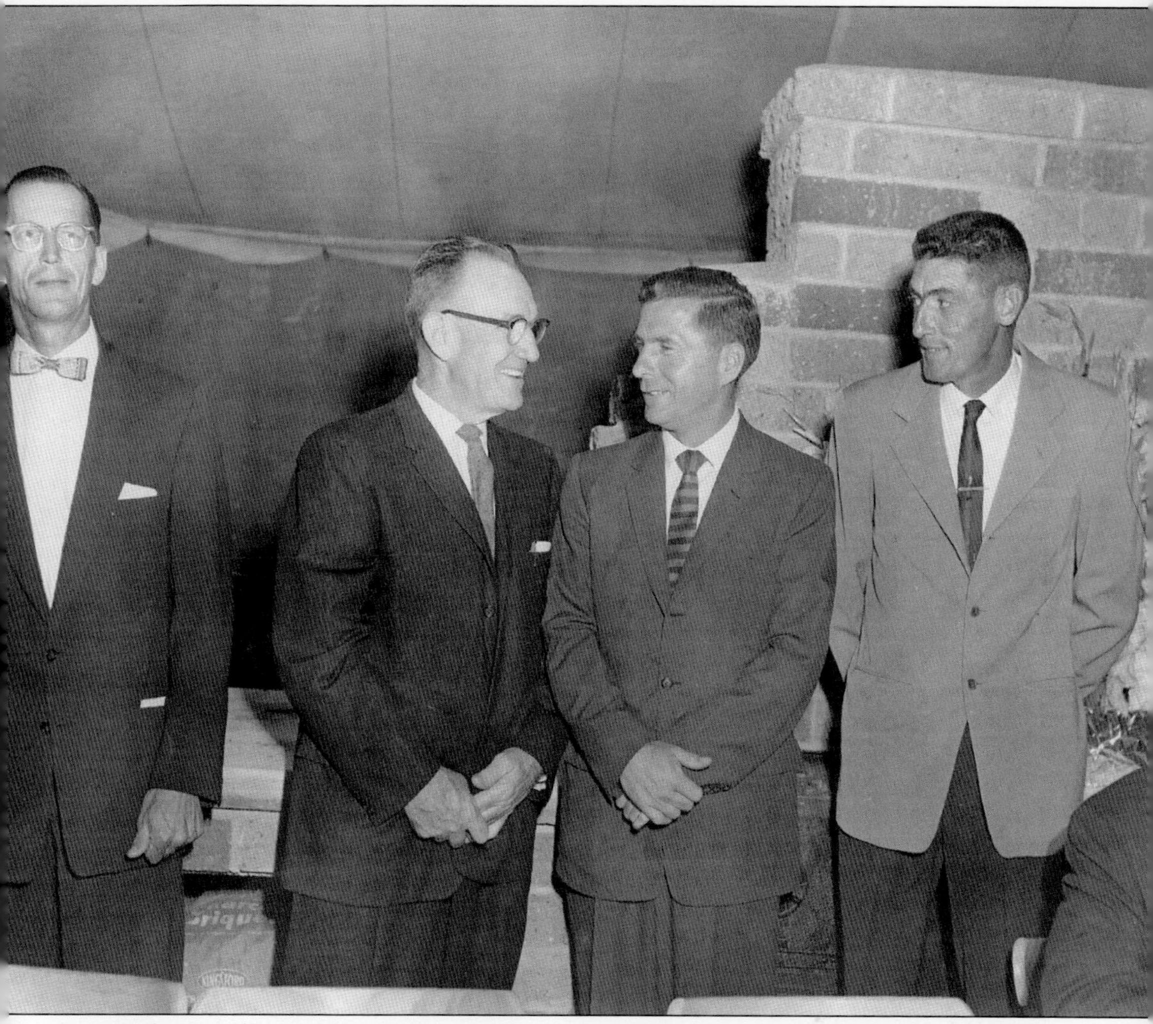

Gov. Wesley Powell (third from left) is seen here at an event in Sandown, flanked by (from left to right) special officer William Dombroski, police chief Ralph Barnes, and deputy chief Chester Tarbox. Barnes served as police chief for 20 years. While Barnes seems to be enjoying a good conversation with the governor, Dombroski and Tarbox are on the job. (Courtesy of the Sandown Police Department.)

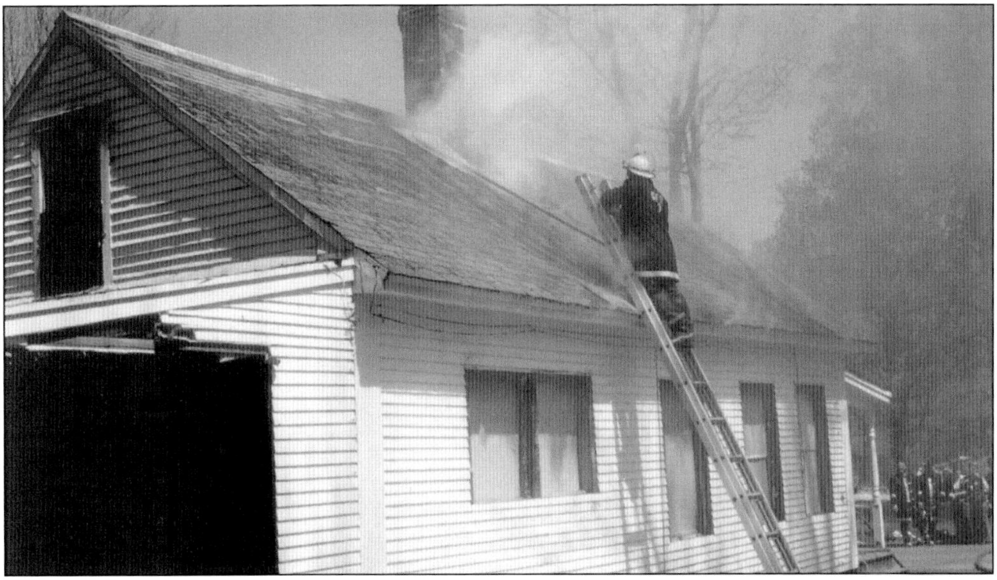

In 1978, the Sandown Fire Department trained on a small cottage on Fremont Road that was slated to be torn down. Throughout the day, different fires were set in the building, and the firemen practiced the best methods for extinguishing the blazes. Volunteers in full gear practiced using their breathing apparatus to go through the smoking structure. At the end of the day, the home was leveled and all were safe. (Courtesy of Gerard Lachance.)

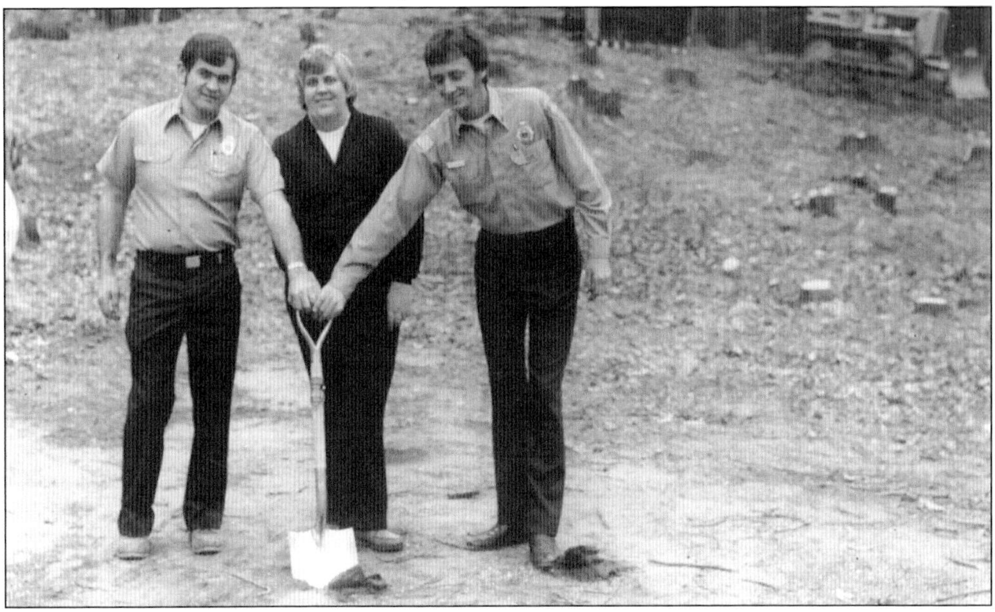

Here, in April 1980, fire station building committee cochairs Irving Bassett (left) and David Burke (right) proudly "dig" the first hole with selectperson Margaret Pskowski during the groundbreaking ceremony for the new fire station. The spirit of cooperation and pride in the building brought the whole town together and also saved taxpayers $140,000 in costs. Sandown's volunteer effort and cost-saving measure garnered regional news articles as Sandown made history. "This has been great public relations for the town and the Fire Department," concluded Irving Bassett. (Courtesy of the Sandown Fire Department.)

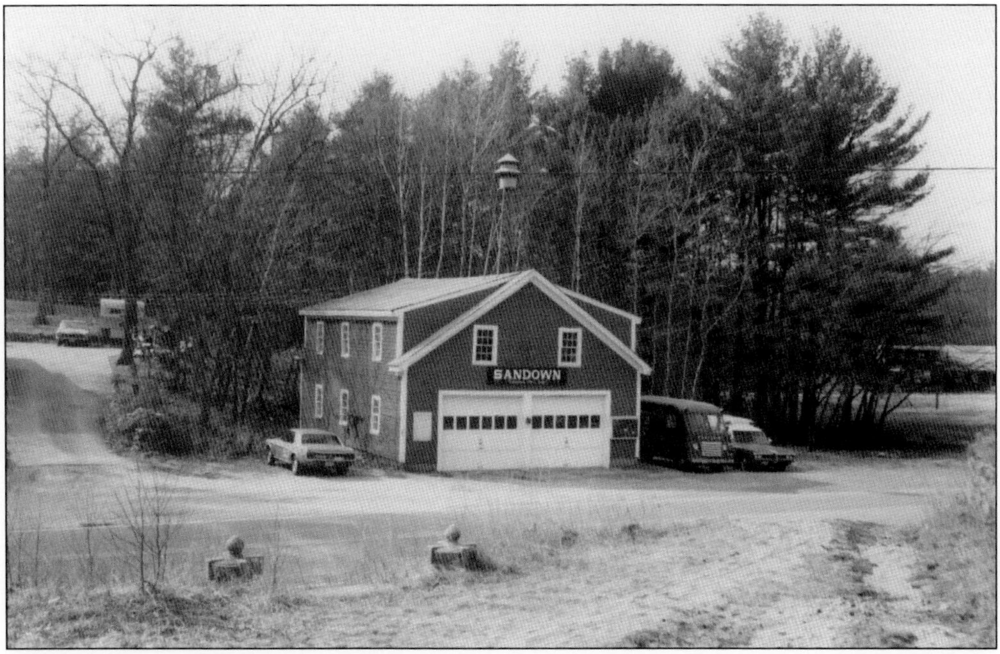

The photograph above is a nostalgic look at the old 1948 fire station, which was torn down in 1980 to make way for the new fire station (below). Both buildings were constructed with volunteer labor and donations, mostly from members of the fire department. During the construction of the new station, town residents also pitched in whenever possible, including town clerk Edward Garvey and Rev. David Watkins, the pastor of St. Matthews United Methodist Church. Women of Sandown served meals to the volunteers at the work parties, and Perrino's Market donated food and beverages. (Both, courtesy of the Sandown Fire Department.)

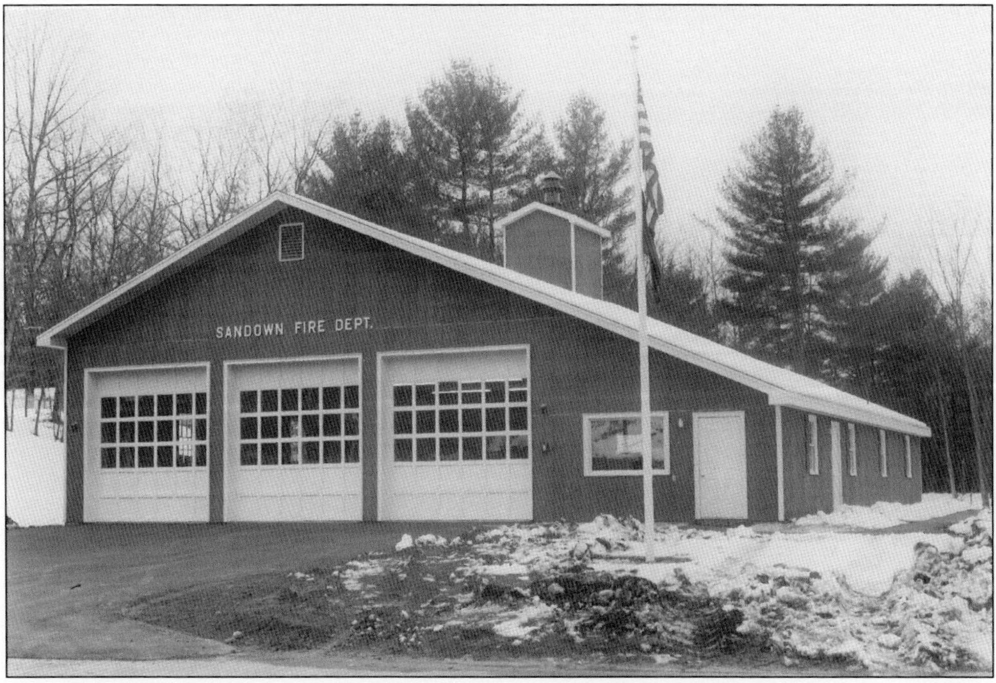

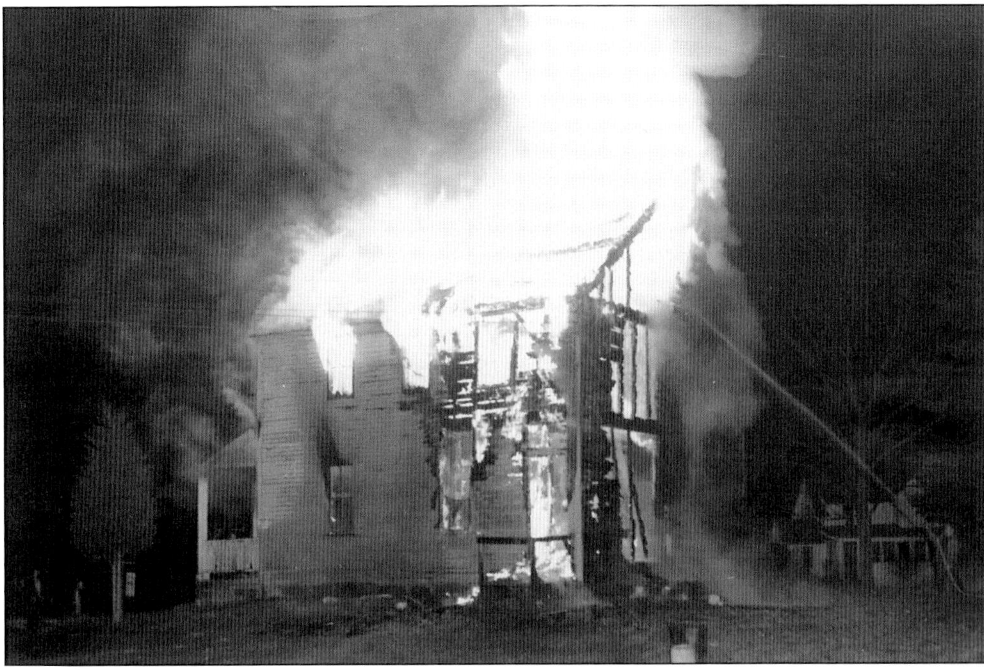

Unfortunately, Sandown has had a number of structure fires over the years. Both businesses and homes have been destroyed despite the best efforts of the volunteer firemen. The 1950s fire seen here destroyed the home of the Andrew Skywinski family, on the corner of Route 121A and Sargent Road. In the right background is the former home of the Ralph and Pearl Drowne family. (Courtesy of the Sandown Fire Department.)

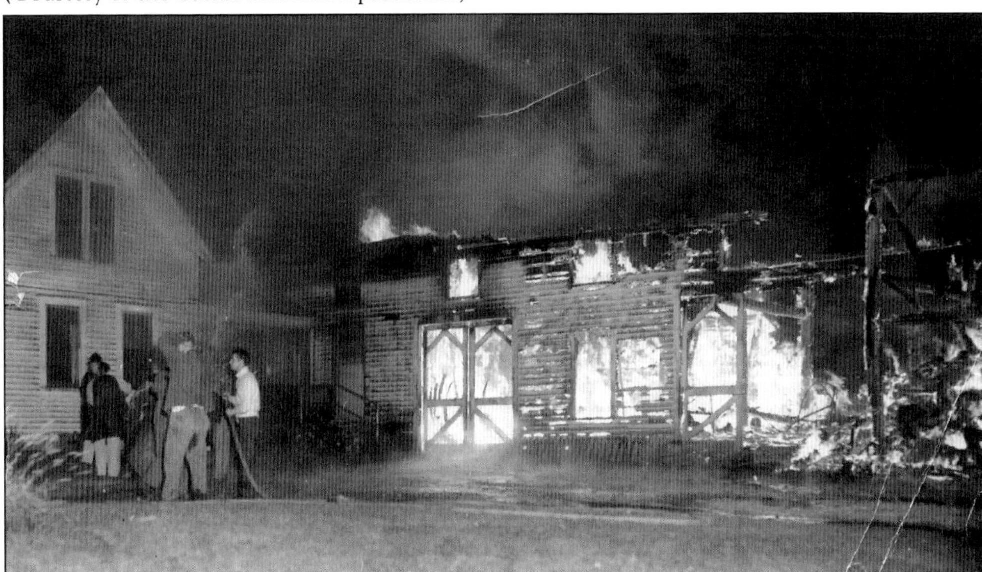

Hilltop Farm, a dairy business on South Main Street, was owned by Arthur and Rose Genualdo. In the 1950s, combustion in one of the big barns started a fire that destroyed the barn and half of the house. After the tragedy, the family built Genualdo's Spaghetti House on the site. The popular restaurant featured homemade pasta and generous portions. A spaghetti and meatball dinner with a side salad cost $1.25, and lasagna was $1.50. (Courtesy of the Sandown Fire Department.)

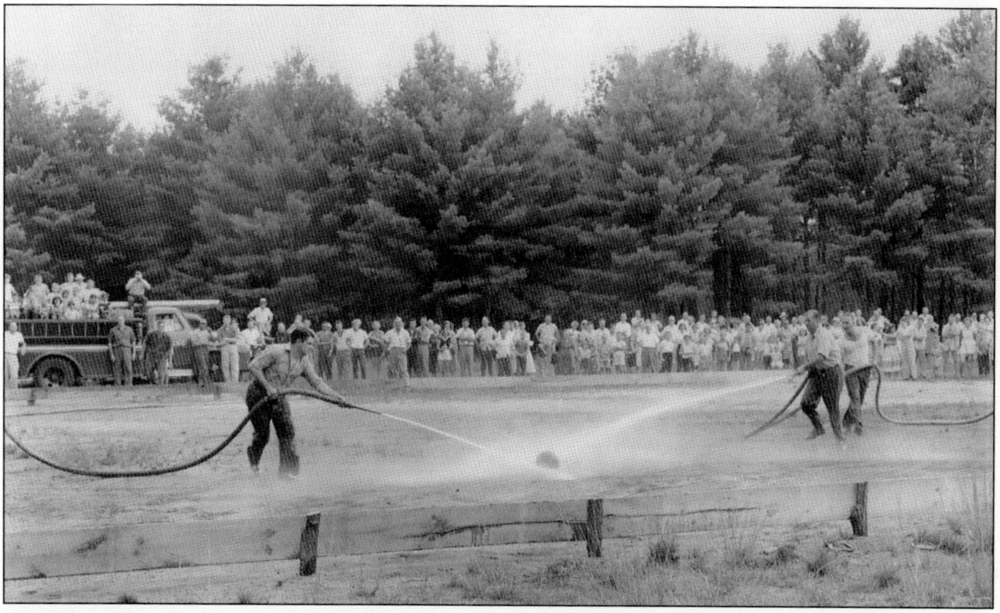

The Chester and Atkinson fire departments were two of the many departments from surrounding towns participating in this "water polo" competition, which was a popular event, as evidenced by the watching crowds during the annual carnival. The competition was held on the playground behind Central School. (Courtesy of the Sandown Fire Department.)

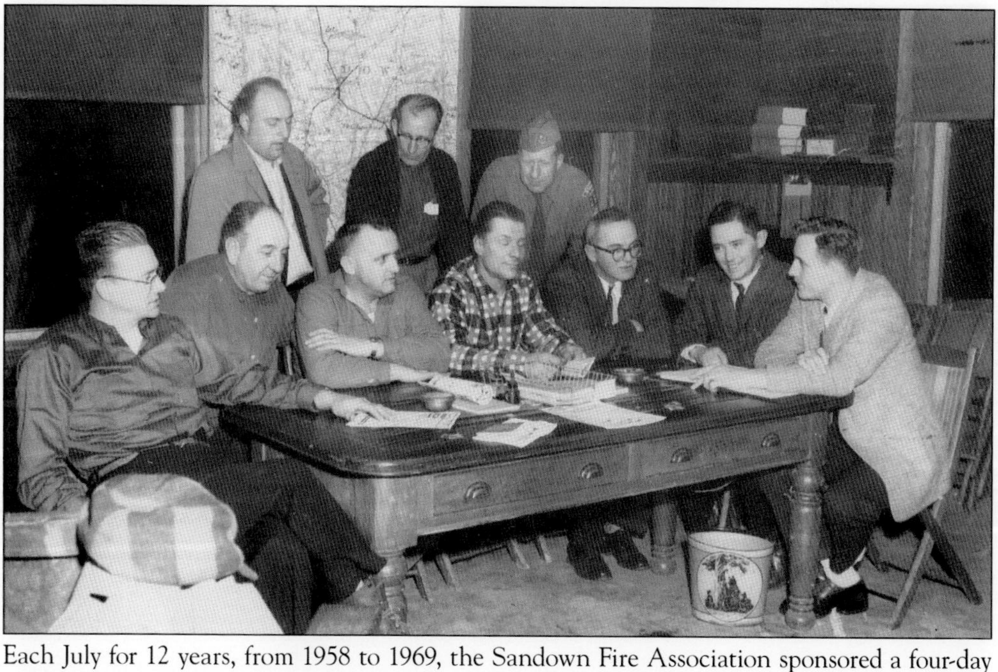

Each July for 12 years, from 1958 to 1969, the Sandown Fire Association sponsored a four-day carnival that attracted thousands of people to town. This fundraising event raised money for fire apparatus, equipment, and supplies. Carnival committee members are seen here discussing plans. They are, from left to right, (first row) Frederick Drowne, Chester Nicolaisen, Edward Deveau, Allen Love, two representative from the carnival company, and David Bauer; (second row) Malcolm MacGregor, John Holmes, and Alpha Learned. (Courtesy of the Sandown Fire Department.)

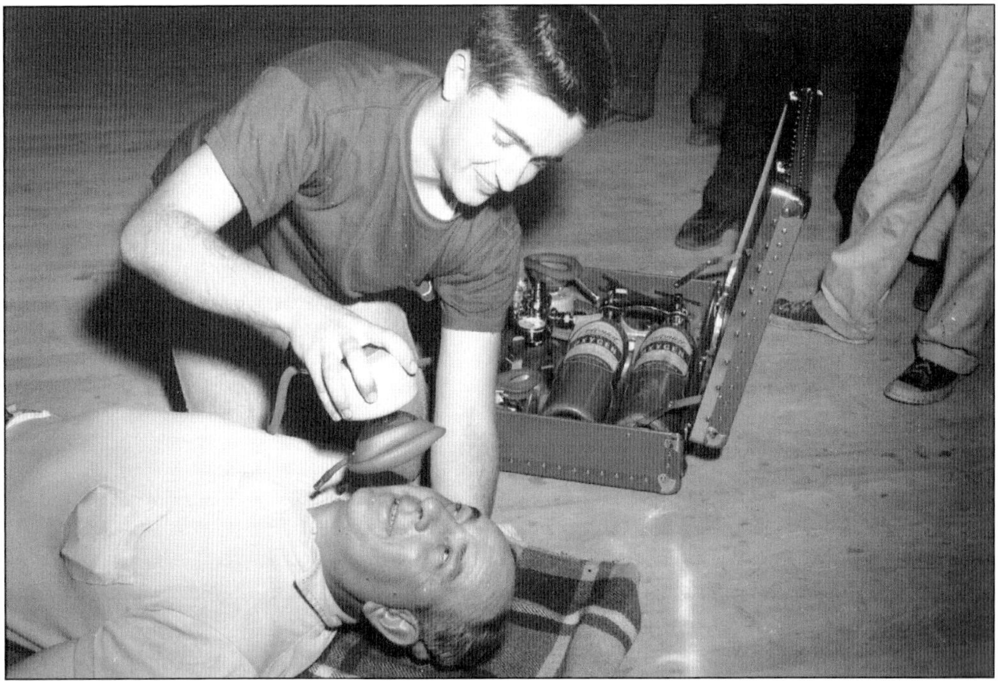

Constant training on new equipment has always been a requirement for members of the Sandown Volunteer Fire Department. Here, around 1955, Robert Holmes "saves" fire chief Chester Nicolaisen as he demonstrates how to use the new resuscitation apparatus. (Courtesy of the Sandown Fire Department.)

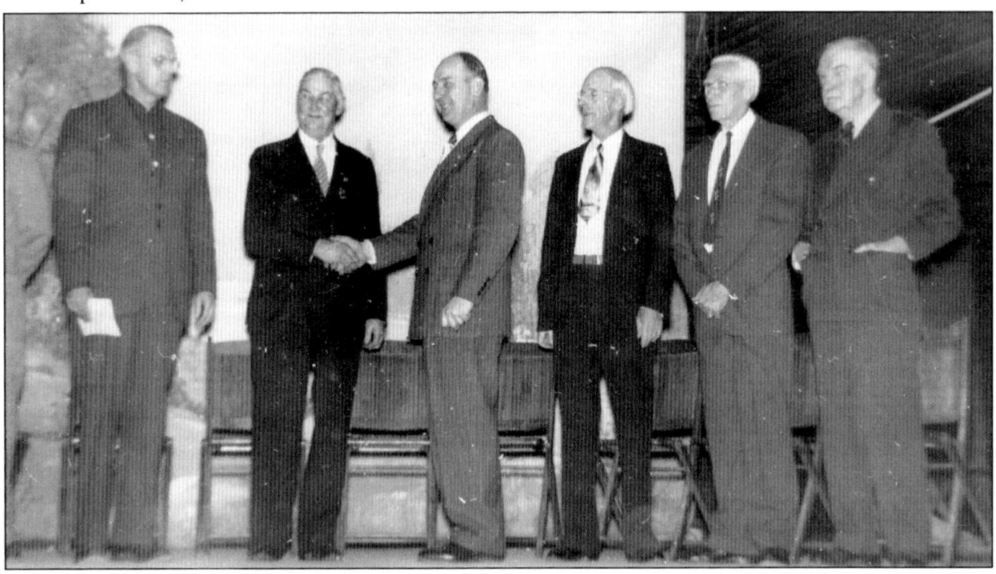

Retiring fire chief Bernard Love (second from left) congratulates newly sworn-in fire chief Chester Nicolaisen (third from left) at a ceremony at the town hall in January 1956. Town clerk Ernest Pillsbury (far left) and selectmen James L. Paine, Charles Burton French, and Adm. Howard Shaw (fourth, fifth, and sixth from left, respectively) witnessed the event. Demonstrating the volunteer spirit so visible in Sandown, Nicolaisen also served as a Boy Scout leader, deputy fire chief, the chairman of the planning board, and a lecturer in the Grange. (Courtesy of the Sandown Fire Department.)

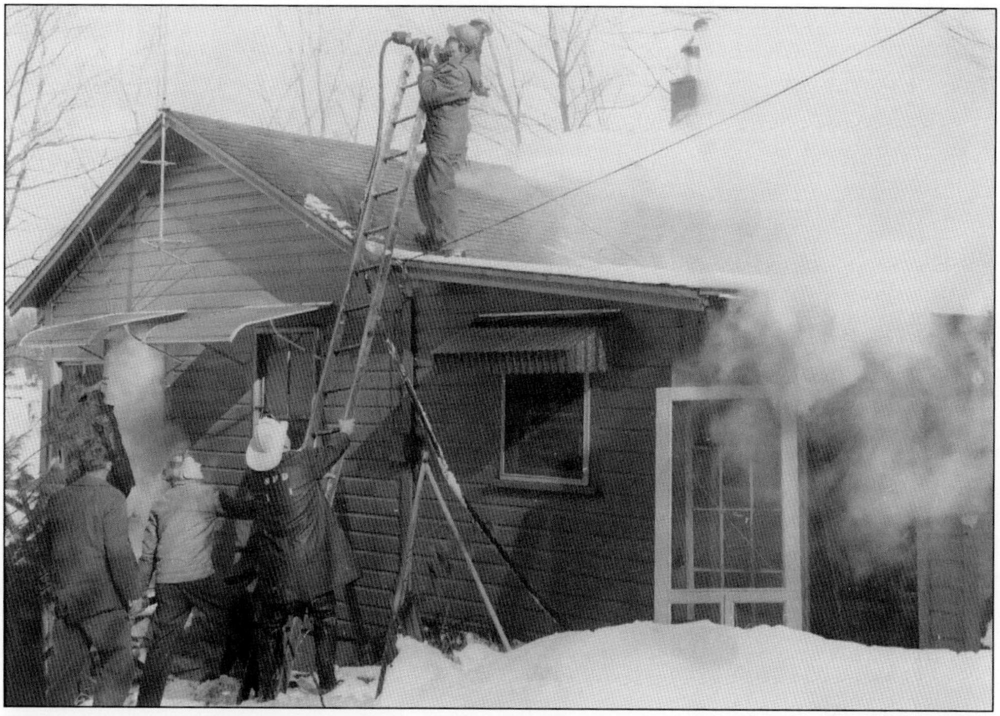

With smoke pouring out, snow on the ground, and no fire gear, volunteer firemen did their best to save the Dustons' cottage on Angle Pond. Fireman William Croteau is on the roof, struggling to set up a water line, while fire chief Chester Nicolaisen (in hat) and firemen Everett "Bud" Holmes and Fred Miller assist from the ground. Saving the structure was the priority for these men, who responded to emergencies in all kinds of weather. (Courtesy of the Sandown Fire Department.)

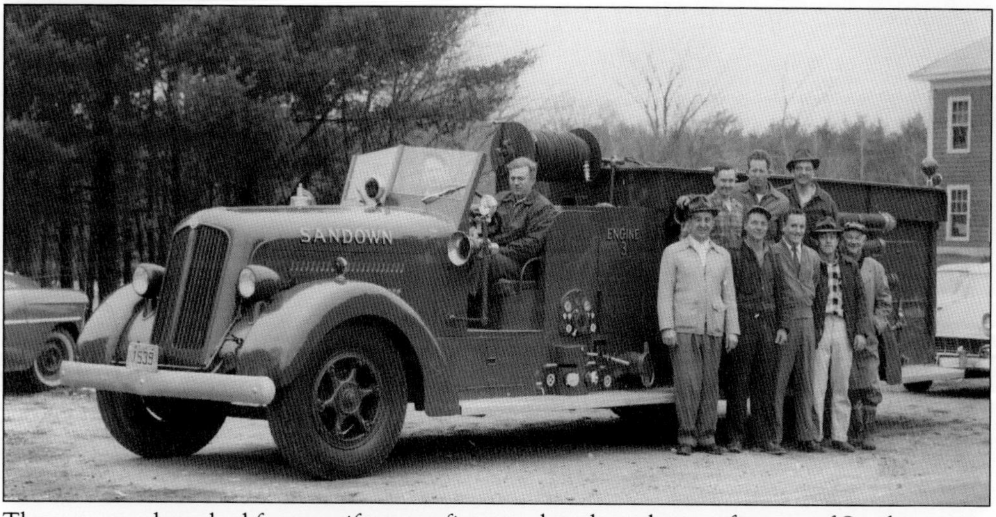

They may not have had fancy uniforms or fire gear, but the volunteer firemen of Sandown were very proud of their department and their equipment. Here, members of the fire department stand next to their newest vehicle, Engine 3. They are, from left to right, (first row) Chester Nicolaisen, Allen Love, David Bauer, Kenneth Bassett, and Bernard Love; (second row) Thomas Spencer, Bud Holmes, and Fred Drowne. Raymond Bassett is in the driver's seat, and Warren Roberts is in the passenger seat. (Courtesy of the Sandown Fire Department.)

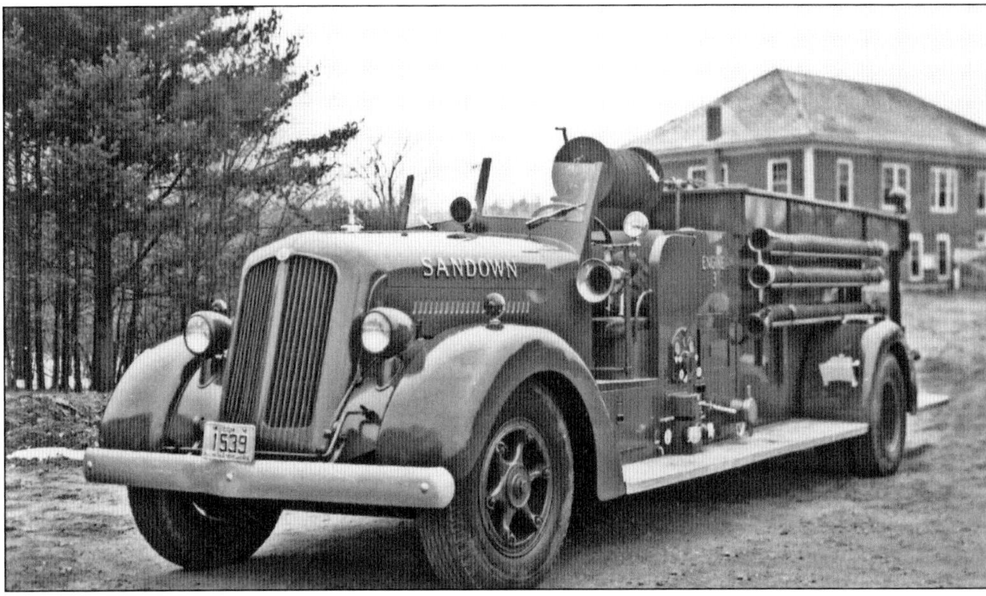

The town approved $500 to create the volunteer fire department and purchase equipment. Bernard Love was named the first fire chief, and a committee of townspeople formed the fire association. Since then, the dedicated volunteers spend hours training and responding to emergency calls. The association has held many fundraisers, including the annual carnival and chicken barbecue during Old Home Day. Their hard work has provided much-needed safety equipment and saved taxpayers thousands of dollars. (Courtesy of John Cameron.)

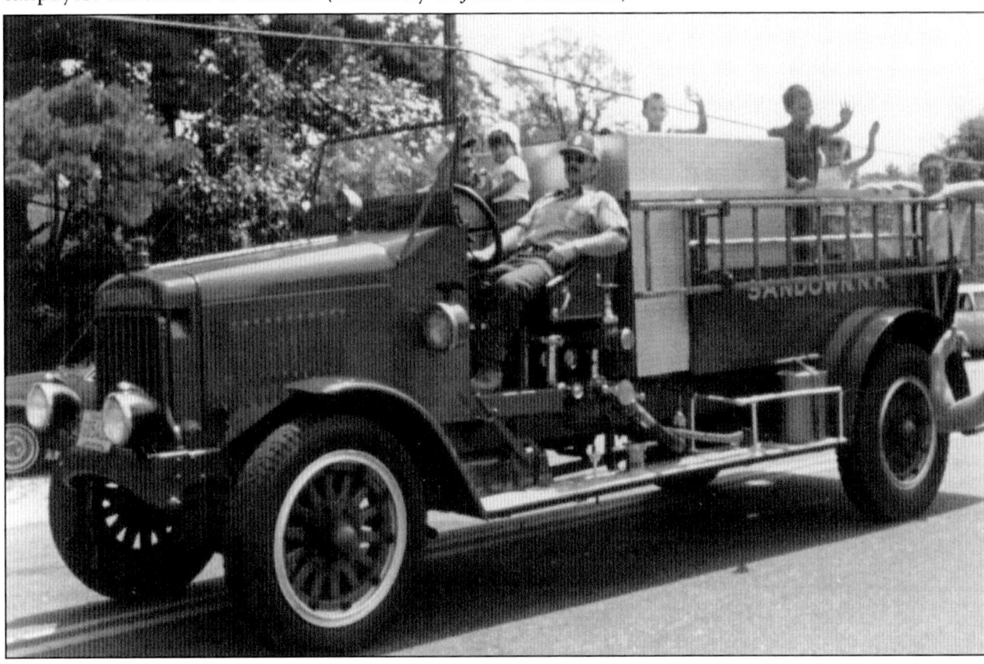

This 1922 International was Sandown's first fire engine. It was purchased in 1948 for $250. Another $190 was spent to outfit the truck for service. It has served Sandown well. It is semiretired now and only used for parades and to give happy children rides during Sandown's summer celebrations. (Courtesy of the Sandown Fire Department.)

Six

COMMUNITY LIFE

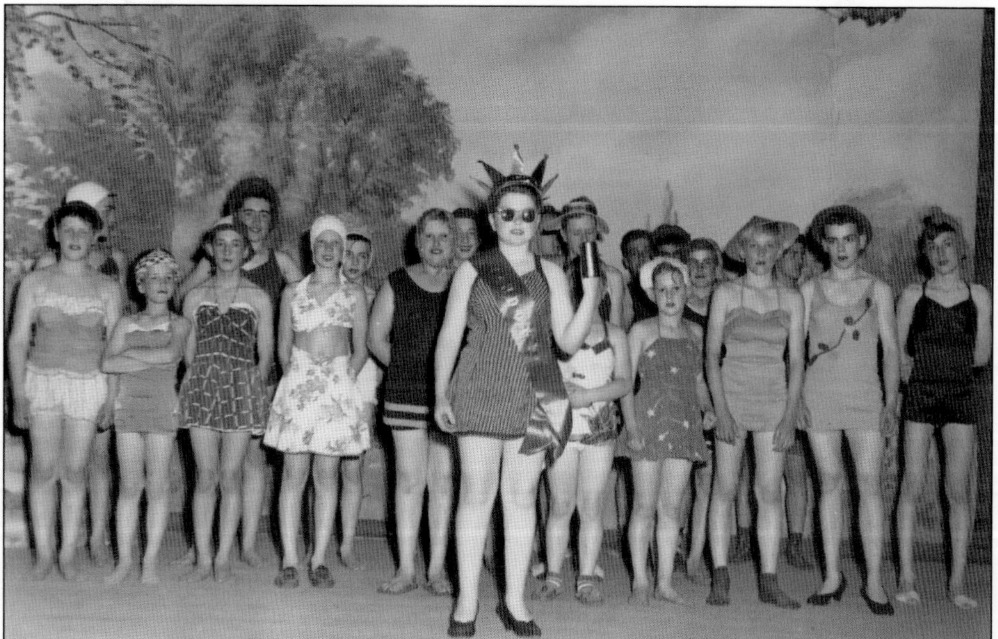

Boy Scout Troop 268 has a long and proud history of service to the community. Fundraising for special events such as camping trips and outings are part of their duties. Demonstrating a good sense of humor and a true commitment to their troop, these 1956 Scouts dressed up as bathing beauties for a fundraiser. Warren Roberts (front and center) won the contest. (Photograph by Mal Cameron; courtesy of Richard Holmes.)

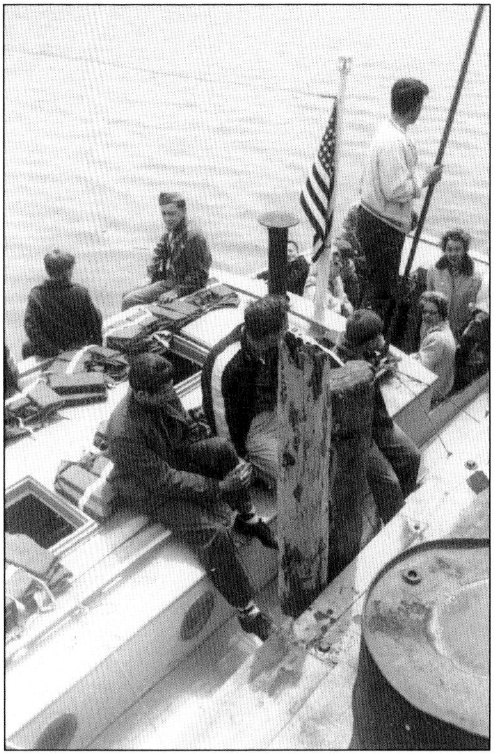

In 1956, the Sandown Boy Scouts were invited to visit the Gloucester, Massachusetts, Sea Scouts, led by William Francis. It was a unique experience for Troop 268, and the weather was perfect for taking the boat out into the harbor. (Courtesy of Carroll Bassett.)

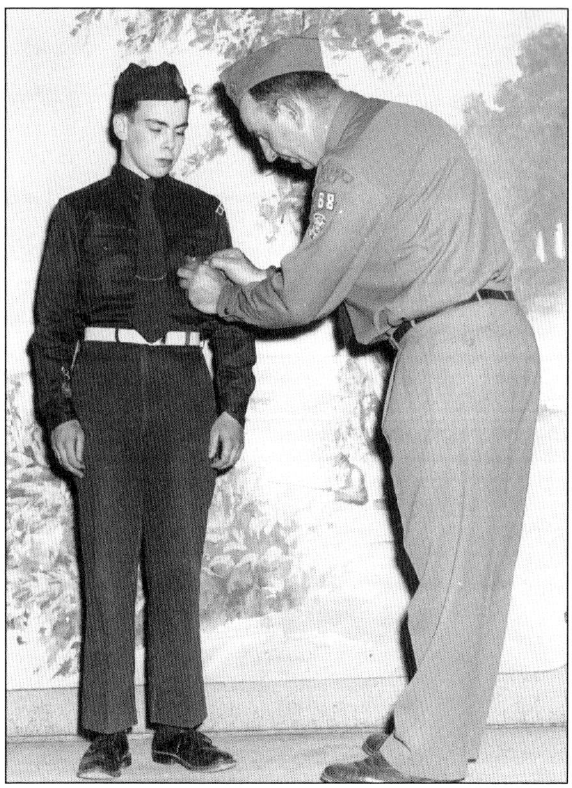

On June 9, 1956, during a special Boy Scout fundraising event, Explorer Scout David Reynolds received the Star Scout Award from Scoutmaster Chester Nicolaisen. (Courtesy of the Sandown Public Library.)

Hiking to Great Rock was an adventure for Sandown children. Girl Scout Troop 297 is seen here preparing for the hike. Great Rock was not a marked trail, and the best way to get there was to walk along the railroad bed until the large cliff appeared. Once at the top, hikers could enjoy a picnic lunch overlooking the woods. Today, there is a well-marked trail to Great Rock in the town forest. (Courtesy of Jacqueline Burke.)

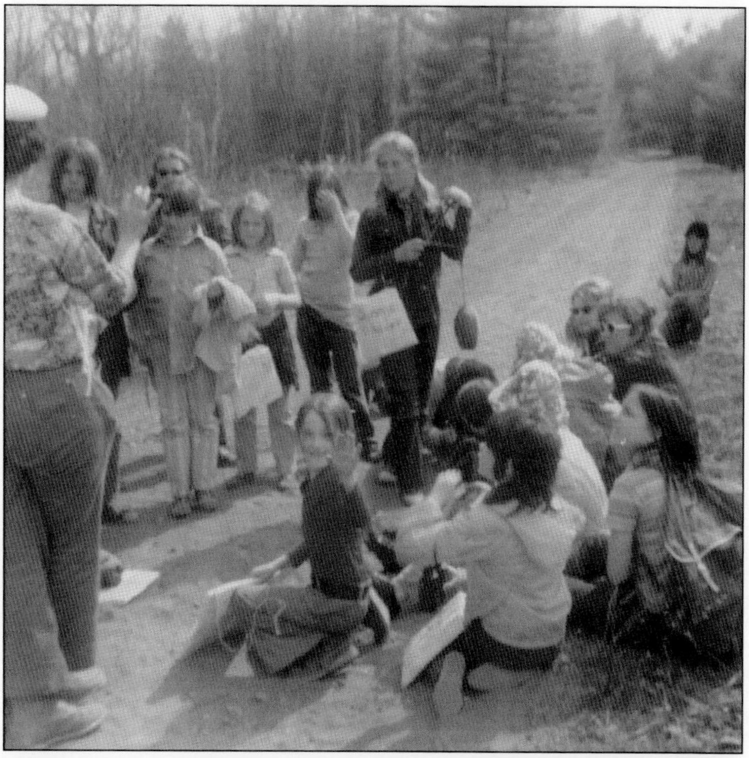

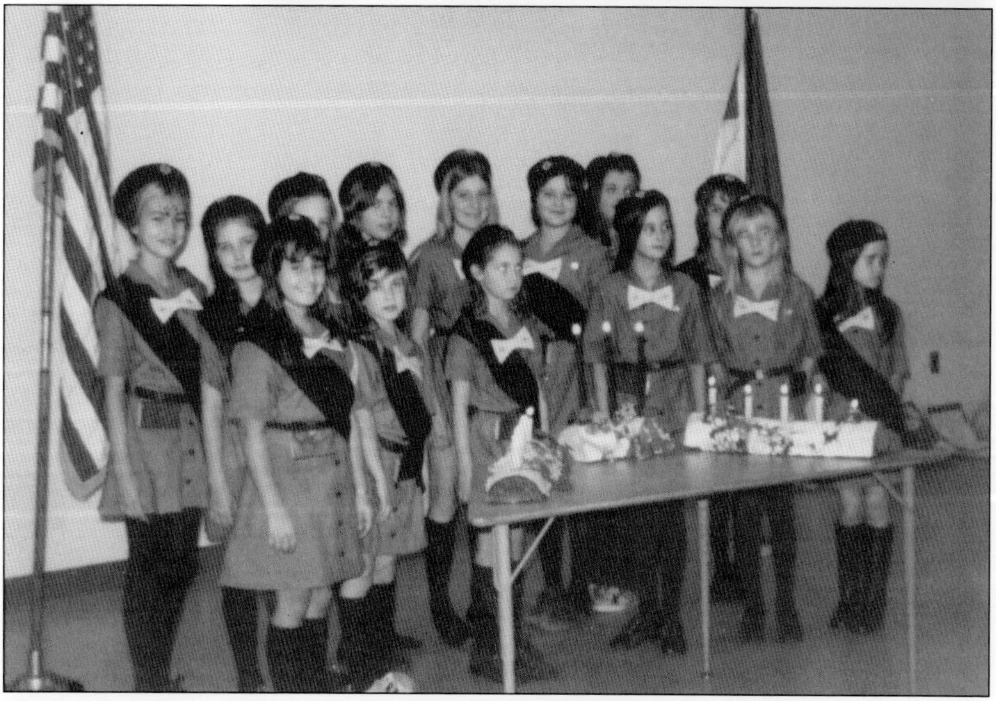

The Candle Lighting and Investiture Ceremony of the Girl Scouts is a tradition that continues today in Scout troops throughout the world. Dressed in their complete uniforms, members of Sandown's Troop 297 stood together in 1972 to participate in the event. (Courtesy of Jacqueline Burke.)

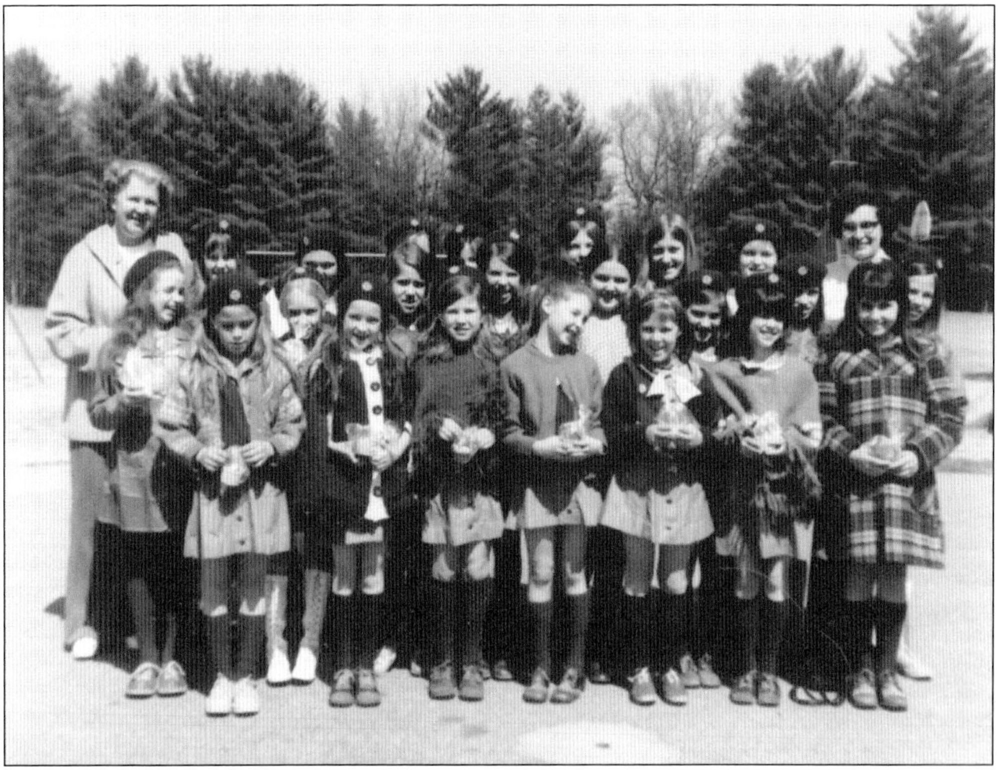

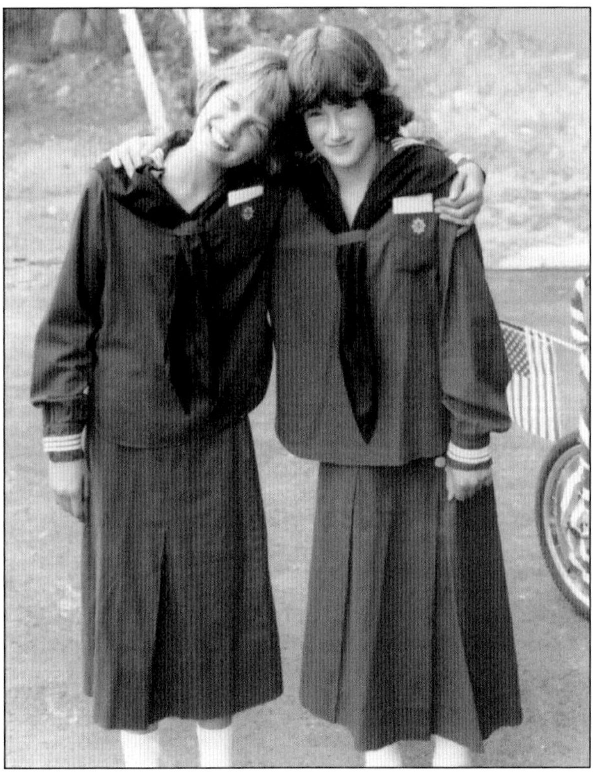

Exemplifying the Girl Scout slogan, "Do a good deed daily," Troop 297 (above) made Easter baskets for the Rockingham County Home in April 1973. From left to right are (first row) Kathleen Kendall, Linda Peterson, Dawn Williams, Kim McCarthy, Kathy Gagnon, Christine Cook, and Betsy Wentworth; (second row) Colleen Coakley, Debbi Batchelder, Elizabeth Johnson, Diana Coakley, Wendy Barker, Cathy Cook, Barbara Fraser, and Linda Cutliffe; (third row) leader Mary Knox, Patricia Knox, Debbi Page, Ramona Zanzegers, Tracy Duston, Dawn Richard, Diane Curran, Carys Kirk, and leader Vera Kirk. (Courtesy of Jacqueline Burke.)

Girl Scouts Stacey Bassett and Rebecca Anderson don antique uniforms in preparation for a parade. (Courtesy of Arlene Bassett.)

4-H Clubs were prevalent in the 1950s and continue today. This group, led by Edith Love, is prepared to leave on a field trip. From left to right are (first row) Louise Deveau, Elizabeth "Betty" Geisser, Suzanne Kendall, and Linda Deveau; (second row) Esther Durling and Gail Spencer; (third row) Carol Ann Oberle and Edith Love. (Courtesy of Arlene Bassett.)

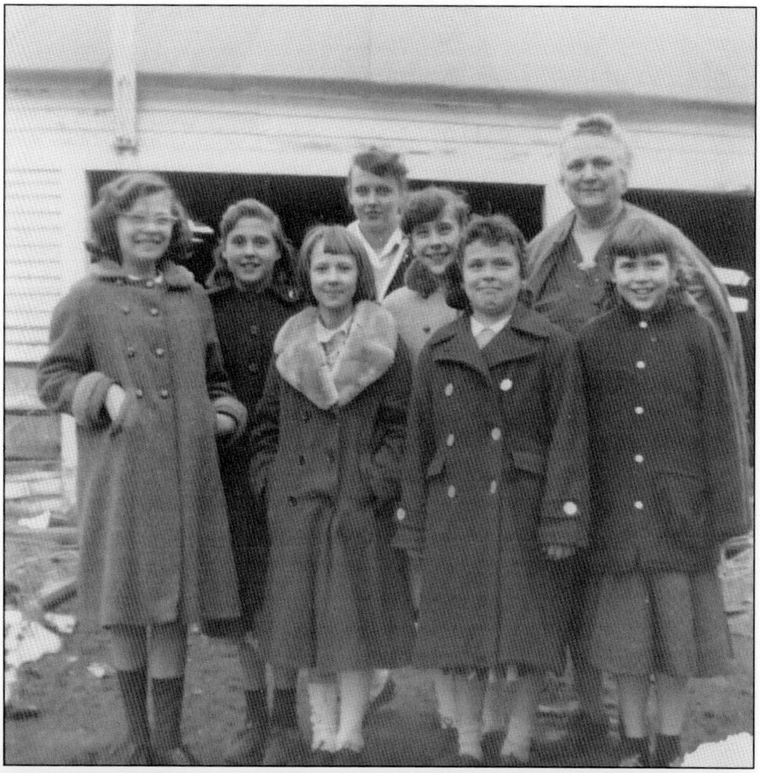

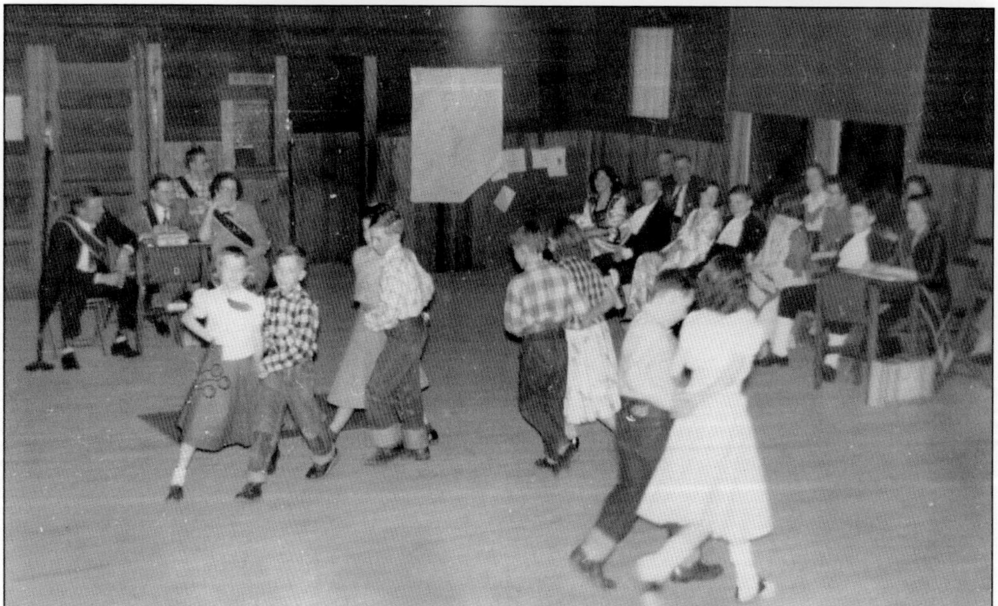

In the early 1900s, square dances were held as fundraisers to help build the Sandown Community Hall. Square dancing continued to be a popular pastime well into the late 1960s. It was quite the social event for teenagers, who, in the 1950s, were known as the Sundown Shufflers. Started by Duaine Steinhoff and F. Edward Deveau, the group took lessons in Chester and won awards and badges for their expertise. (Courtesy of the Sandown Public Library.)

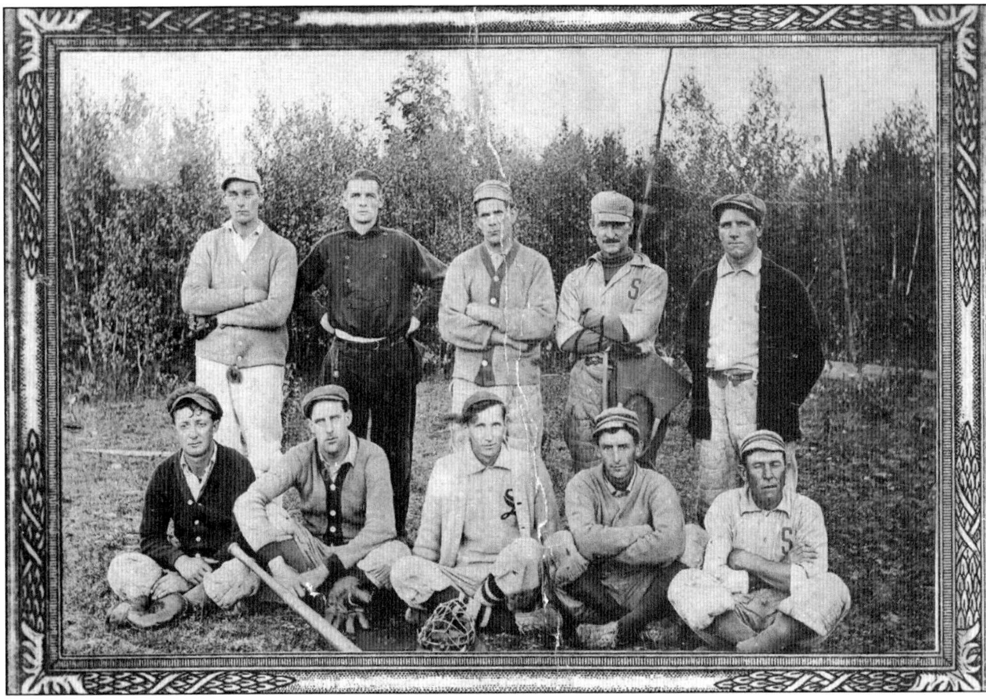

Baseball was alive and well in the early 1900s in Sandown. The Fessenden mill had half-days on Saturdays so workers could play in the afternoon. From the looks on the faces of the team members in these two photographs, they were serious about the game. Seen above are, from left to right, (first row) Roy Clark, H. Mills, Beverly Seeley, Charles Merrick, and Archie Beaubien; (second row) Phillip Knights, ? Ayer, two unidentified players, and Ernest Nye. The 1912 team below included, from left to right, (first row) Beverly Seeley, Louis Bunker, Ernest Baker, and Archie Beaubien; (second row) Phillip Knights, Ralph S. True, Herbert Mills, Charles Merrick, and Ernest Nye. (Both, courtesy of the Sandown Historical Society.)

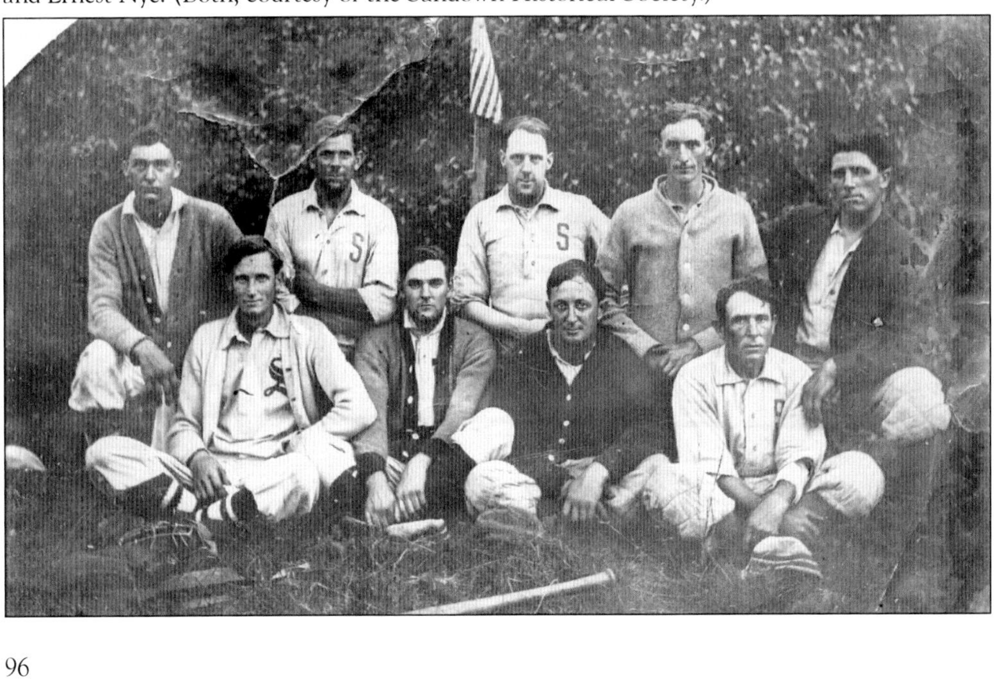

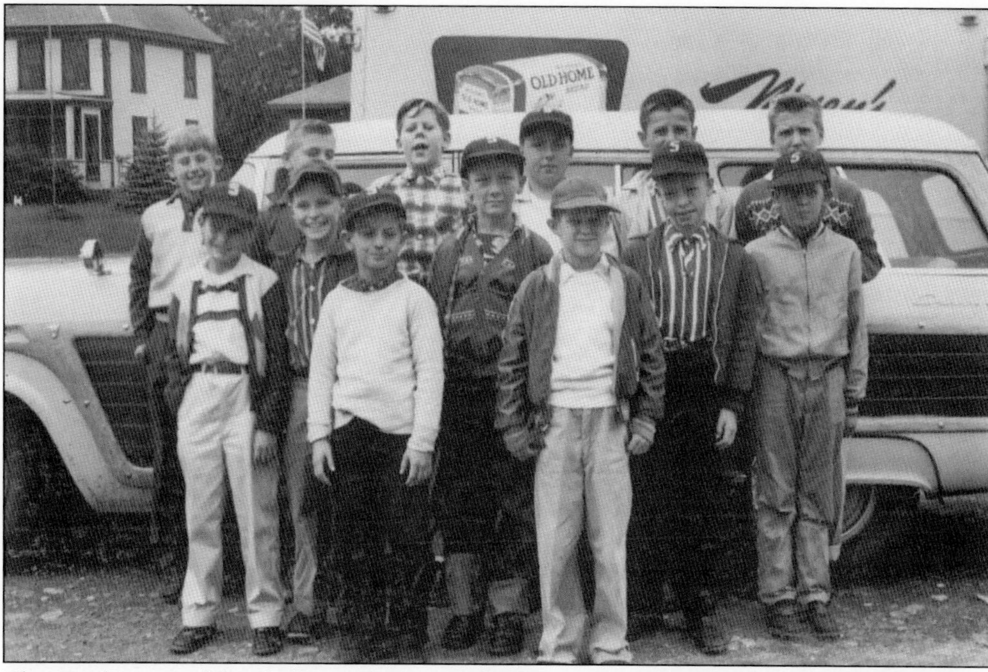

This Sandown youth baseball team from around 1955 is heading to Boston to see a Red Sox game. Seat belts were not an issue at the time, as the boys piled into the station wagon. From left to right are (first row) Ralph Huckins and William Love; (second row) Gerald Steinhoff, Malcolm MacGregor, Allen Love, David Drowne, and Richard Lessard; (third row) Charles Holmes, Eugene Kachuck, Ronald Pinard, Richard Nicolaisen, Richard Drowne, and Vincent Humphrey. (Photograph by Mal Cameron; courtesy of John Cameron.)

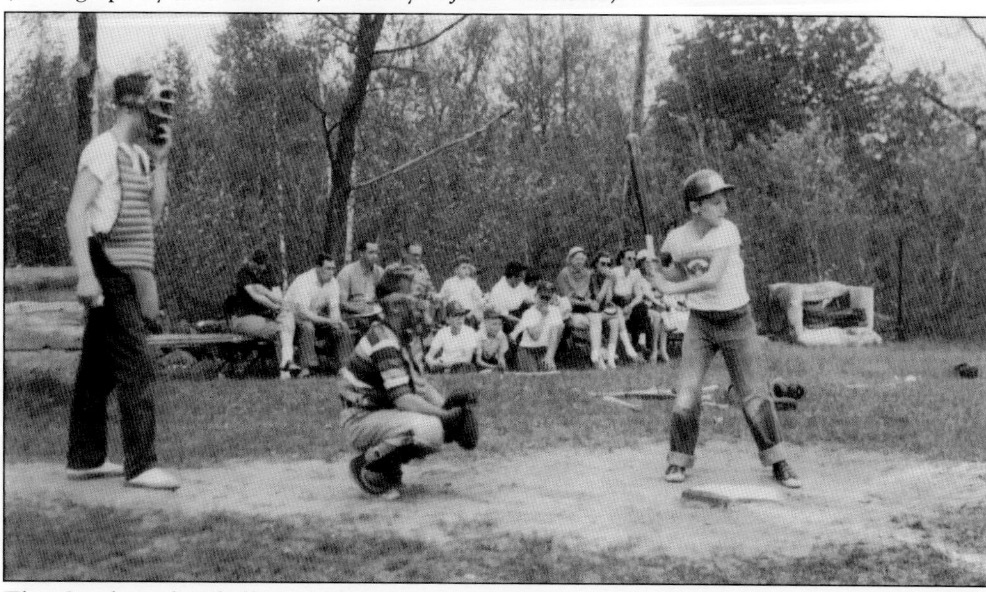

This Sandown baseball team played its home games at the playground behind the Central School around 1955. The ball field was bumpy and crude, but they had team spirit and they played their best. At bat is Charles "Chuck" Holmes. (Photograph by Mal Cameron; courtesy of John Cameron.)

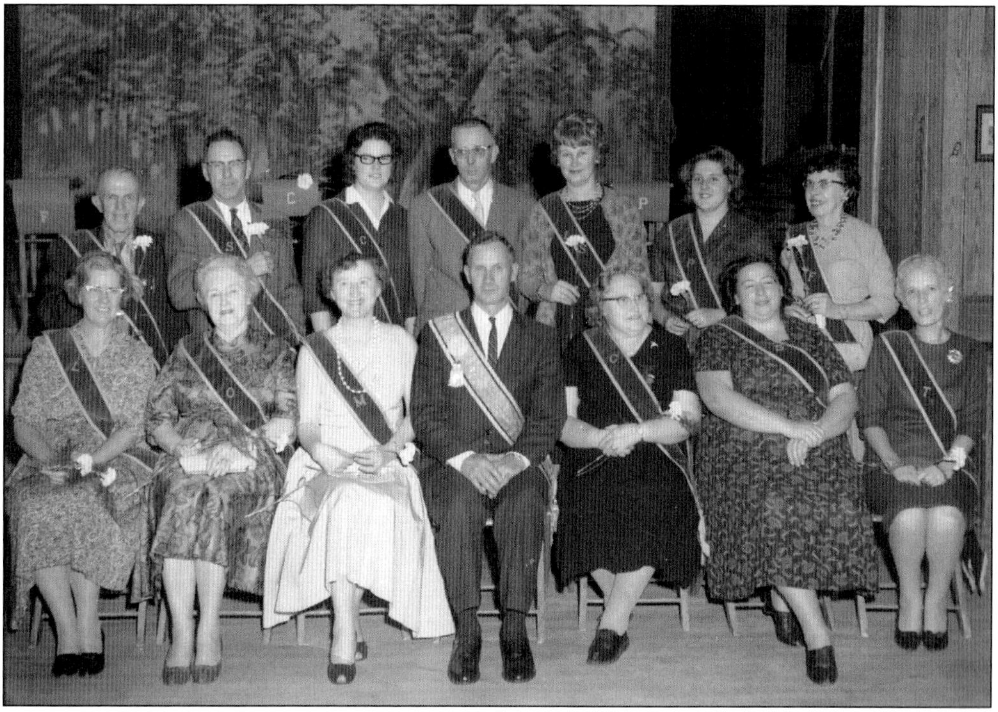

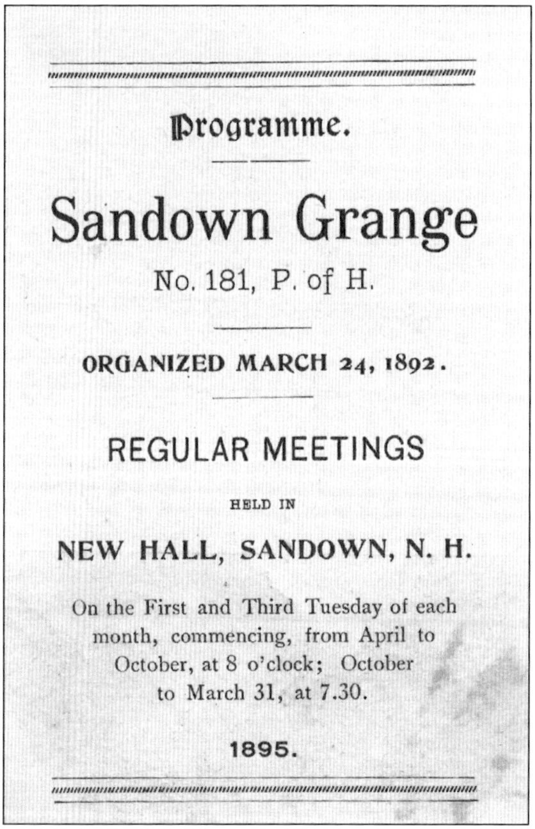

Programme.

Sandown Grange

No. 181, P. of H.

ORGANIZED MARCH 24, 1892.

REGULAR MEETINGS

HELD IN

NEW HALL, SANDOWN, N. H.

On the First and Third Tuesday of each month, commencing, from April to October, at 8 o'clock; October to March 31, at 7.30.

1895.

Sandown Grange No. 181 officially began on March 24, 1892, with the motto "We strive to do well." By supporting other town groups and offering many social events, the Grange attracted members of all ages. Seen above are, from left to right, (first row) Hazel Rogan, Margaret Phillips, Angela "Nell" Cameron, an unidentified man, Lena Durling, Virginia Lessard, and Harriet Sousa; (second row) Raymond K. Bassett, Charles Durling, Suzanne Drowne, Rudolph True, Jeanne Humphrey, Esther Durling, and an unidentified woman. (Courtesy of June McNally.)

Inside this 1895 foldout brochure is a list of dates of all of the Grange meetings for the year. The Grange had everything, including fairs, fellowship, pageantry, fun, and even some mystery. The cover reads "No. 181, P. of H." The initials stand for Patrons of Husbandry. The Grange was a farmers' organization, and one definition of husbandry is "the cultivation or production of plants or animals." (Courtesy of Richard Holmes.)

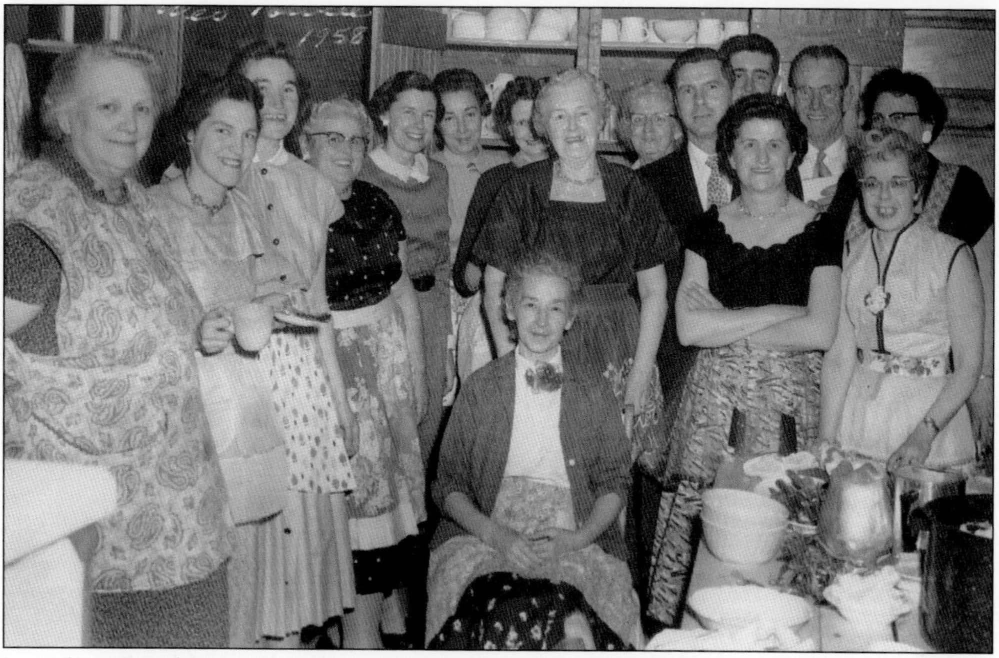

In 1958, a Republican Club dinner was held in honor of Wesley Powell, a New Hampshire gubernatorial candidate. From left to right are (seated) Olive Follansbee; (second row, behind Olive) Margaret Phillips, Irene Barnes, and Marjorie Holmes; (third row) Edith Love, Frances Love, Josephine Carpenter, Gertrude Millard, Beverly Powell, Pam Nicolaisen, Joyce Kennedy, Maude Holmes, candidate Wesley Powell, Robert Holmes, Ralph Barnes, and Lillian Butt. (Courtesy of Richard Holmes.)

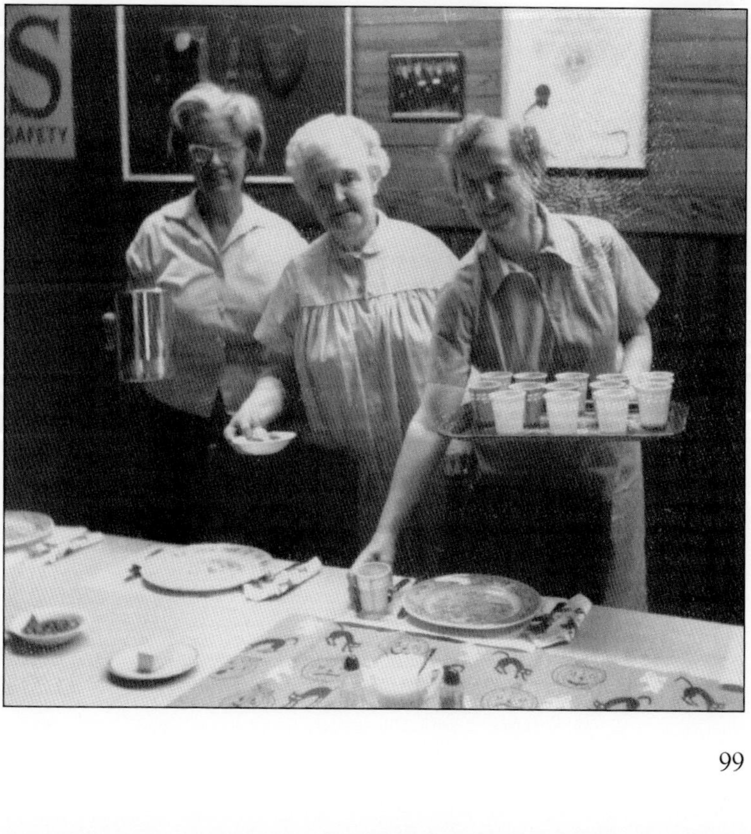

Public suppers at the town hall were very popular in the 1950s and 1960s. Here, from left to right, Hazel (True) Rogan, Margaret Phillips, and Angela "Nell" Cameron prepare the tables for the annual Fall Harvest Supper. (Courtesy of Dorothy Batchelder.)

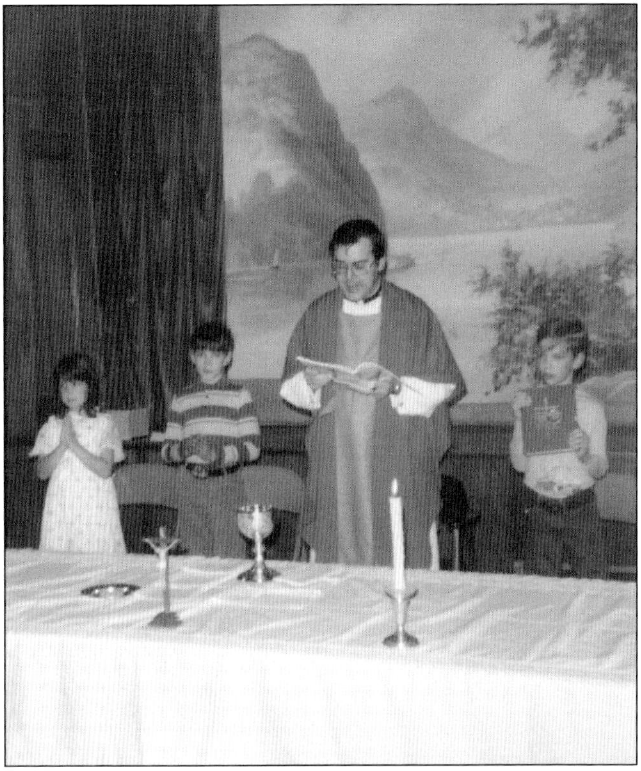

In July 1977, the Catholic community in Sandown formed St. Michael's Station. After holding Sunday mass at St. Matthews United Methodist Church during the summer, the community moved their worship services to the town hall. For the next 23 years, Catholics gathered there every Sunday, setting up the town hall as a church for Catholic worship. After mass, everything was stored away in a closet until the next week. Seen at left are, from left to right, Jennifer Cabral, Thomas Sceggell, Fr. Paul Daneault, and Michael Moynihan. Below, the children of St. Michael's Station perform a Christmas pageant at the town hall. Angels, shepherds, wise men, and a real live baby were all part of the play. (Both, courtesy of Ann Cabral.)

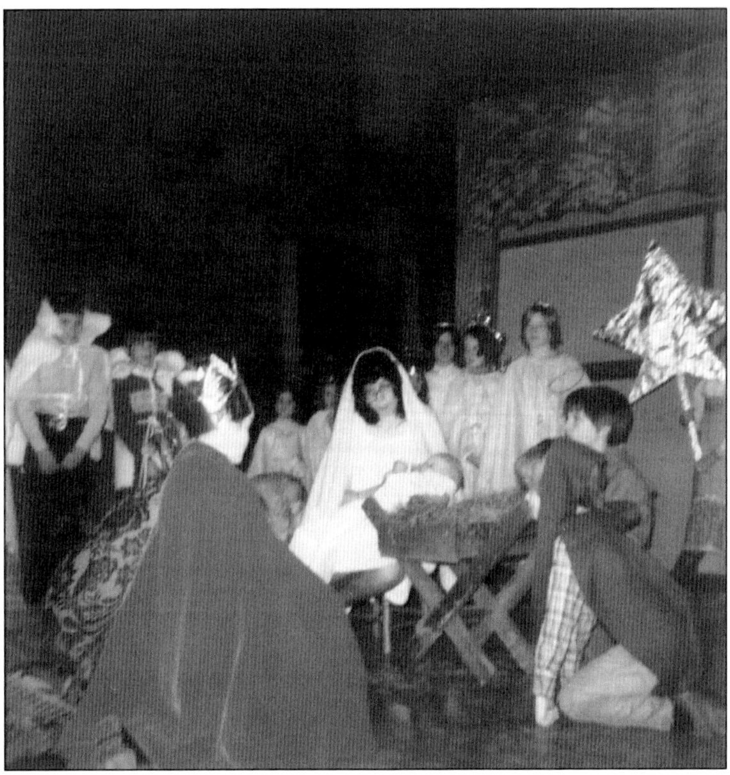

St. Matthews United Methodist Church was built in 1835 and has served the spiritual needs of its parishioners ever since. Even when the building temporarily closed in 1909 for repairs and renovations, the congregation simply moved to the Old Meeting House so services would not be interrupted. (Photograph by Ralph Bonner; courtesy of Arlene Bassett.)

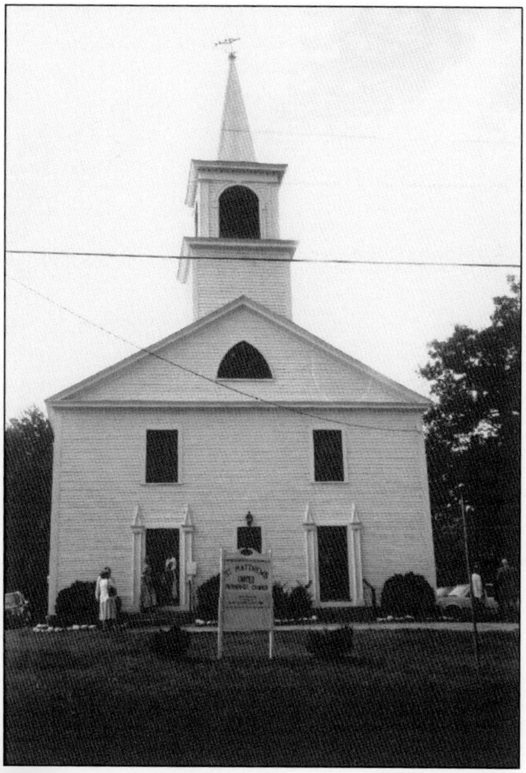

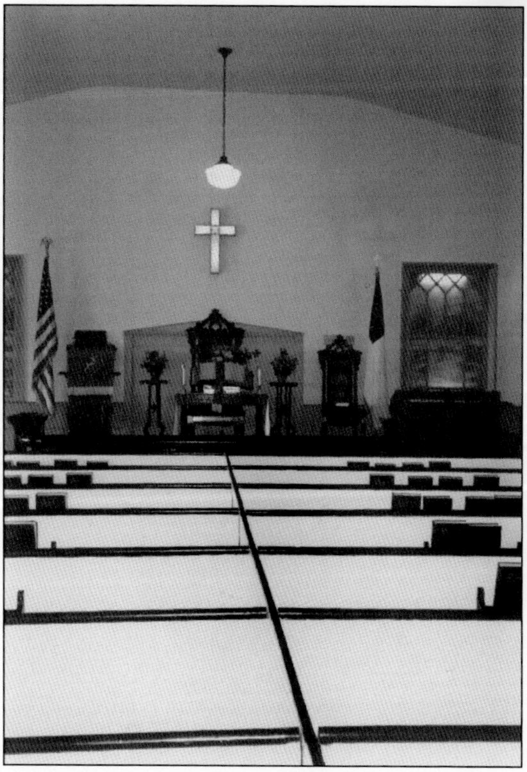

This photograph shows the interior of St. Matthews Church around 1950. It looks much the same today, except that the two windows have been removed and the cross is now a wooden one. Two exit doors replaced the windows, resulting in three avenues of escape from this second-story sanctuary. (Photograph by Ralph Bonner; courtesy of Arlene Bassett.)

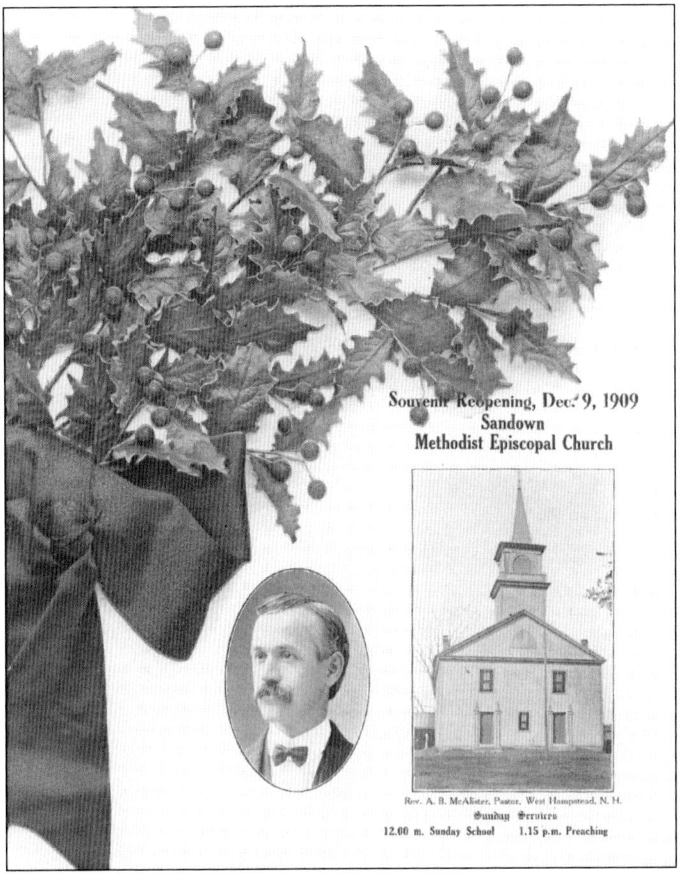

After St. Matthews Church went through a renovation in 1909, it celebrated its reopening on December 9. This souvenir poster was distributed on that day. Pastors were shared with the West Hampstead Methodist Church, and the parsonage was located in that town. Pastor Ambrose B. McAllister served the two churches from 1907 through 1909. (Courtesy of St. Matthews Church.)

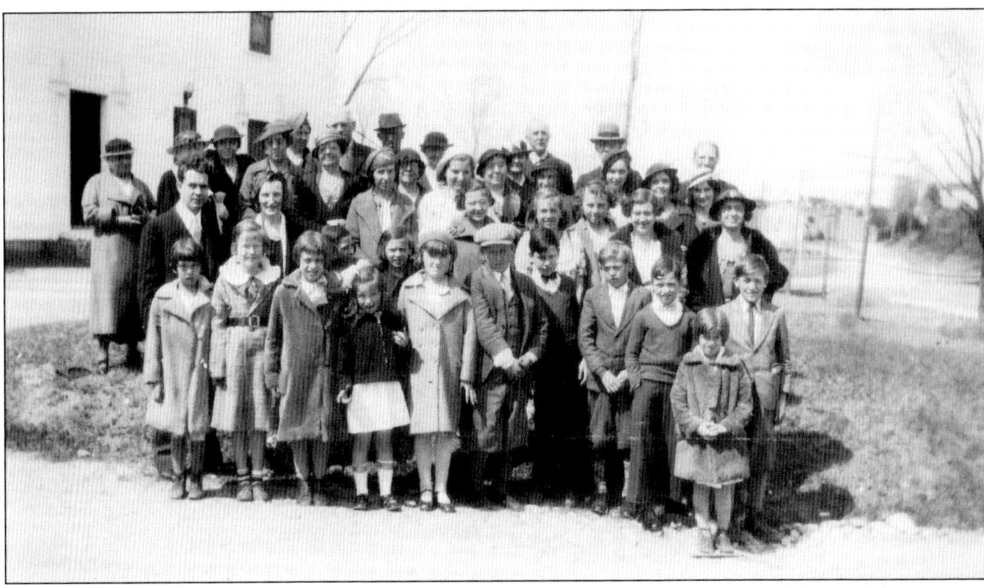

In 1934, the pastor of St. Matthews United Methodist Church was Rev. Donald H. Baldwin. Here, on Reverend Baldwin's final Sunday at the church, the entire congregation posed for a farewell photograph. (Courtesy of Dorothy Batchelder.)

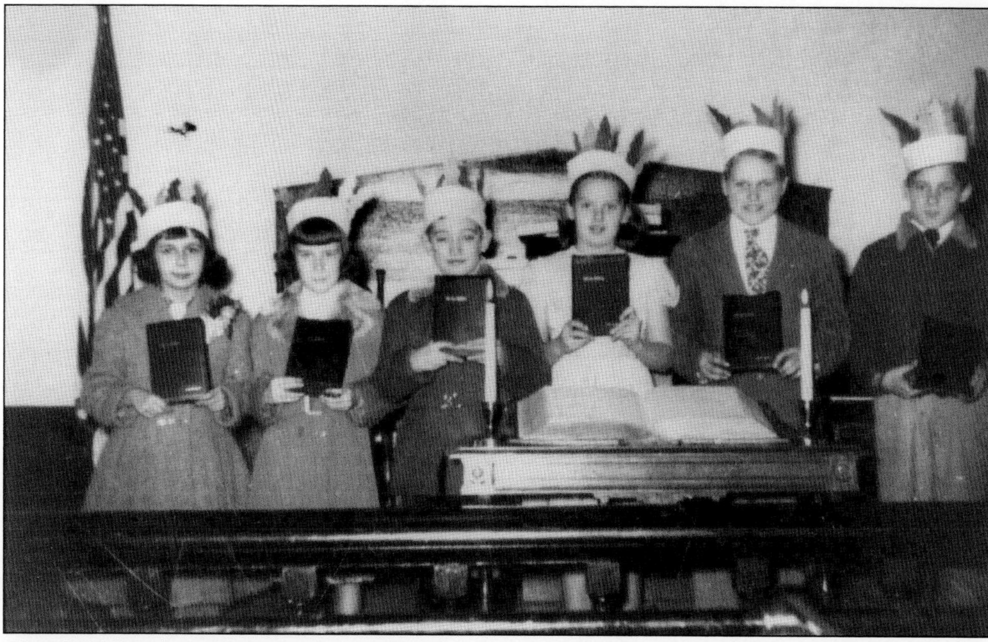

This 1955 Sunday school class learned the books of the Bible in order. For every half-dozen books learned, students earned a feather in their cap. They then received Bibles as a reward for a job well done. Seen here from left to right are Nancy Noyce, Gail Spencer, Richard Holmes, Arlene Holmes, Clifford Durling, and Bernard Kelley. (Courtesy of Arlene Bassett.)

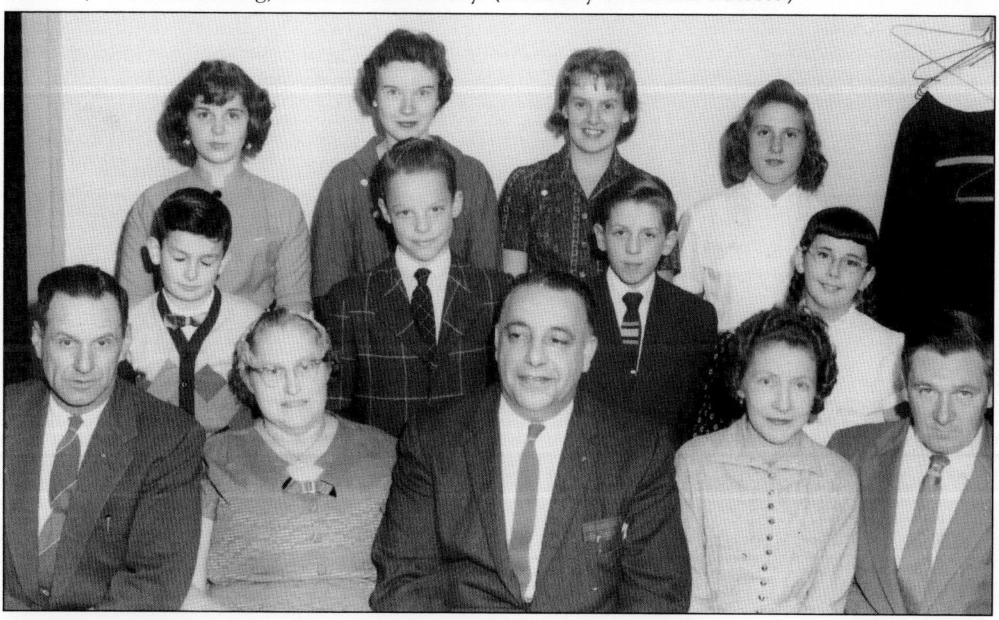

Involving young people in church activities was a hallmark of St. Matthews United Methodist Church. The youth group volunteered for fundraisers and church activities. The 1955 officers and leaders were, from left to right, (first row) Charles Durling, Lena Durling, Rev. John Torosian, Virginia Spencer, and Thomas Spencer; (second row) Jerry Steinhoff, David Drowne, Richard Lessard, and Robin Noyce; (third row) Dorothy Pinard, Jean Spencer, Arlene Holmes, and Esther Durling. (Courtesy of Richard Holmes.)

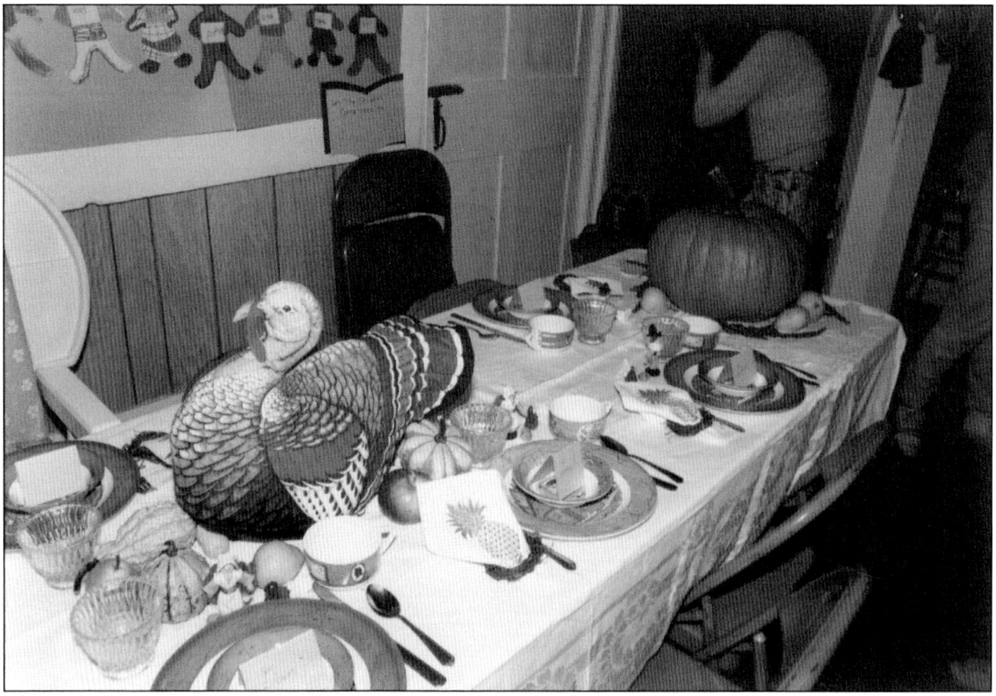

The Calendar Supper was a popular event at St. Matthews United Methodist Church. A group of 24 parishioners would pair up to decorate 12 tables, each representing a month of the year. Each pair tried to outdo the others with themed table settings, centerpieces, favors, appetizers, and dessert. Another group of volunteers cooked a pot roast meal that was served to everyone. Seen here is the November table, depicting Thanksgiving. (Courtesy of Arlene Bassett.)

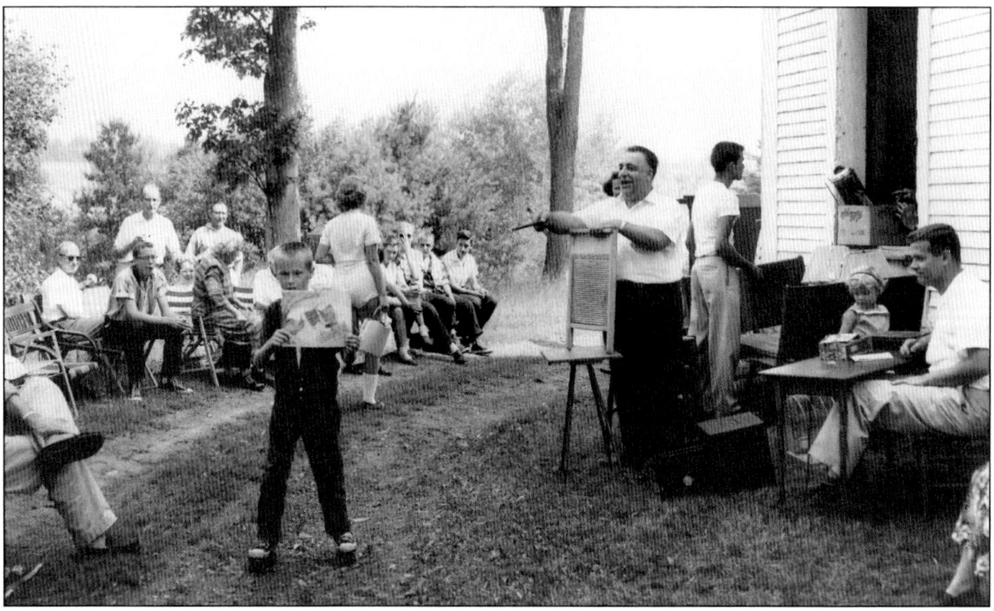

This young St. Matthews Methodist Church parishioner participated in the 1959 church auction, with Rev. John Torosian serving as auctioneer. This fundraiser was one of many church events that served as both a social activity and a means to raise money. (Courtesy of Richard Holmes.)

Seven

Roads and Waterways

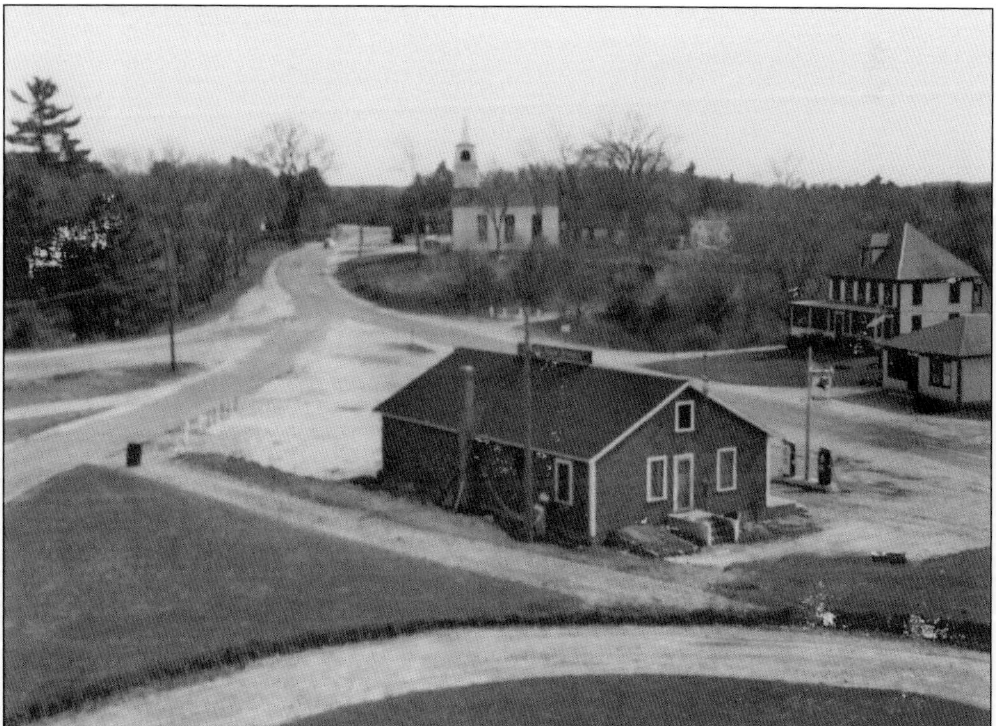

This 1956 photograph, taken from an attic window of a home on Fremont Road, looks down to the town center and Main Street (Route 121A), with St. Matthews United Methodist Church in the background and the Dinsmore store in the foreground. The home of Edna and Charles Burton French and the post office are across the street. Note the gas pumps in the store parking lot. With the railroad no longer in service, fuel for the automobile was in demand. (Courtesy of John Cameron.)

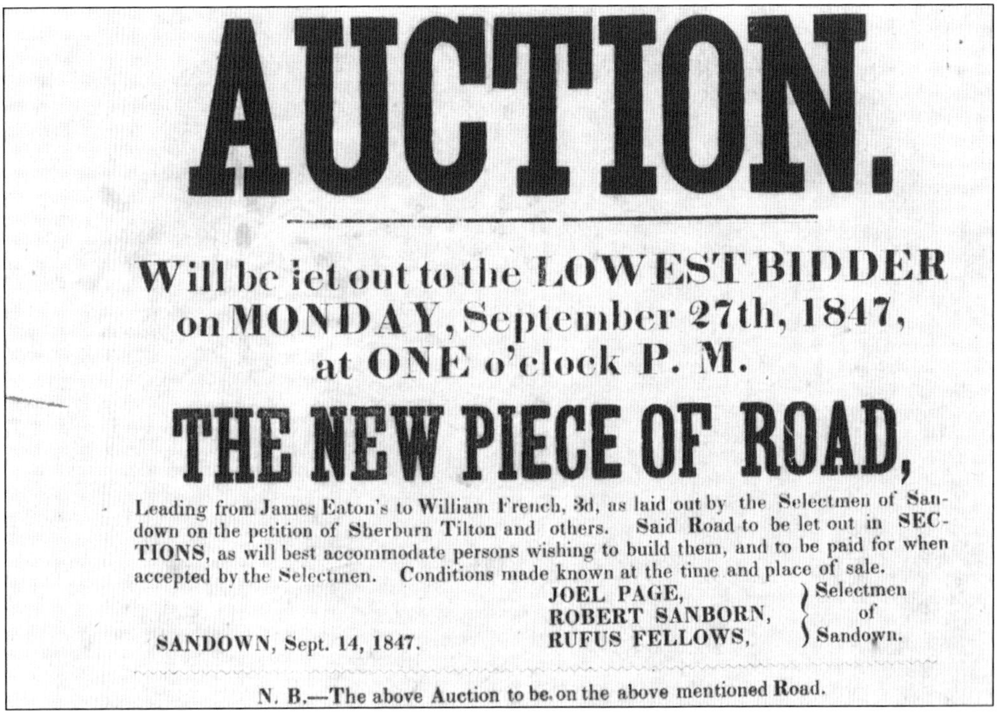

AUCTION.

Will be let out to the LOWEST BIDDER on MONDAY, September 27th, 1847, at ONE o'clock P. M.

THE NEW PIECE OF ROAD,

Leading from James Eaton's to William French, 3d, as laid out by the Selectmen of Sandown on the petition of Sherburn Tilton and others. Said Road to be let out in SECTIONS, as will best accommodate persons wishing to build them, and to be paid for when accepted by the Selectmen. Conditions made known at the time and place of sale.

JOEL PAGE,
ROBERT SANBORN,
RUFUS FELLOWS, } Selectmen of Sandown.

SANDOWN, Sept. 14, 1847.

N. B.—The above Auction to be on the above mentioned Road.

This flyer advertises an auction for bids to build sections of the new road. It states that the lowest bidder will be selected, but it also appears that the road will be divided into sections and will be built by more than one bidder. The bids were to be in the hands of the selectmen by September 27, 1847. (Courtesy of the Sandown Historical Society.)

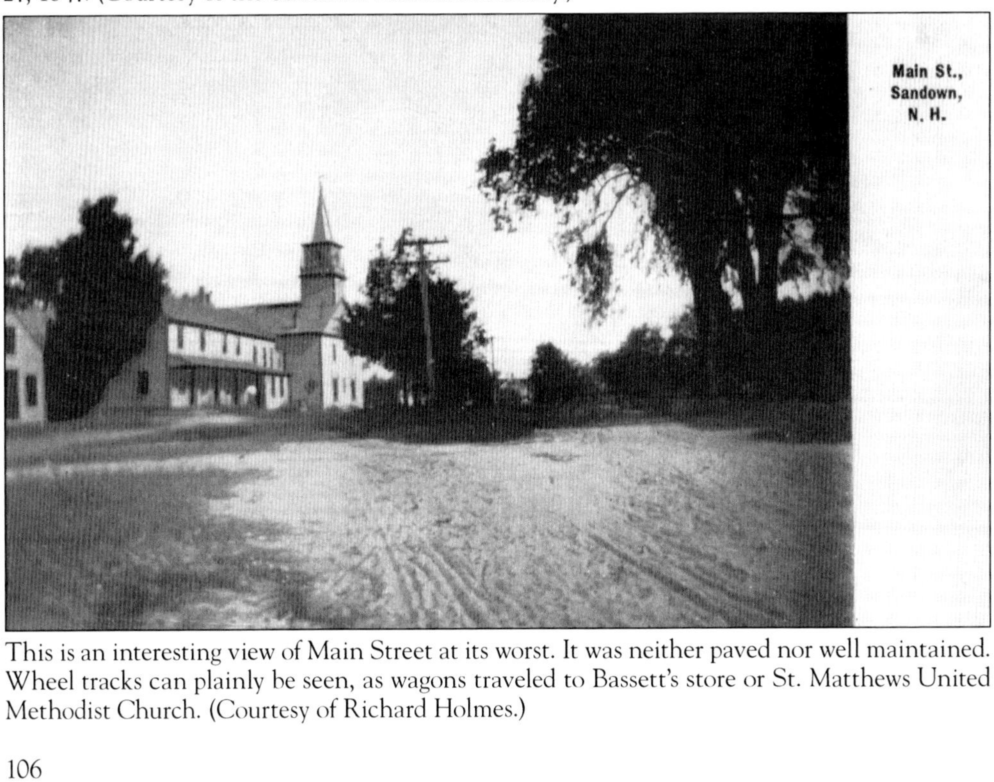

This is an interesting view of Main Street at its worst. It was neither paved nor well maintained. Wheel tracks can plainly be seen, as wagons traveled to Bassett's store or St. Matthews United Methodist Church. (Courtesy of Richard Holmes.)

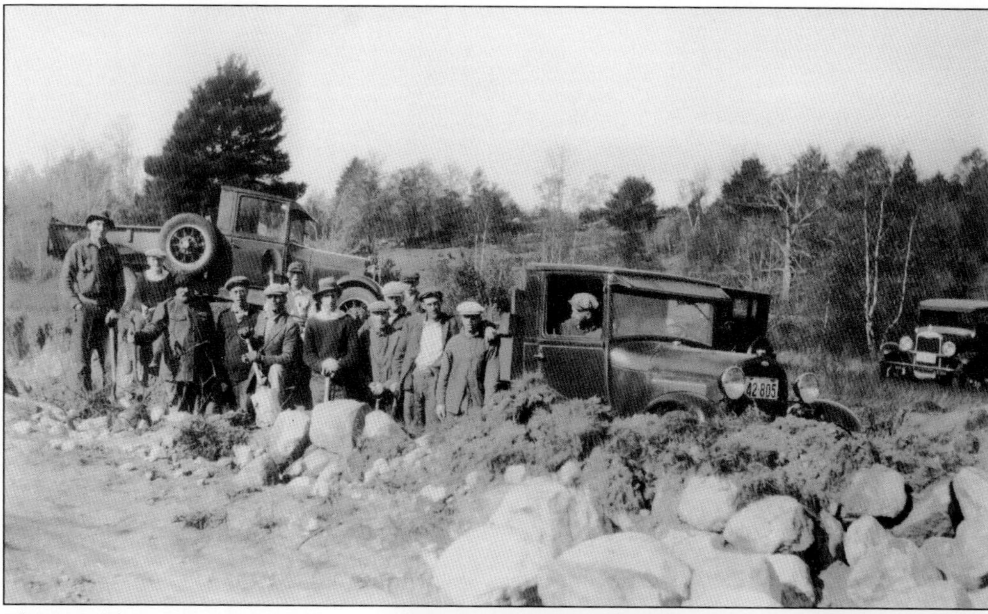

The men above were part of a Works Progress Administration (WPA) road crew in Sandown around 1935. Shovels in hand, they are ready to work. Except for their trucks, shovels and jackhammers were the only available construction equipment, so progress was slow. (Courtesy of June McNally.)

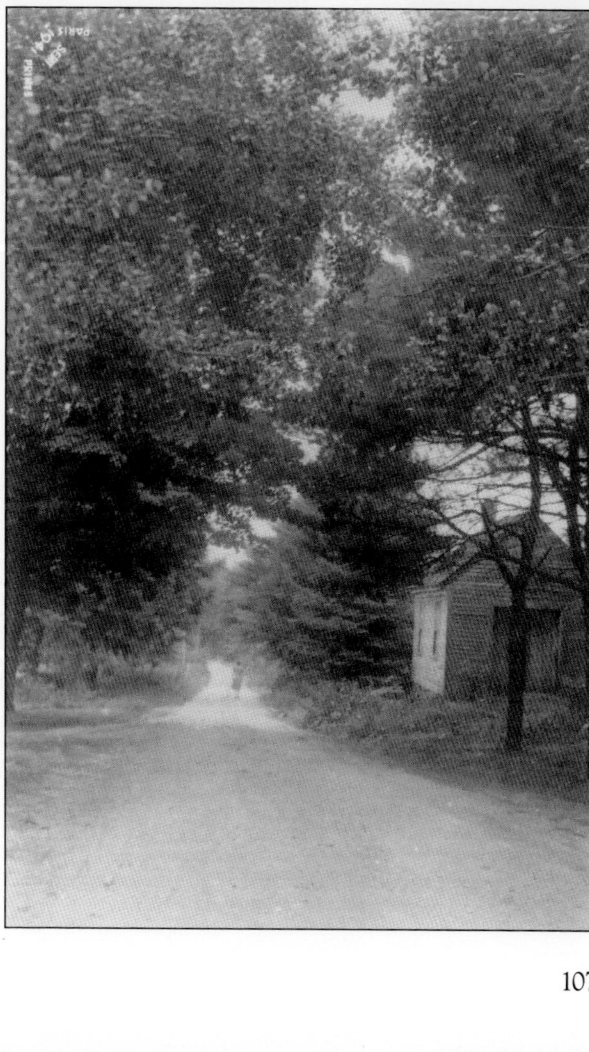

This photograph shows an unpaved North Road as it wanders past the apple and peach orchard. The small building on the right was known as the "old shop." It was no doubt the location of one of the multitude of cottage industries so prevalent in the town's early years. (Courtesy of Alden True.)

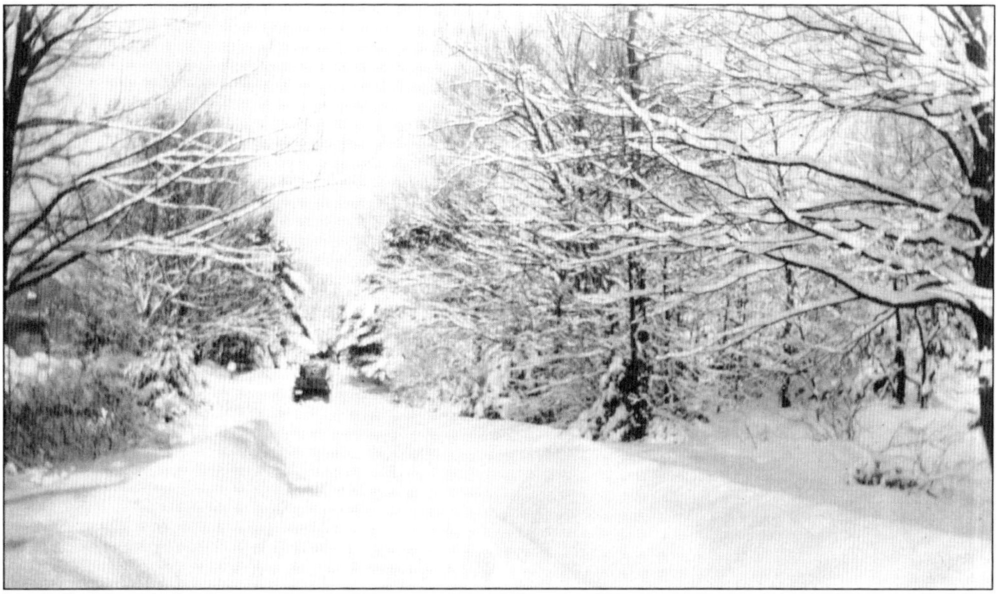

Sandown's Main Street (Route 121A) looks much different today than it does here, when it was barely passable after a big snowstorm. One lone vehicle with a brave driver is in the distance. (Courtesy of Linda Torre.)

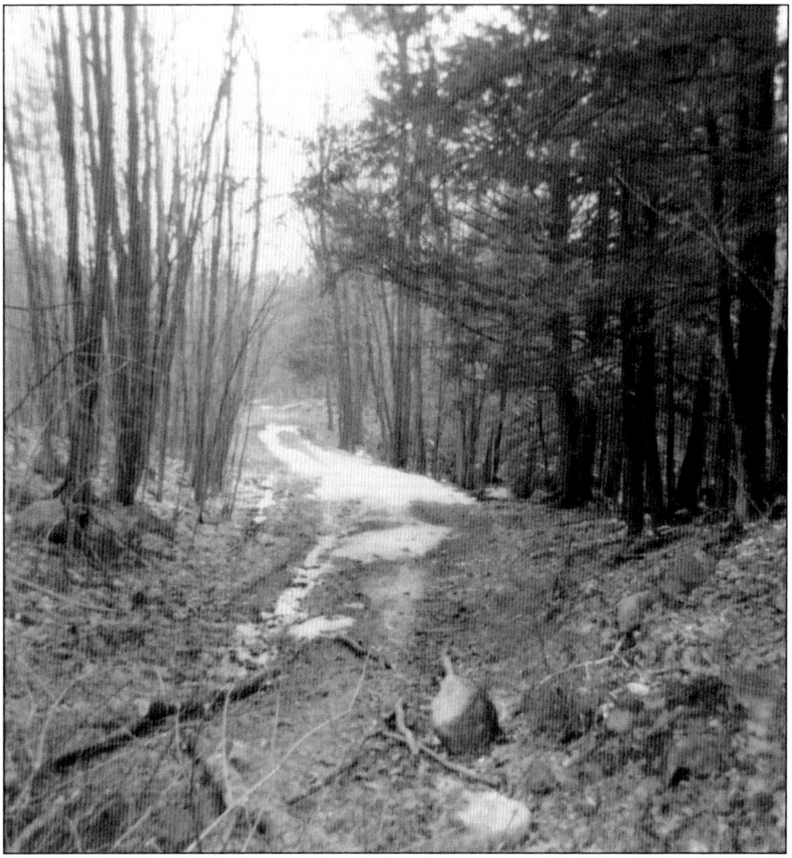

As late as 1956, there were still no houses on Little Mill Road. The road was not paved, and most of the way was inaccessible by any kind of vehicle. (Courtesy of Ruth Holmes.)

From the late 1800s to the 1960s, Sandown's population increased with the arrival of summer residents and tourists, which supplemented the local economy. Postcards were used to advertise Sandown as a place to visit. Fishing along the bank of the Exeter River, with its abundance of wildlife and open spaces, was considered "having a good time in Sandown" and was a great way to enjoy the peace and quiet of small-town life. (Courtesy of Richard Holmes.)

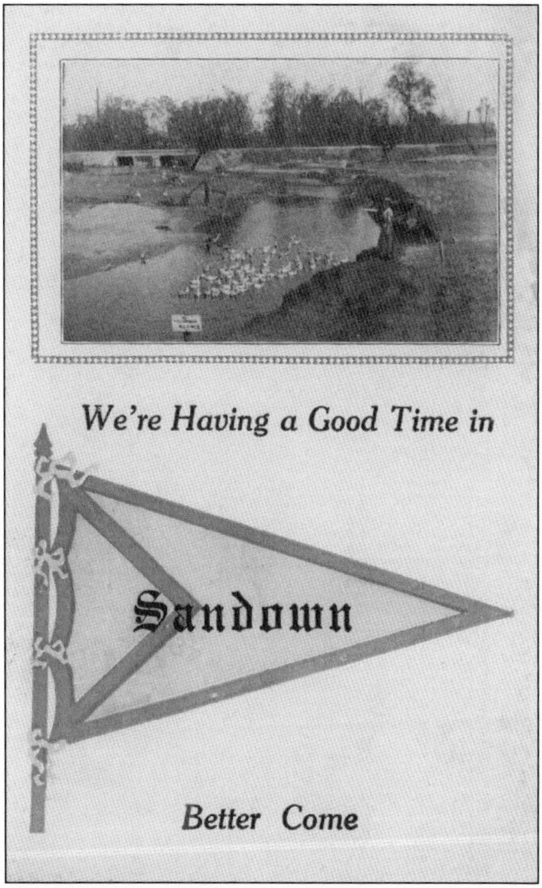

Lake Phillip (below), located near the town center, was named for Native American chief King Phillip. In 1906, Wampanoag Camp was advertised as a "summer camp for boys on the shores of Lake Phillip." Today, the 85-acre lake is known as Phillips Pond, and town residents take advantage of the public beach area during the summer months, when a lifeguard is on duty. (Courtesy of the Sandown Historical Society.)

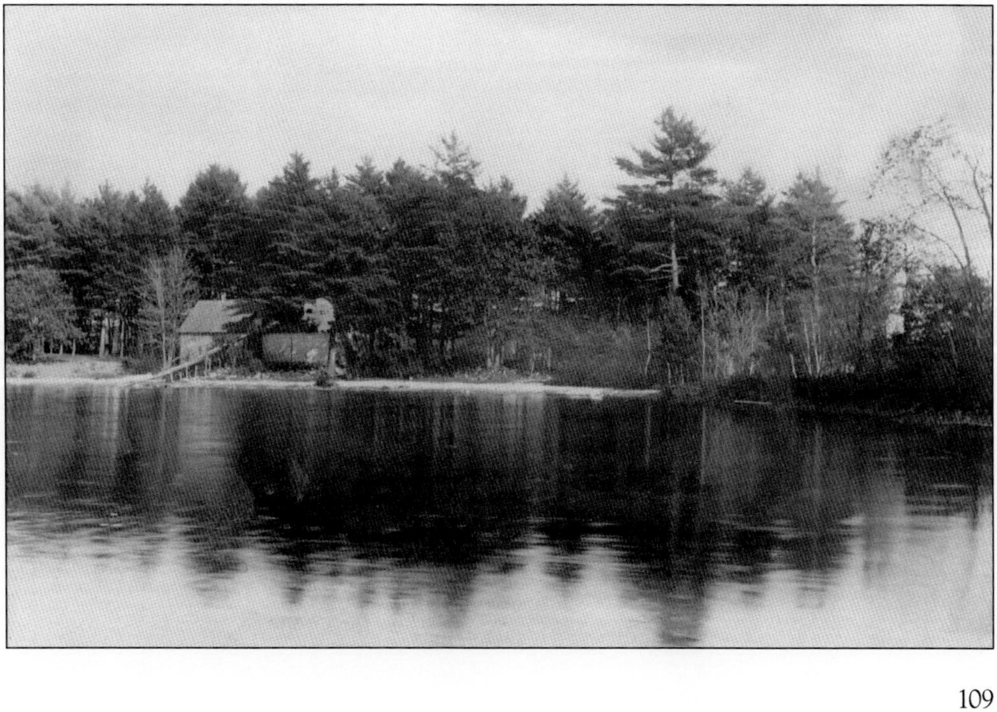

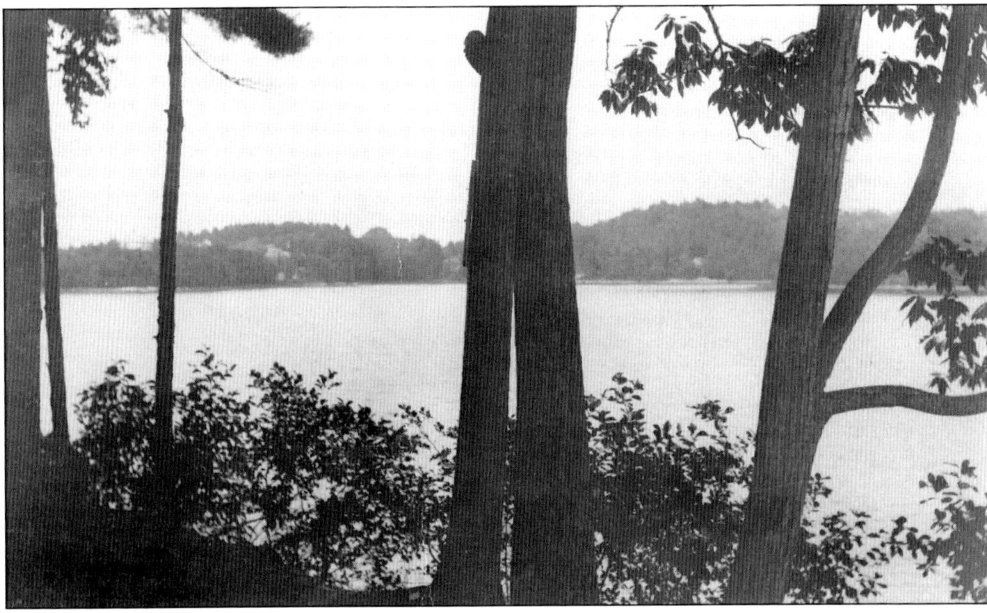

Picture postcards highlighting the beauty and tranquility of the lakes and ponds in Sandown attracted summer residents to the area. In 1908, Mrs. G.W. Ladd sent the postcard above to Mrs. J.W. Fellows of Cambridgeport, Massachusetts, with the message, "Wanted—summer boarders—fine lake, boating, canoeing, bathing and fishing. Pine grove. Plenty of fresh eggs and milk and vegetables in season. Prices according to room and pocketbook." The postcard below shows Longfellow Pier, which was located at Holts Point Road on Angle Pond. (Above, courtesy of Richard Holmes; below, courtesy of Eleanor Bassett.)

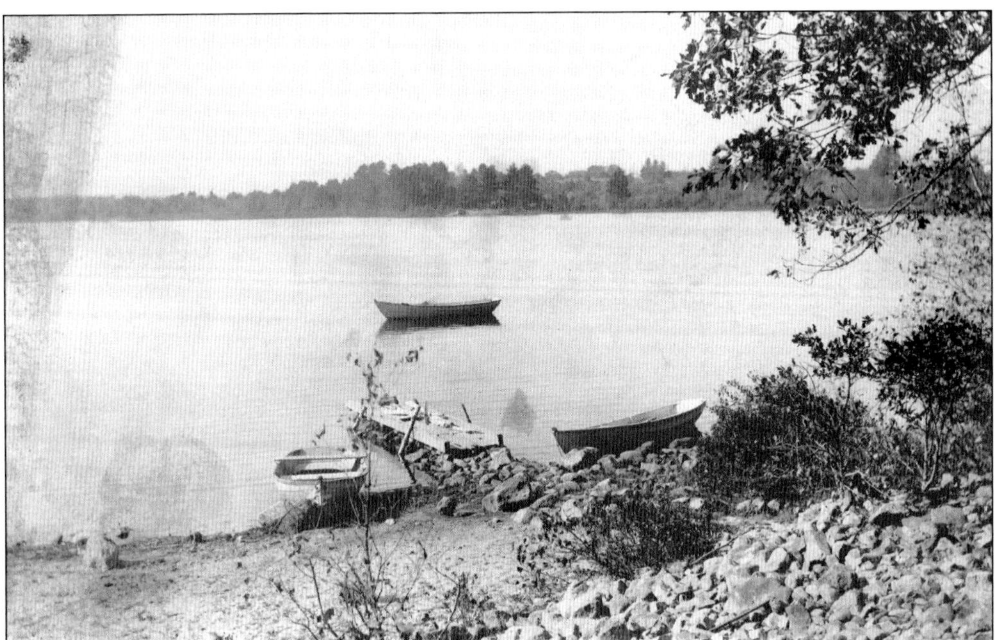

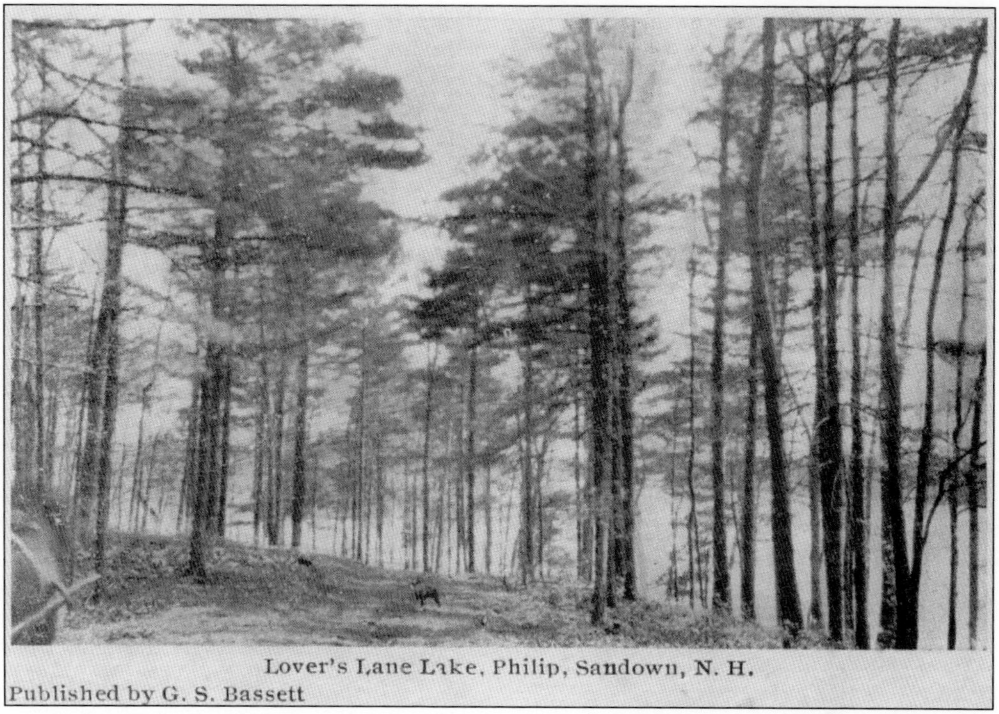

Local merchants used all sorts of advertisements to attract tourists to Sandown. Taking full advantage of the beauty of the area and its close proximity to the railroad depot, Lover's Lane on Lake Phillip must have been a popular spot, as both of these postcards suggest it as a romantic getaway. (Both, courtesy of Richard Holmes.)

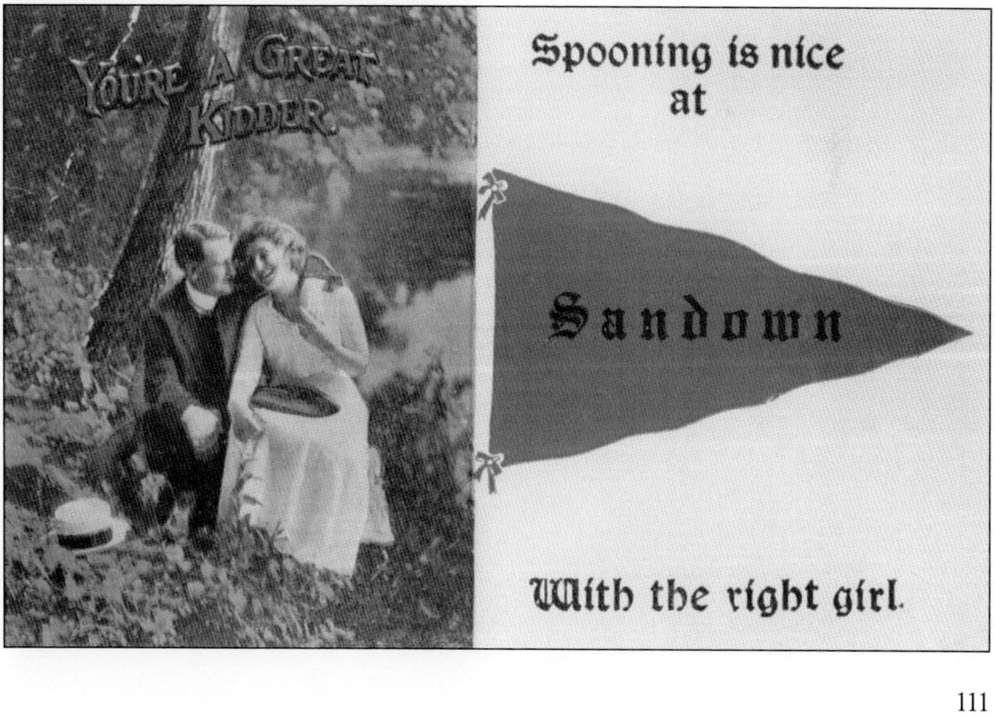

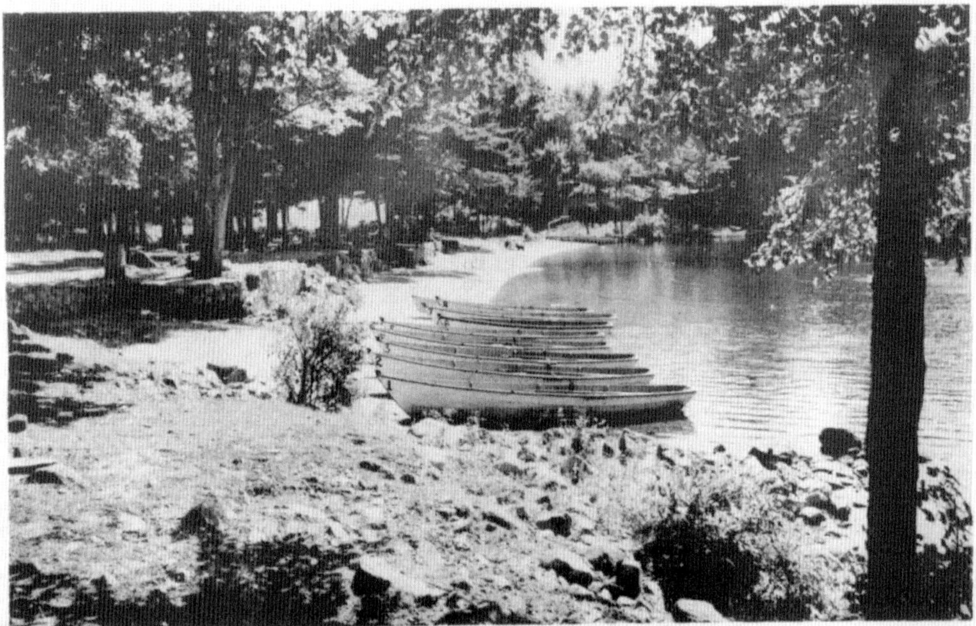

Shore View at Angle Pond

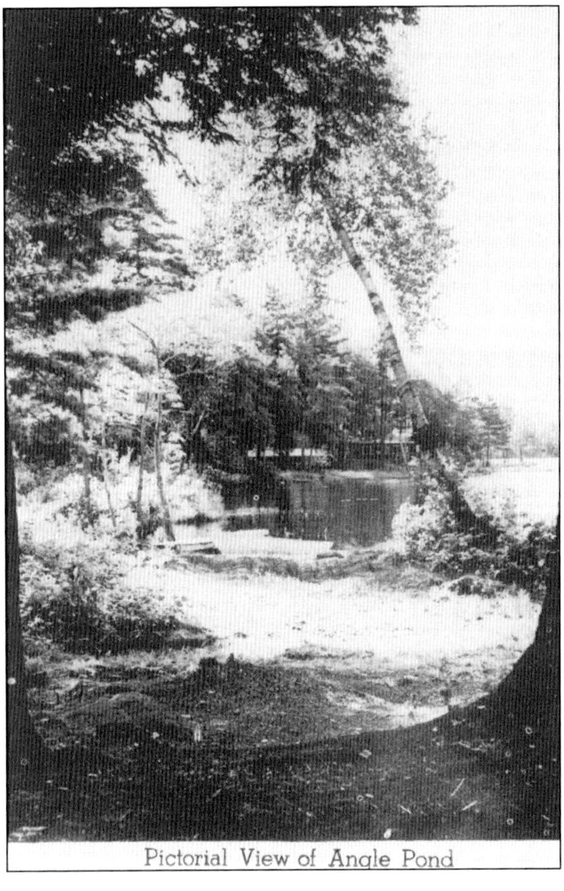

Pictorial View of Angle Pond

With water temperature much warmer than the ocean, a nice beach area (above), and lots of shady spots, Angle Pond was an ideal getaway. Today, campers still enjoy the campground and the beautiful sunsets over the pond. The lake is also the home of many seasonal cottages and year-round private homes that dot the shoreline. The camps of the Correlle and Provost families are seen at left. (Both, courtesy of Jacqueline Burke.)

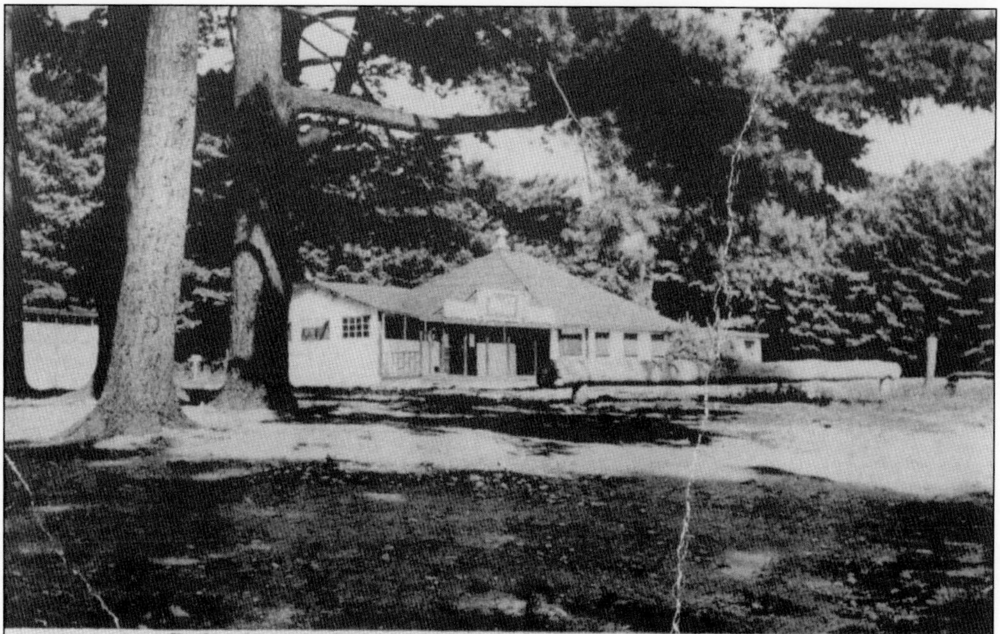

Refreshment Stand and Dance Hall at Angle Pond

The largest of the lakes in Sandown is Angle Pond, which attracted many tourists and summer residents. Campsites, cottages, and hotels were available for visitors. A refreshment stand and dance hall also provided entertainment for guests and year-round residents. (Courtesy of the Sandown Public Library.)

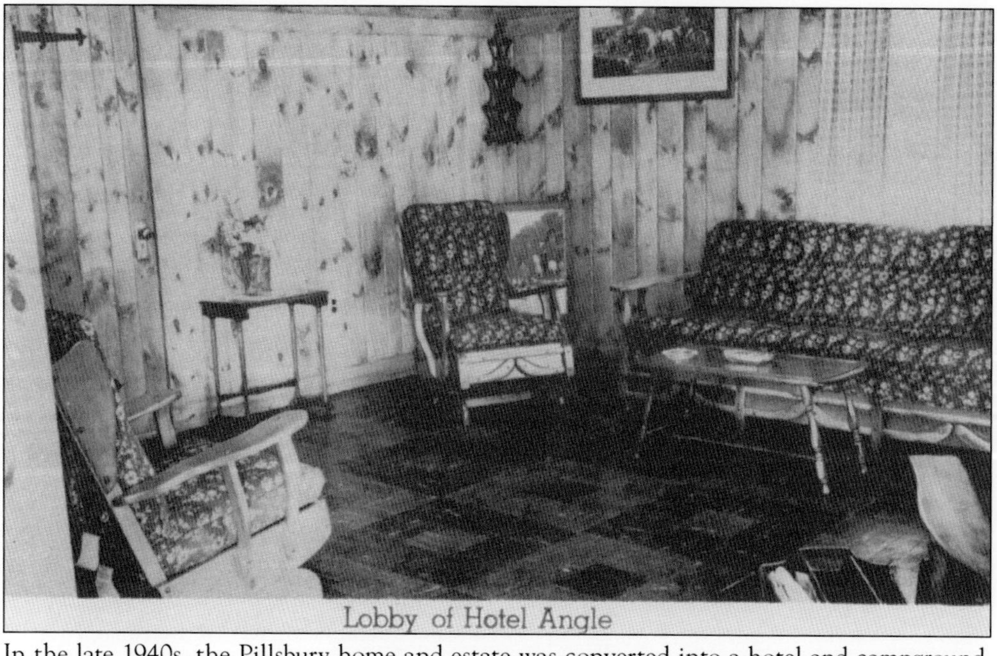

Lobby of Hotel Angle

In the late 1940s, the Pillsbury home and estate was converted into a hotel and campground. Summer guests felt right at home in the lobby of the Angle Pond Hotel, which featured comfortable rustic furniture. The hotel was destroyed by a fire in 1962. Today, Angle Pond Campground offers seasonal sites for camping and day visits. (Courtesy of Jacqueline Burke.)

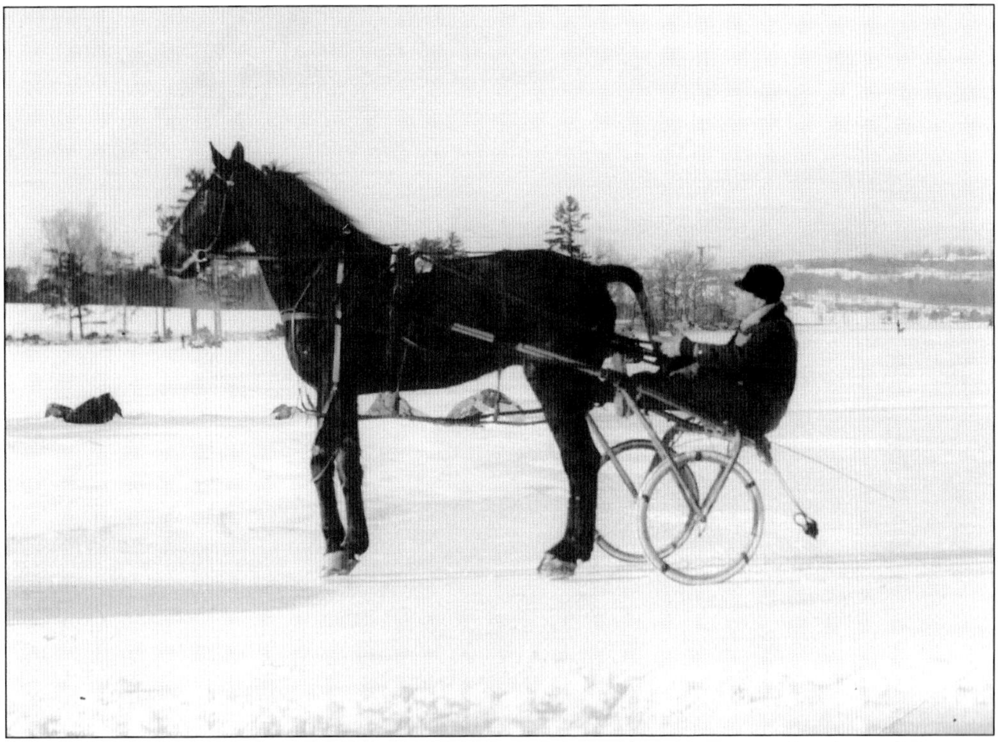

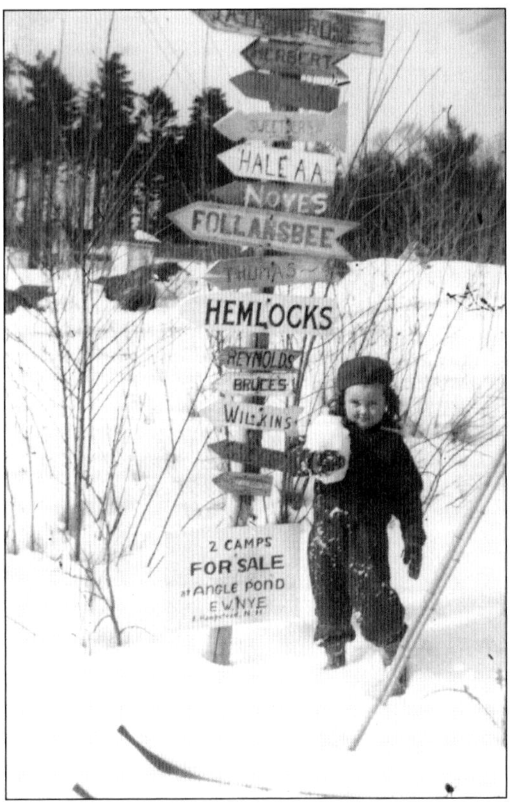

During the winter months, frozen lakes and ponds provided outdoor recreational fun, including ice fishing, ice-skating, cross-country skiing, and snowshoeing. Harness racing on the ice (above) was a more unique but popular event in New England. Today, snowmobiling and ice sailing have replaced the horses and sulkies that used to trot across the frozen water. (Photograph by Harold J. Piper; courtesy of Robert and Lois MacKinnon.)

Although Angle Pond was known more as a summer attraction, it did not stop three-year-old Jacqueline Provost and her family from enjoying some winter fun. They would leave their vehicle near the end of the road and use skis and snowshoes to hike into their camp. This post shows the names of some of the camp owners in 1939. (Courtesy of Jacqueline Burke.)

Eight

Celebrating Good Times

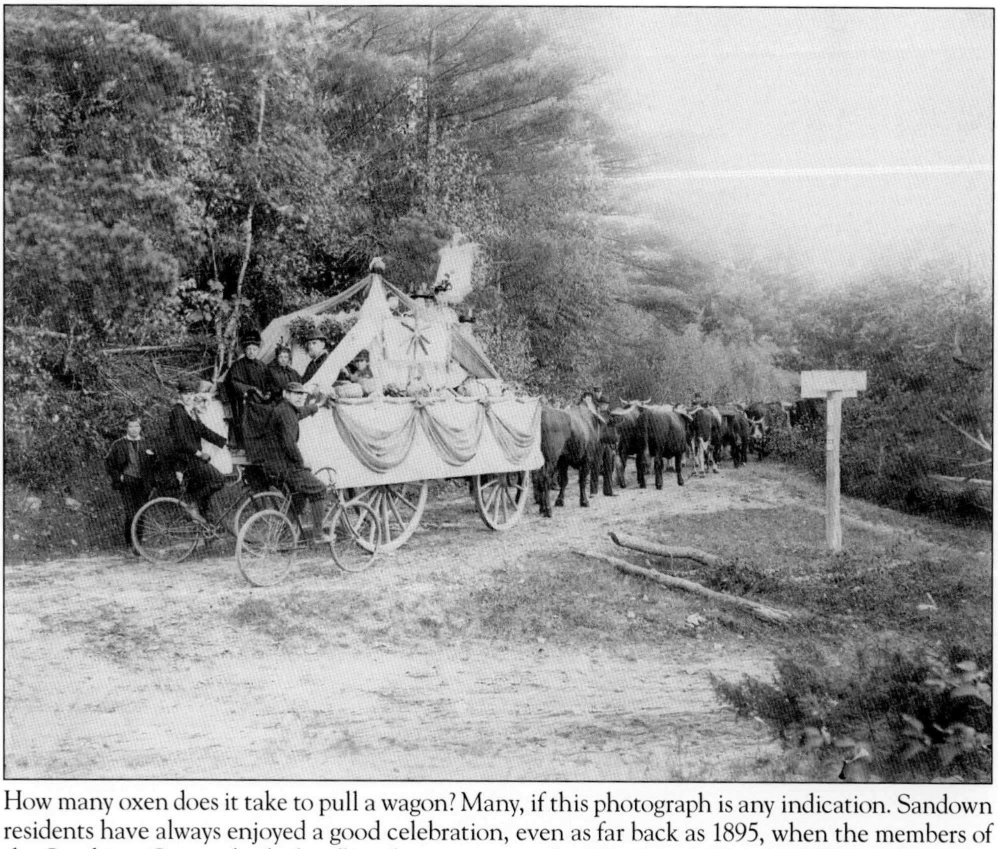

How many oxen does it take to pull a wagon? Many, if this photograph is any indication. Sandown residents have always enjoyed a good celebration, even as far back as 1895, when the members of the Sandown Grange built this float for a town parade. (Courtesy of Lois MacKinnon.)

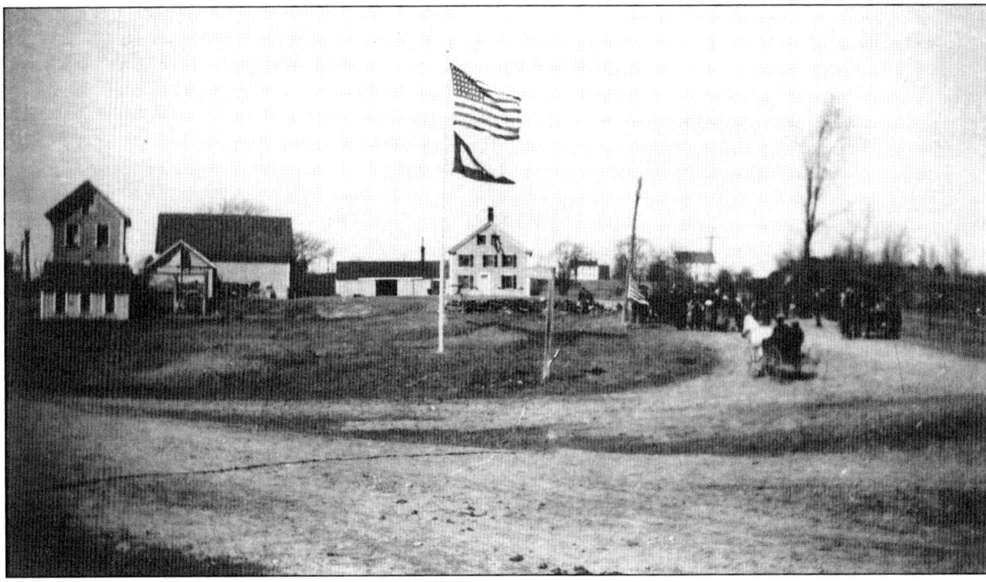

This photograph was taken in 1918, when World War I was raging. Several young men from Sandown were involved in the fighting. The citizens showed their support as they gathered to raise the town's service flag. The ceremony took place at the depot end of Fremont Road, in front of the parsonage. (Courtesy of Eleanor Bassett.)

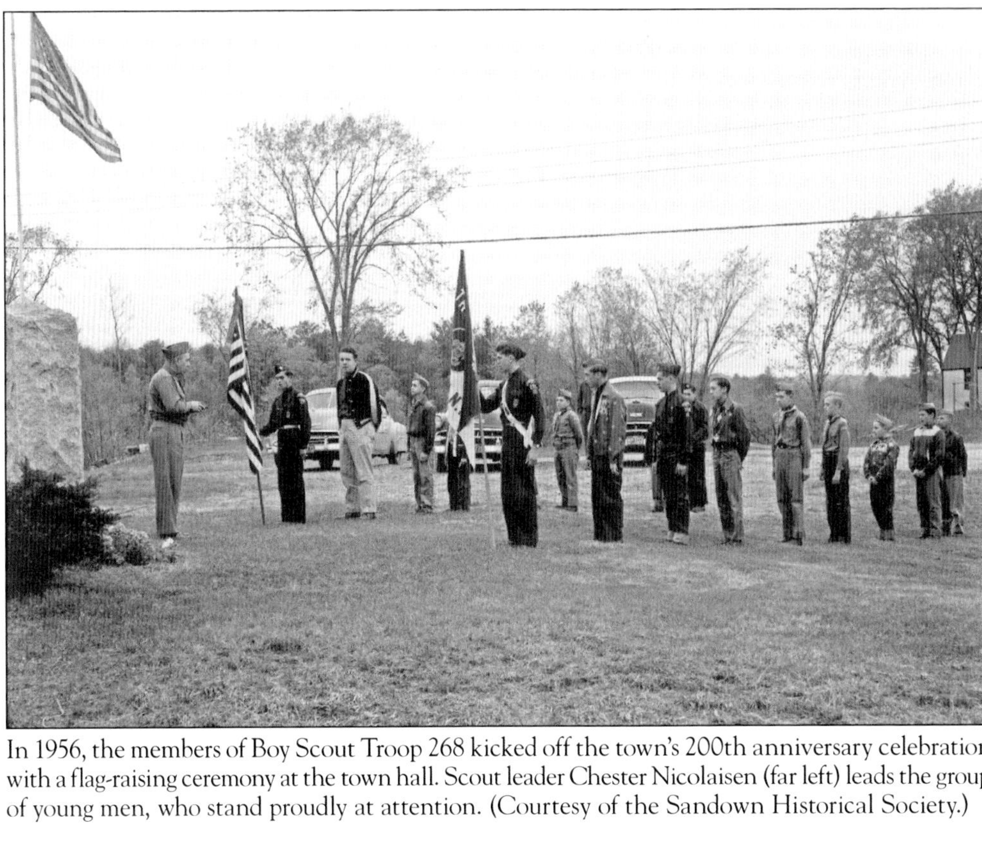

In 1956, the members of Boy Scout Troop 268 kicked off the town's 200th anniversary celebration with a flag-raising ceremony at the town hall. Scout leader Chester Nicolaisen (far left) leads the group of young men, who stand proudly at attention. (Courtesy of the Sandown Historical Society.)

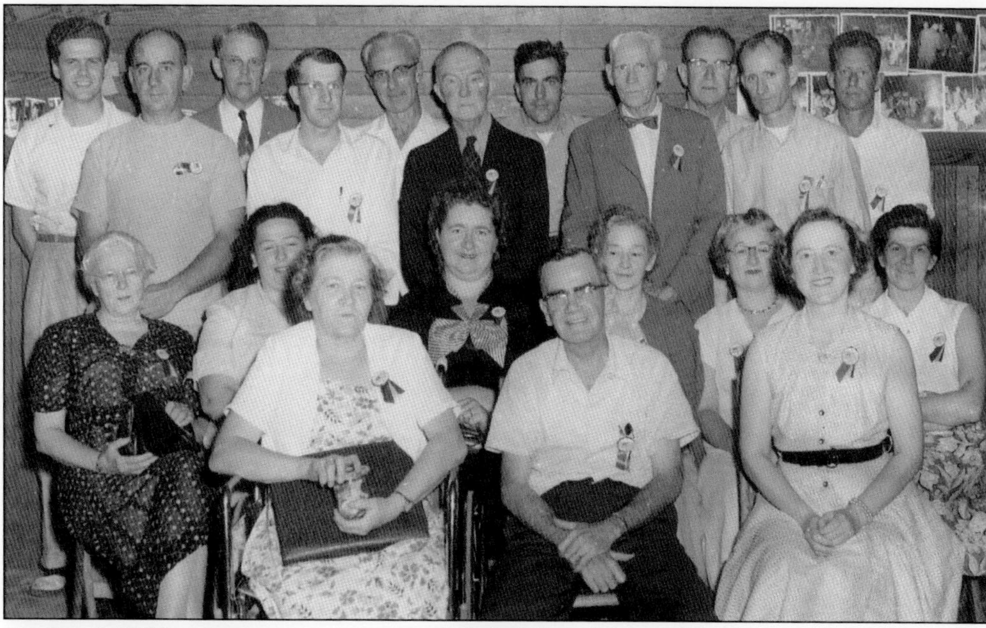

Sandown's 200th anniversary committee included, from left to right, (first row) Priscilla Bassett, Delbert Shepard, and Angela "Nell" Cameron; (second row) Bertha Follansbee, Virginia Lessard, Alice Tarbox, Olive Follansbee, Olga Stenzel, and Eleanor Bassett; (third row) Chester Nicolaisen, Lloyd Lessard, Adm. Howard R. Shaw, Charles Burton French, and John Holmes Jr.; (fourth row) Stanley Kennedy, Ernest Pillsbury, William Croteau, William Hutchinson, Ralph Barnes, and Everett "Bud" Holmes. (Courtesy of the Sandown Historical Society.)

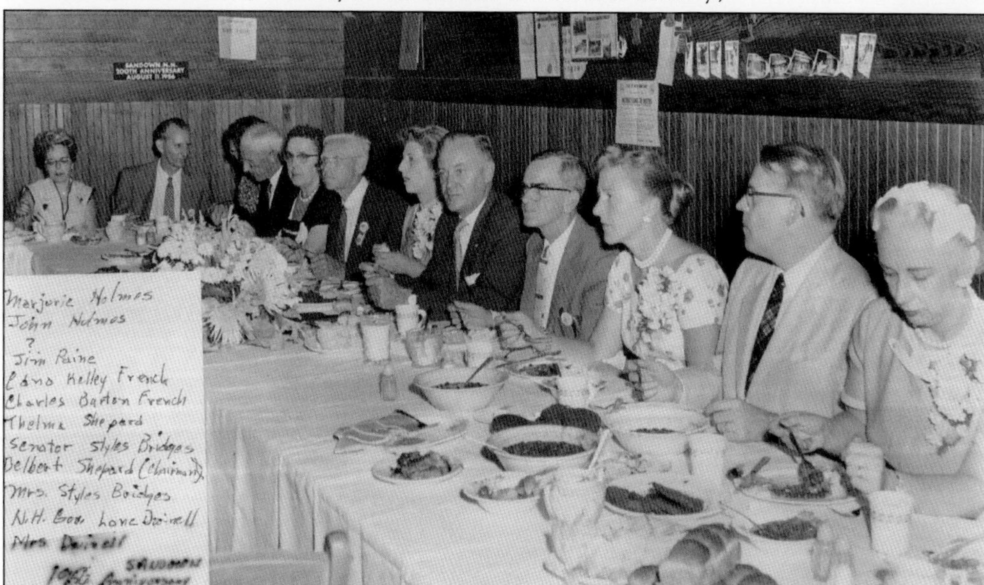

Invited guests Gov. Lane Dwinell, Sen. Styles Bridges, and their wives enjoyed a catered dinner as part of the 200th anniversary celebration in 1956. Joining them were a number of Sandown's prominent citizens. From left to right are Marjorie and John Holmes, Charlotte and James Paine, Edna and Charles Burton French, Thelma Shepard, Senator Bridges, Delbert Shepard, Delores Bridges, Governor Dwinell, and Elizabeth Dwinell. (Courtesy of the Sandown Historical Society.)

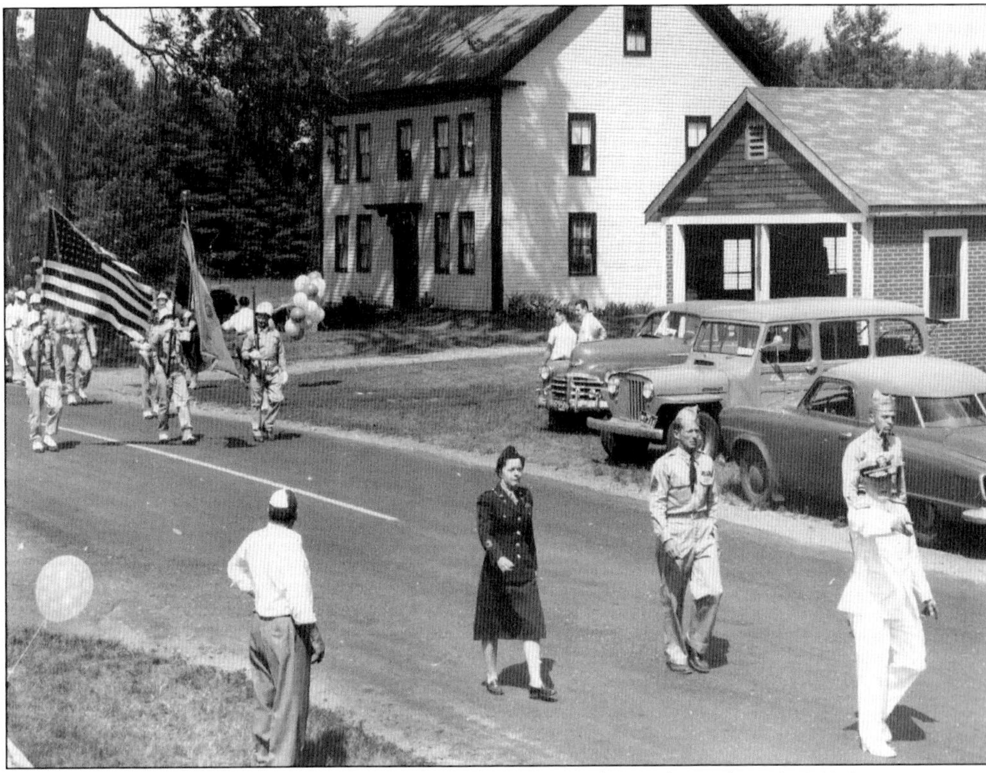

Honoring the military is an important part of any parade, and Sandown's 200th anniversary celebration in 1956 was no exception. Leading this group is Adm. Howard R. Shaw. Behind him are, from left to right, Ruth Phillips, Everett "Bud" Holmes, and William Bassett. (Photograph by Mal Cameron; courtesy of the Sandown Historical Society.)

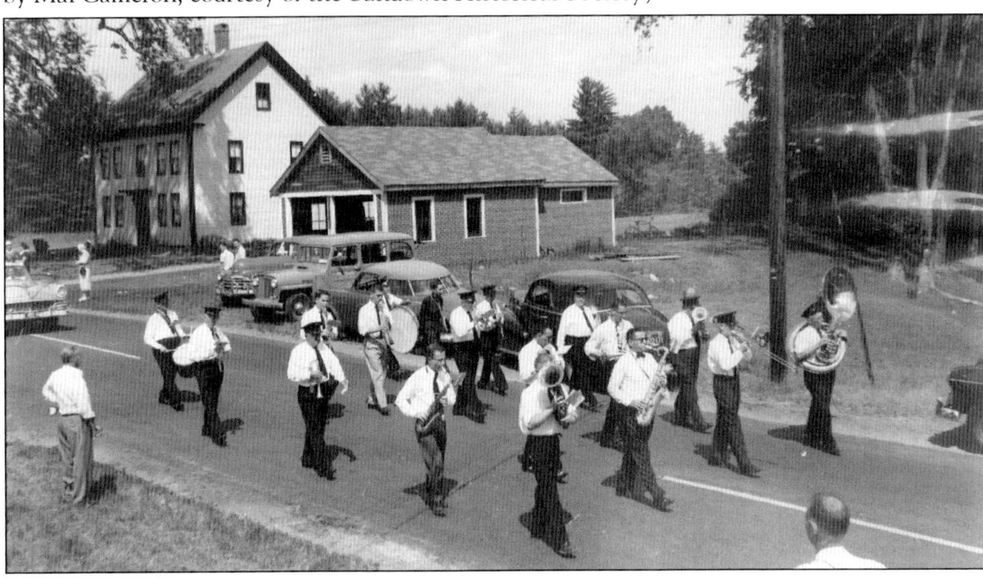

No parade would be complete without a military band. This band from Derry was in perfect step at Sandown's 200th anniversary celebration as they marched through the center of Sandown past the former Triple Elms Hotel. (Courtesy of the Sandown Historical Society.)

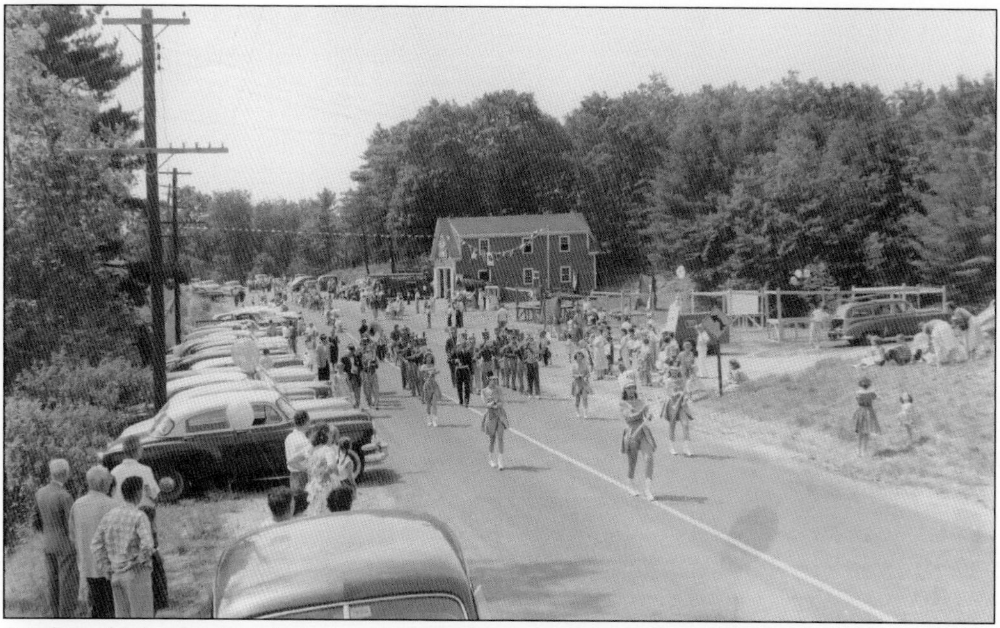

Sandown high school students were among the majorettes and band members in this marching band from Sanborn Seminary in Kingston, which participated in the 200th anniversary celebration parade. Since there was no high school in Sandown, teenagers could choose between the area's high schools. Because of their close proximity, Pinkerton Academy, in Derry, and Sanborn Seminary, in Kingston, were the popular choices. (Photograph by Mal Cameron; courtesy of the Sandown Historical Society.)

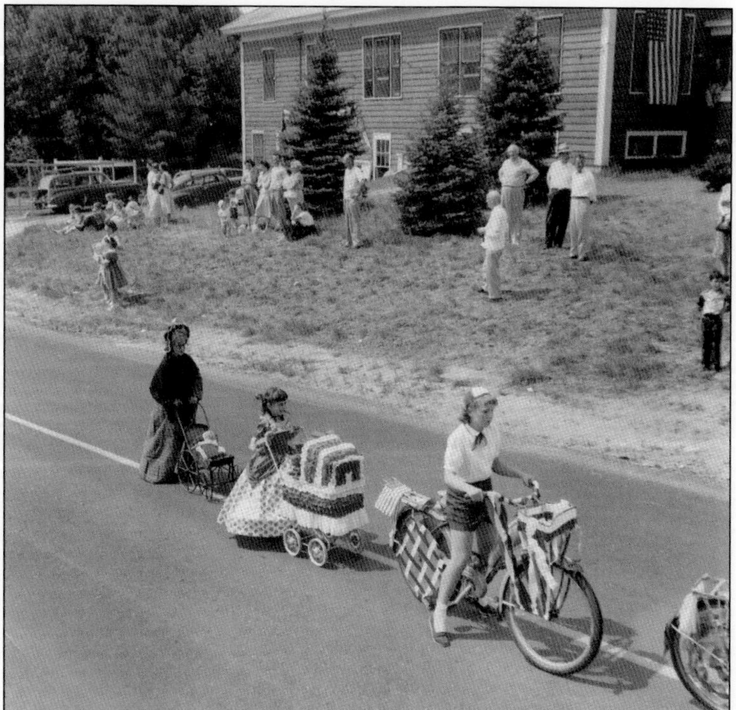

One fun activity at the 200th anniversary celebration was this children's parade. In front, on the bicycle, is Arlene Holmes, and pushing the decorated doll carriage is Robin Noyce. The "girl" in the old-fashioned costume pushing the antique stroller is Charles "Chuck" Holmes. (Photograph by Mal Cameron; courtesy of the Sandown Historical Society.)

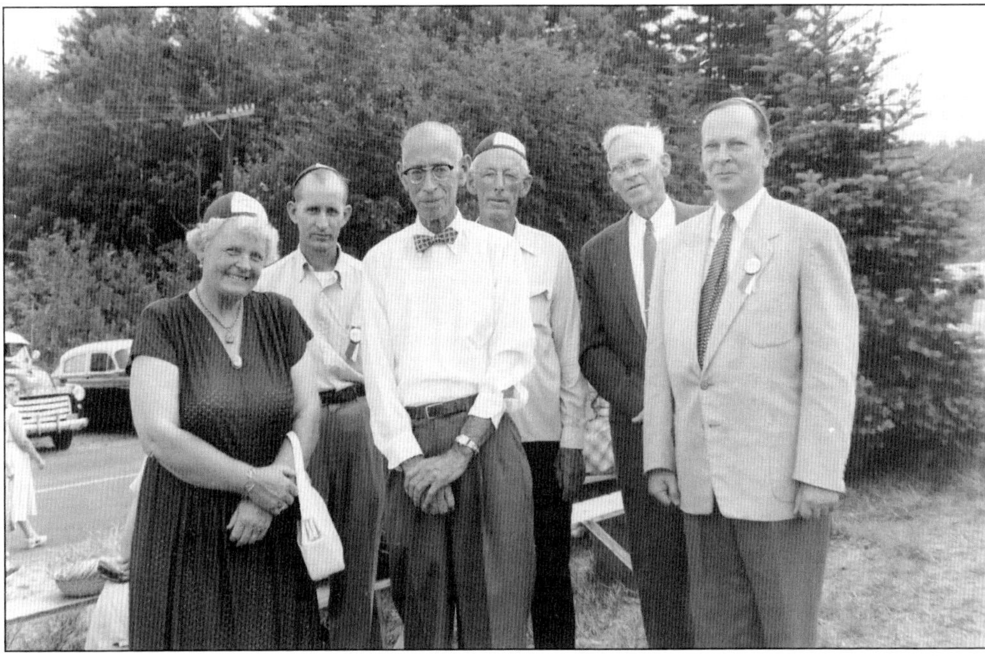

The 200th anniversary children's parade took place in the morning, but the main parade was held in the afternoon. The judges for the main parade were, from left to right, (first row) Doris Spollet of Hampstead, Edward Clark of Kingston, and Rev. John Rea Chapmen of Sandown; (second row) Sandown selectmen John B. Holmes Jr., James L. Paine, and Charles Burton French. (Photograph by Mal Cameron; courtesy of the Sandown Historical Society.)

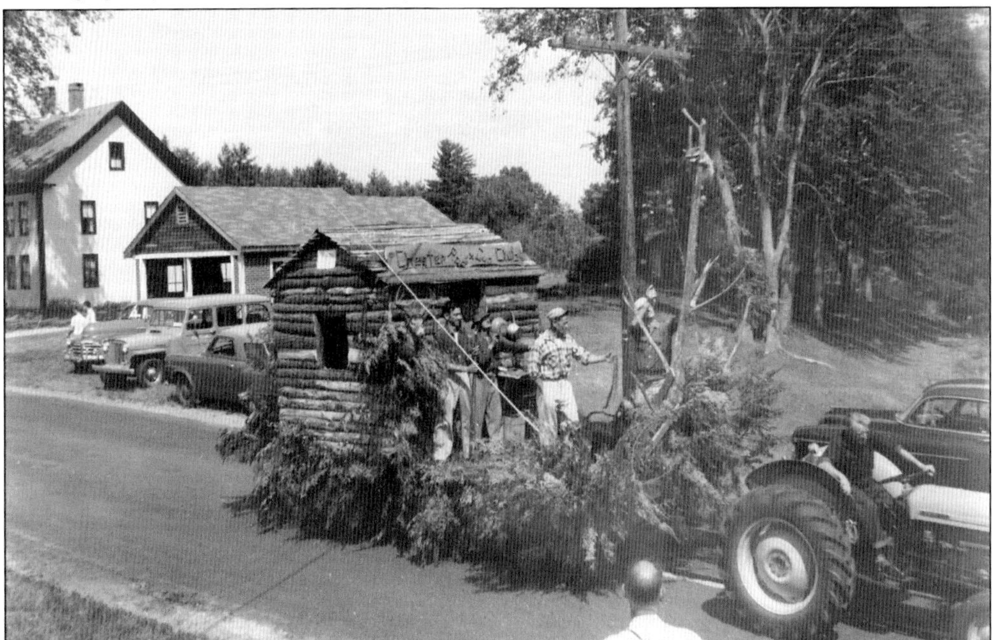

This float won first prize in the 200th anniversary parade. It was sponsored by the Chester Rod & Gun Club. Pulling the float is a tractor driven by Eugene Tenney. Note the raccoon perched in the tree. (Photograph by Mal Cameron; courtesy of the Sandown Historical Society.)

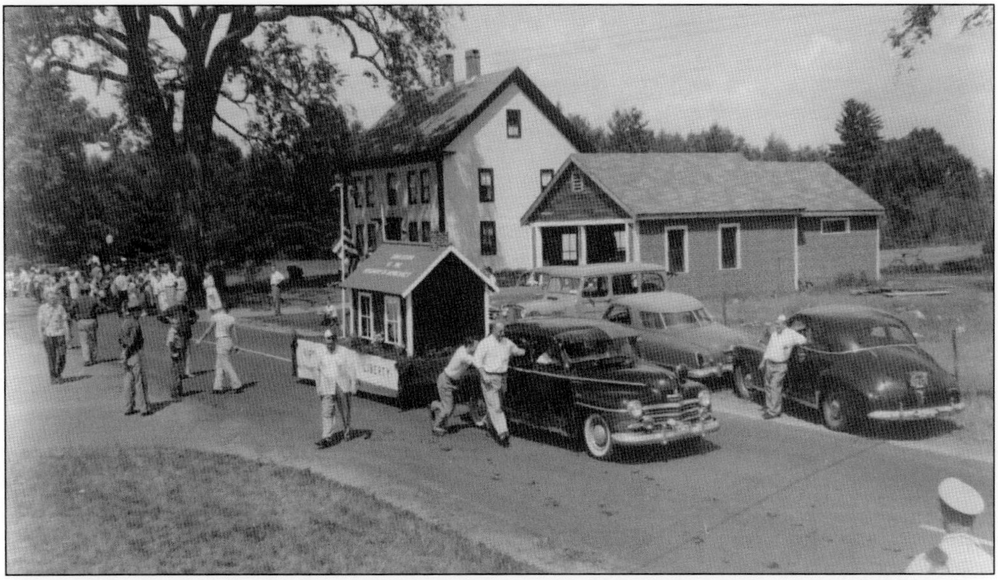

The 200th anniversary parade's second-place winner is seen here. It was entered by the Junior Order of United American Mechanics. Ironically, the car broke down and had to be pushed past the judges' stand. (Photograph by Mal Cameron; courtesy of the Sandown Historical Society.)

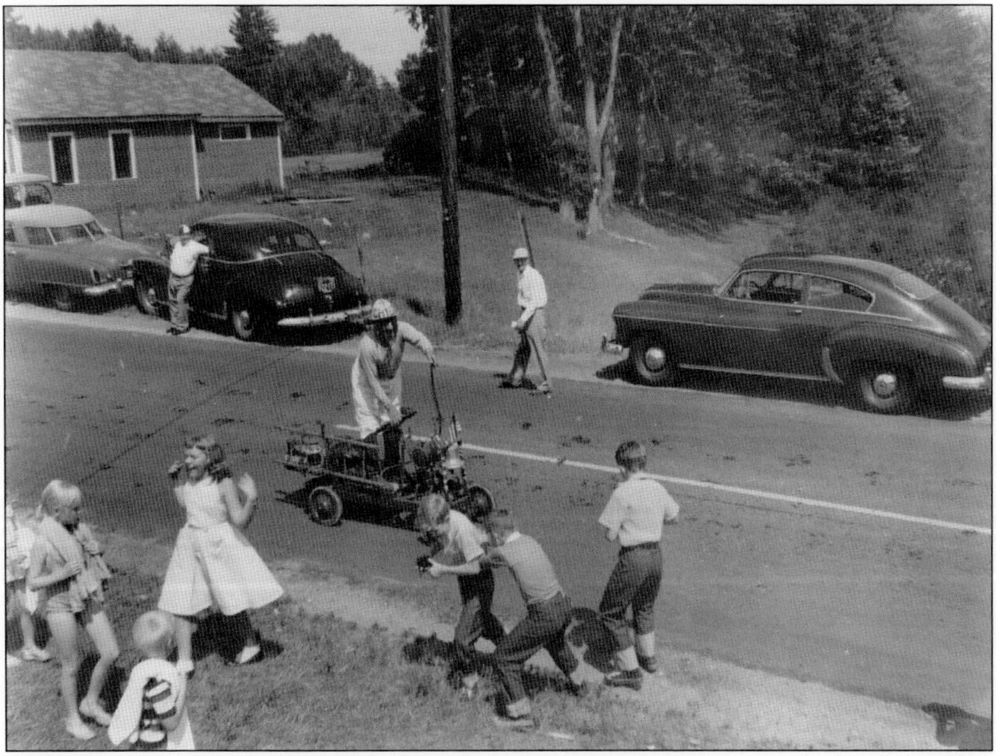

Fremont resident Albert "Pokey" Fuller tied for third prize in the 200th anniversary parade with his tiny fire truck. Fuller was a popular bus driver who transported high school students from Sandown, Chester, Fremont, and Brentwood to Sanborn Seminary in Kingston. He also served as county commissioner. (Photograph by Mal Cameron; courtesy of the Sandown Historical Society.)

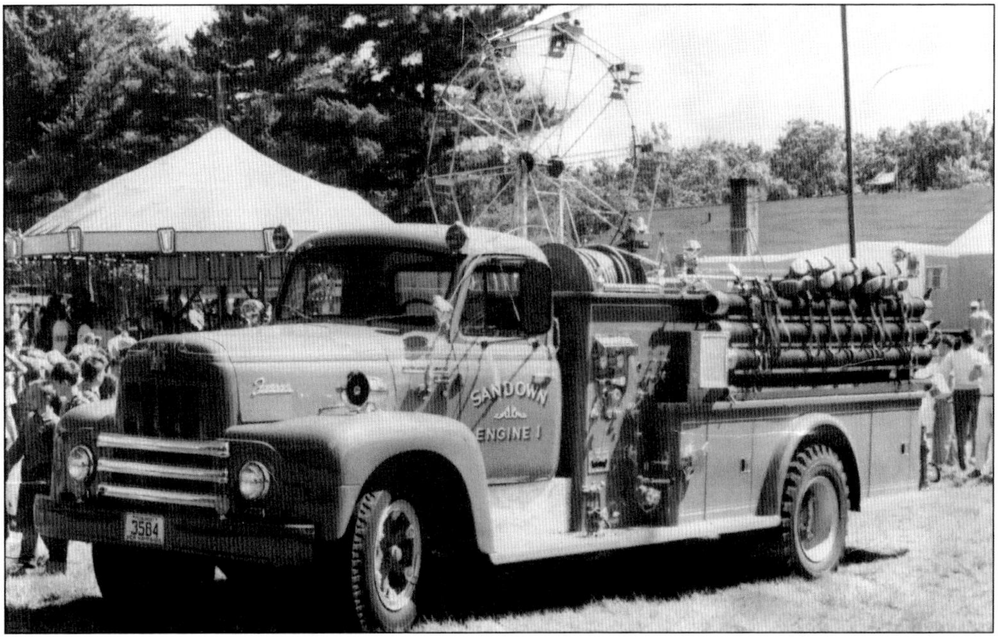

Sandown's Engine 1 is proudly on display at the fire association's Fourth of July carnival as a reminder of the purpose for the fundraising event. Crowds of people from all over the region came for the festivities, which included a Ferris wheel and a merry-go-round. (Courtesy of the Sandown Fire Department.)

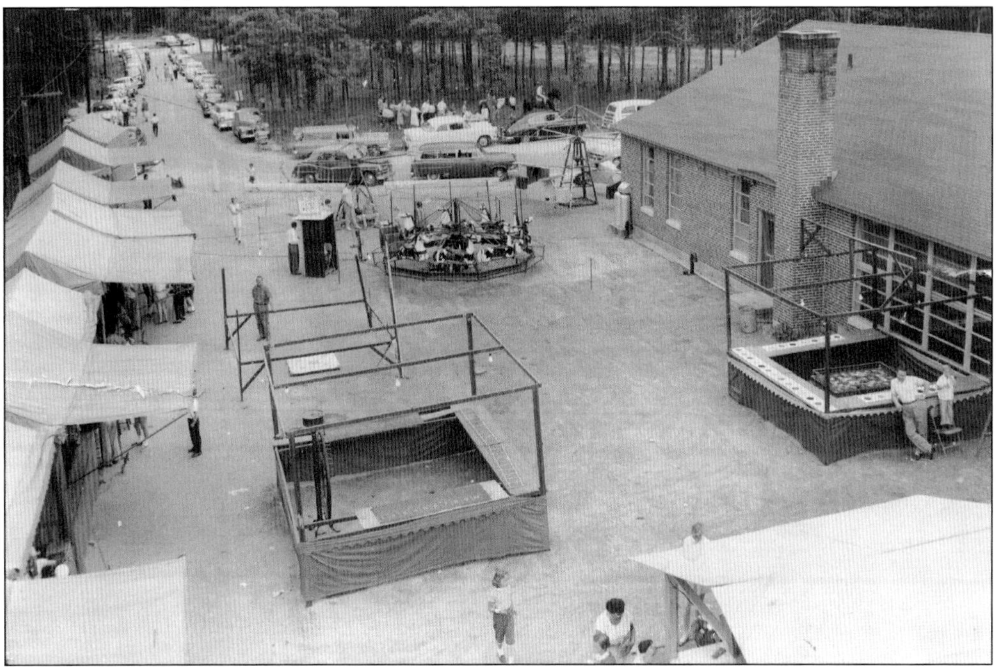

Carnival rides, games of chance, and food booths were set up on the midway behind the original Central School. Nightly entertainment took center stage during the four day event, including dancing by the Huckins Huskers led by Evelyn Huckins and square dancing led by Edward Deveau, Duaine Steinhoff, and Malcolm Cameron. (Courtesy of the Sandown Fire Department.)

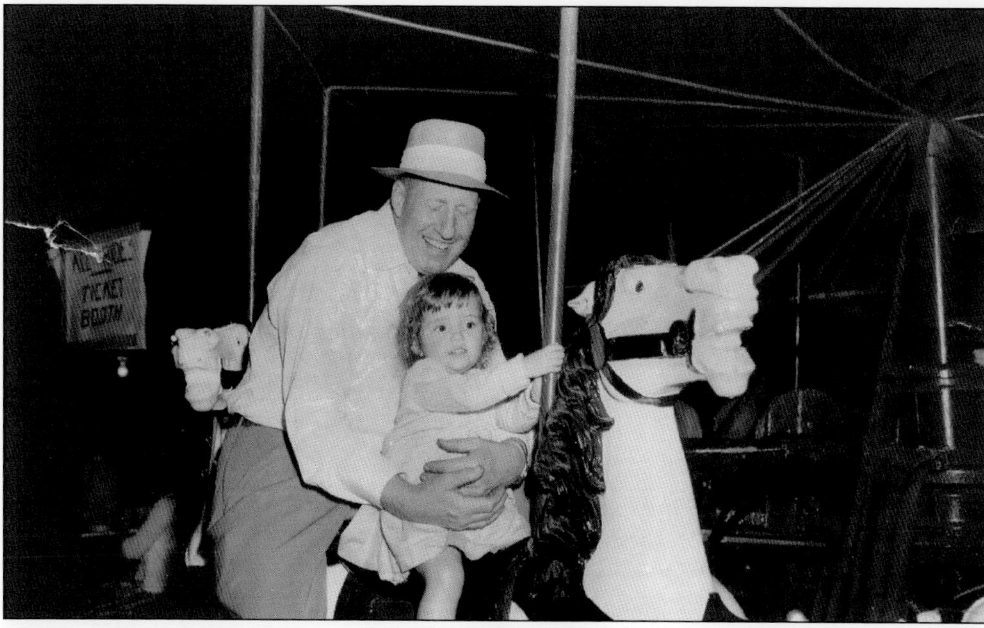

For 12 years, from 1958 to 1969, the Sandown Fire Association held a four-day carnival over the Fourth of July to raise money for needed equipment. Not only did this fundraiser save the town thousands of dollars in taxes, it also provided a strong community event that promoted the small town and brought thousands of visitors to the area. Each year, the carnival was set up at the Central School with a midway, a parade, rides, fireworks, and plenty of food. A bonfire was built in the pit next to the school, where the public library is now located. Somehow, a car was at the top of the bonfire. Above, Alpha Learned and his foster child enjoy the merry-go-round. Below, people try their luck "gambling," which was all in good fun. (Both, courtesy of the Sandown Fire Department.)

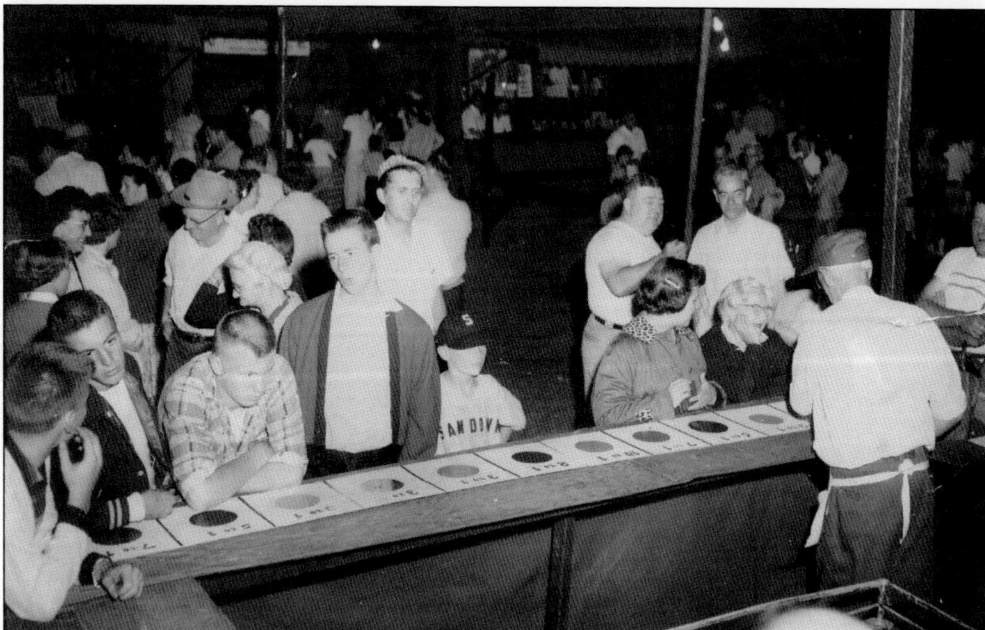

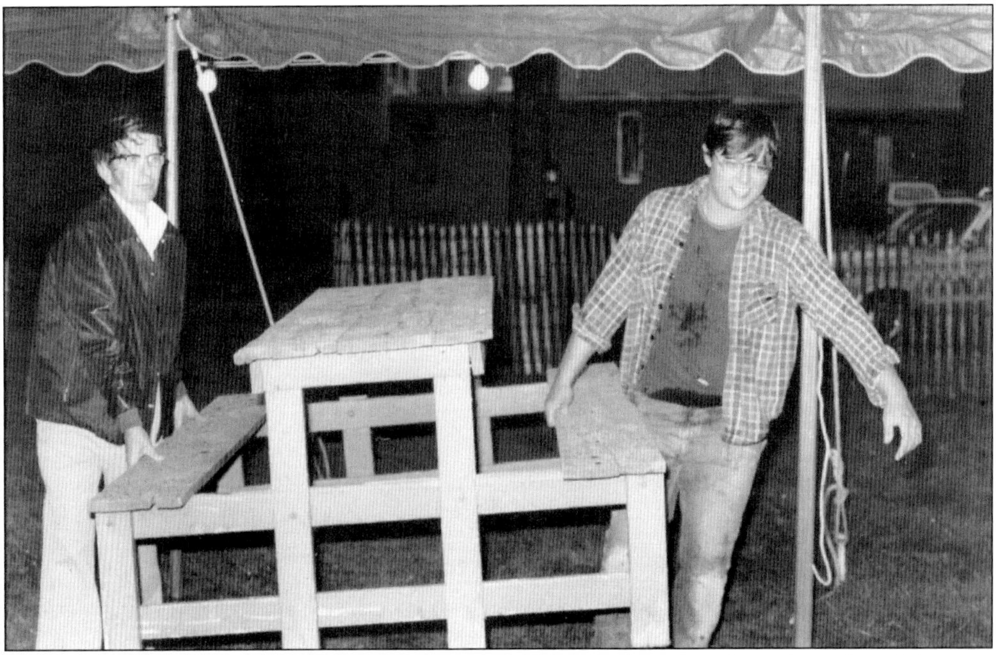

Setting up the tables under the tent for the annual Oktoberfest was a big job, as the tables were quite heavy. Here, Sandown Civic Association members Gary Batchelder and Richard Drowne are hard at work. (Courtesy of David Drowne.)

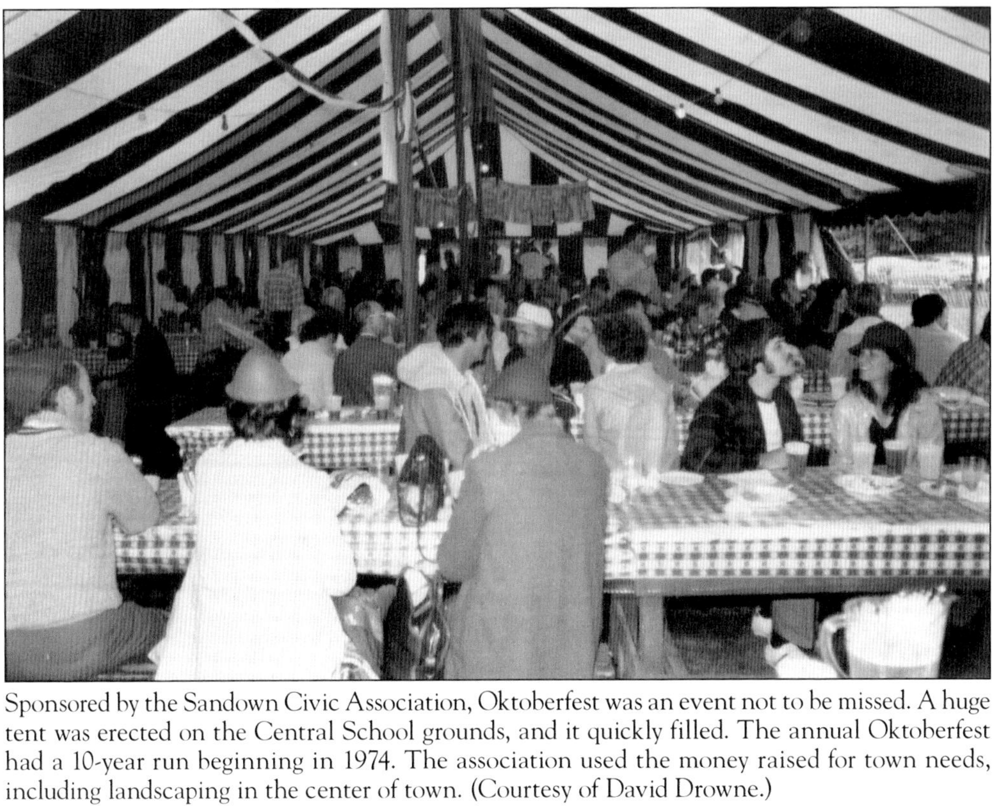

Sponsored by the Sandown Civic Association, Oktoberfest was an event not to be missed. A huge tent was erected on the Central School grounds, and it quickly filled. The annual Oktoberfest had a 10-year run beginning in 1974. The association used the money raised for town needs, including landscaping in the center of town. (Courtesy of David Drowne.)

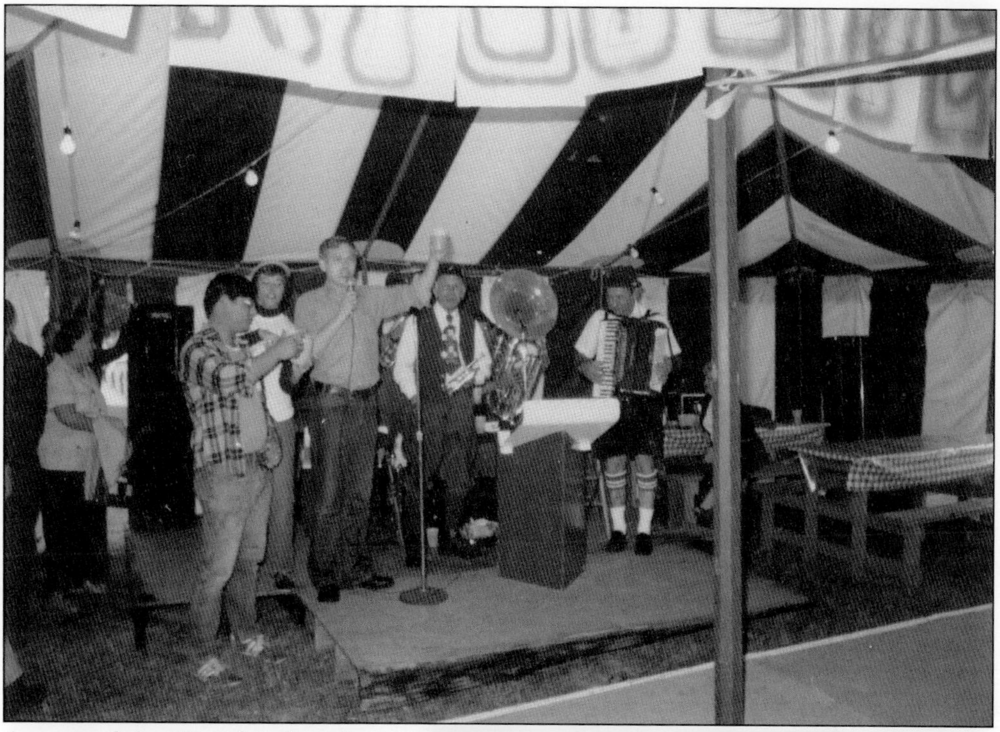

An oompah band was hired to play at the annual Oktoberfest. They are seen above as a toast is made, one of many throughout the day and evening. Everything came to a halt when a toasting song was sung in German, and everyone took a sip of beer. (Courtesy of David Drowne.)

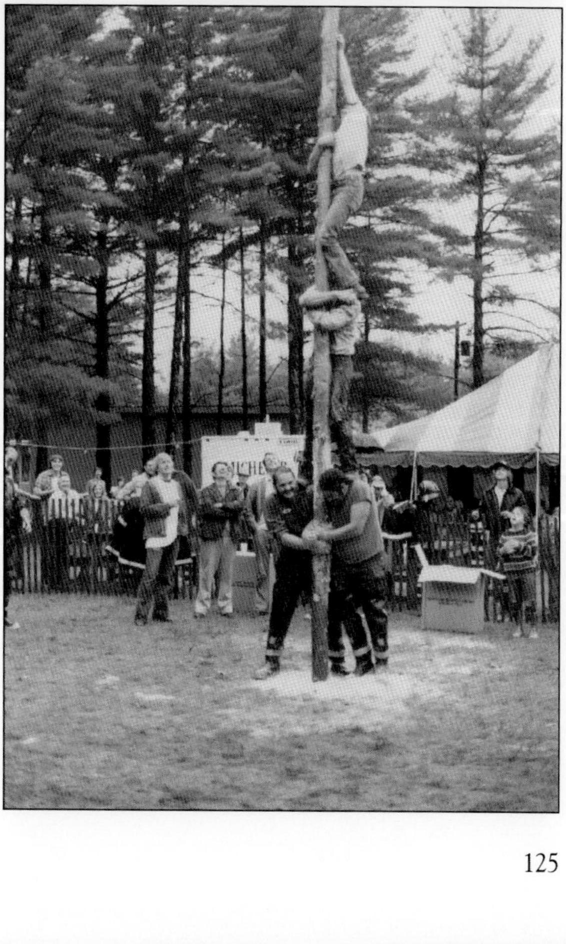

Many contests of strength and endurance were part of Oktoberfest. Here, a team of men attempt to climb a greased pole by any means possible. They stood on shoulders and pushed each other up through the slippery grease to claim the prize at the top. (Courtesy of David Drowne.)

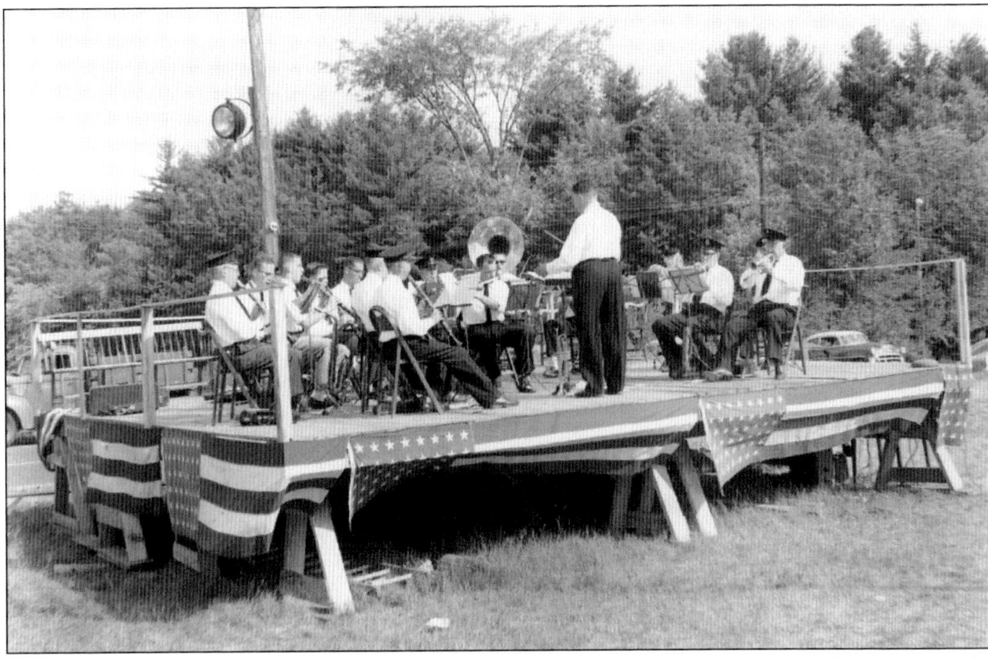

This outdoor band concert was performed as part of the 200th anniversary celebration in 1956. (Photograph by Mal Cameron; courtesy of John Cameron.)

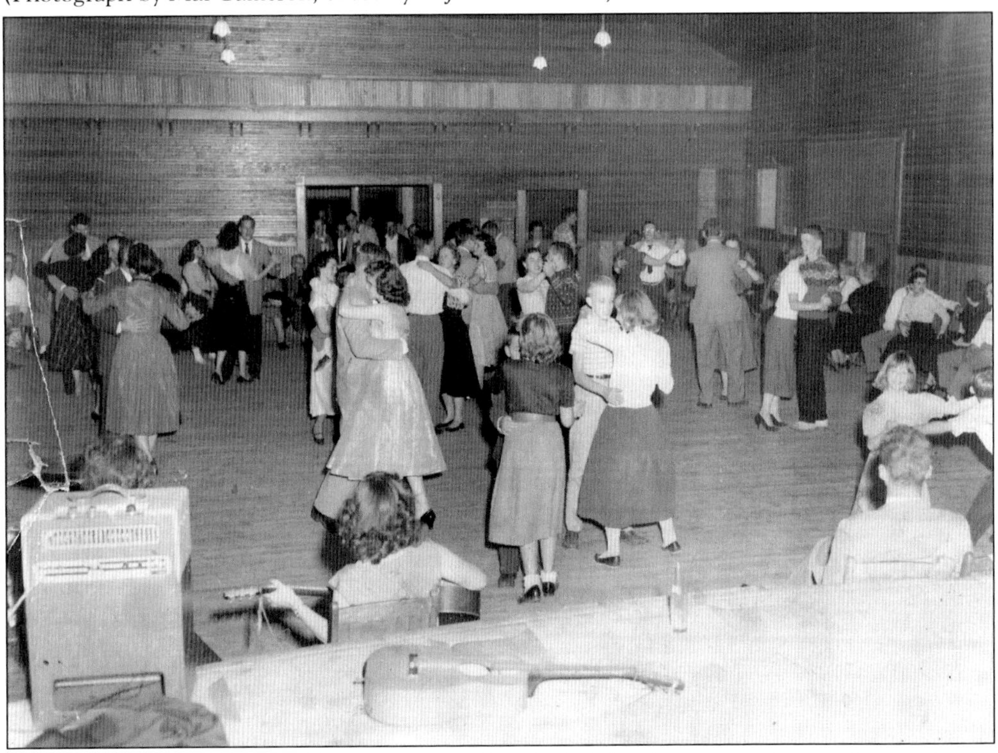

Dances at Sandown Town Hall were very popular. Both old and young can be seen here enjoying the evening. Sandown was a small town and there was little to do, so most of the population would turn out for any event held at the town hall. (Courtesy of the Sandown Fire Department.)

The 225th anniversary parade, on August 8, 1981, was filled with dignitaries, bands, and floats. Among those participating was the New Hampshire Brigade of Colonial Forces, which held a mock militia battle later in the day. Color guards and marching units from the USS *Constitution*, Fort Devens, and the Air Force participated as well. Former US senator Warren Rudman and former governor Meldrim Thomson were among the dignitaries in the parade. (Courtesy of the Sandown Historical Society.)

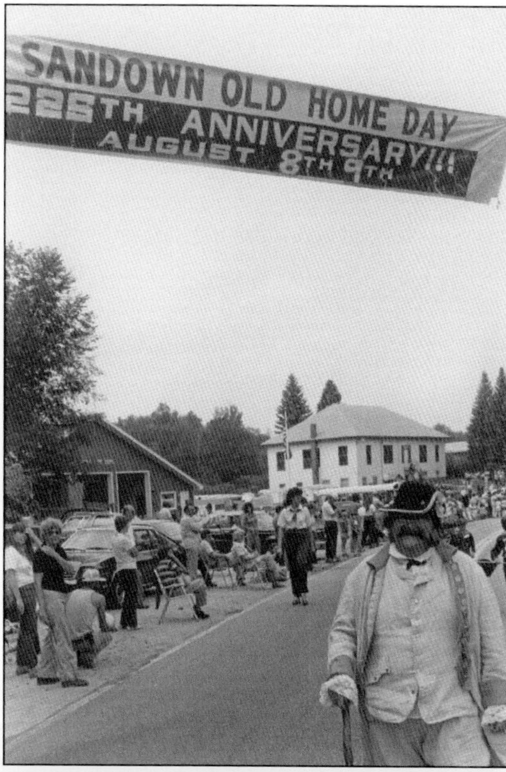

The Rockingham County Home float (below) was one of seven floats participating in the 225th anniversary celebration parade. The Saturday festival included two different parades, Ronald McDonald, a militia battle, square dancing, and fireworks. On Sunday, Old Home Day services were held at the Old Meeting House with Rev. John Rea Chapman as the guest minister, followed by a beef dinner at St. Matthews United Methodist Church. (Courtesy of Linda Torre.)

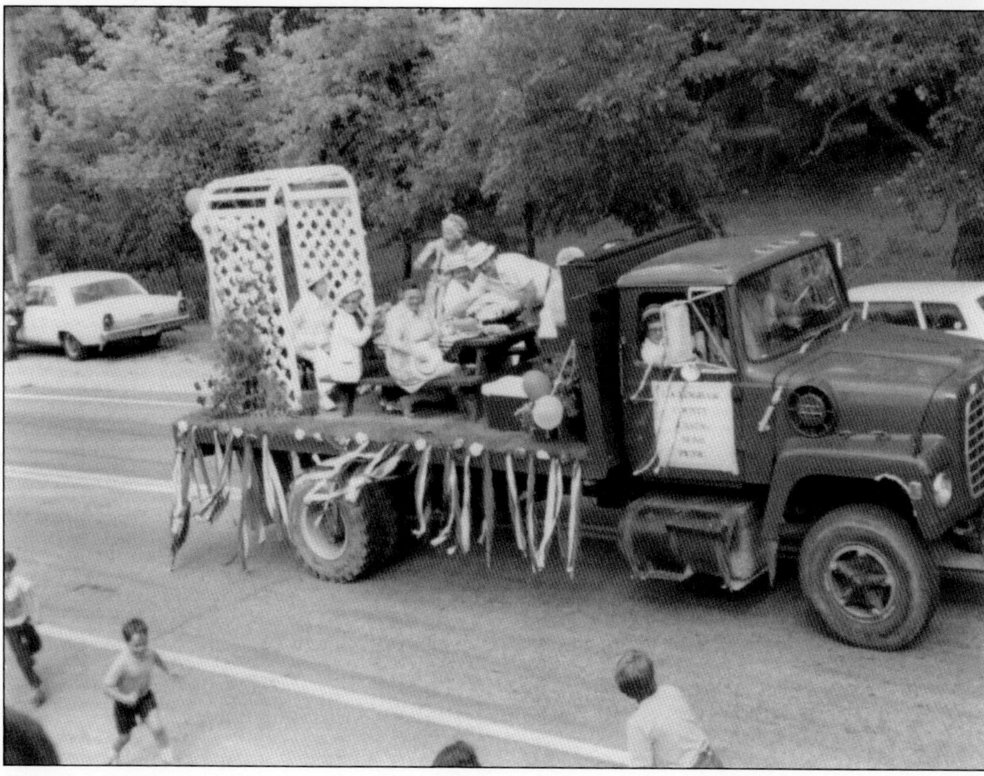